REGENTS CRITICS SERIES

General Editor: Paul A. Olson

SAMUEL JOHNSON'S
LITERARY CRITICISM

Other volumes in the Regents Critics Series are:

Joseph Conrad on Fiction
Edited by Walter F. Wright

Critical Writings of Ford Madox Ford
Edited by Frank MacShane

Literary Criticism of George Henry Lewes
Edited by Alice R. Kaminsky

Literary Criticism of Alexander Pope
Edited by Bertrand A. Goldgar

Literary Criticism of Edgar Allan Poe
Edited by Robert L. Hough

Russian Formalist Criticism: Four Essays
Translated with an introduction by
Lee T. Lemon and Marion J. Reis

Literary Criticism of William Wordsworth
Edited by Paul M. Zall

Shelley's Critical Prose
Edited by Bruce R. McElderry, Jr.

Literary Criticism of John Dryden
Edited by Arthur C. Kirsch

Sir Philip Sidney's Defense of Poesy
Edited by Lewis Soens

*The Author's Craft and Other Critical Writings
of Arnold Bennett*
Edited by Samuel Hynes

Literary Criticism of Oscar Wilde
Edited by Stanley Weintraub

Literary Criticism of James Russell Lowell
Edited by Herbert F. Smith

Ben Jonson's Literary Criticism
Edited by James D. Redwine, Jr.

Literary Criticism of Sainte-Beuve
Translated and edited by Emerson R. Marks

Bernard Shaw's Nondramatic Literary Criticism
Edited by Stanley Weintraub

Literary Criticism of Dante Alighieri
Translated and edited by Robert S. Haller

Samuel Johnson's
Literary Criticism

Edited by

R. D. STOCK

UNIVERSITY OF NEBRASKA PRESS · LINCOLN

Copyright © 1974 by the University of Nebraska Press

All Rights Reserved

Library of Congress Cataloging in Publication Data

Johnson, Samuel, 1709–1784.
  Samuel Johnson's literary criticism.

  (Regents critics series)
  Bibliography: p.
  1. Literature—Addresses, essays, lectures. 2. English philology—Addresses, essays, lectures. I. Stock, Robert D., ed. II. Title.
PR3523.S8   820'.9   73–91398
ISBN 0–8032–0469–8
ISBN 0–8032–5467–9 (pbk.)

MANUFACTURED IN THE UNITED STATES OF AMERICA

Regents Critics Series

The Regents Critics Series provides reading texts of significant literary critics in the Western tradition. The series treats criticism as a useful tool: an introduction to the critic's own poetry and prose if he is a poet or novelist, an introduction to other work in his day if he is more judge than creator. Nowhere is criticism regarded as an end in itself but as what it is—a means to the understanding of the language of art as it has existed and been understood in various periods and societies.

Each volume includes a scholarly introduction which describes how the work collected came to be written, and suggests its uses. All texts are edited in the most conservative fashion consonant with the production of a good reading text; and all translated texts observe the dictum that the letter gives life and the spirit kills when a technical or rigorous passage is being put into English. Other types of passages may be more freely treated. Footnoting and other scholarly paraphernalia are restricted to the essential minimum. Such features as a bibliographical check-list or an index are carried where they are appropriate to the work in hand. If a volume is the first collection of the author's critical writing, this is noted in the bibliographical data.

PAUL A. OLSON

University of Nebraska

Contents

Introduction

To introduce concisely the "essence" of Johnsonian criticism is neither easy nor desirable. So alembicated, it might well appear deceptively systematic or, like that of "Dick Minim," inanely platitudinous. It has therefore seemed more suitable to provide separate introductions for the several parts of this collection, to which, by way of prelude, may be added these few remarks.

Neoclassicism used commonly to be dismissed as a perverse and deplorable obsession which fastened on the English mind in 1660 with the advent of Charles II and Gallicism, and was dispelled in 1800 by the homely pen of Wordsworth. But such criticism as we have from the Renaissance—that of Sidney and Ben Jonson, for instance—can as properly be styled neoclassical as any, and that criticism lingers intelligently on into the nineteenth century in the commentaries of, say, Walter Scott and Francis Jeffrey. Nevertheless, it is true that in Dryden it found its first vigorous and comprehensive expression, and in Johnson a century later its last. This criticism at its finest, as executed by Dryden, Addison, Pope, and Johnson, is generally resilient and pragmatic. The influence of French classicism, more systematic and obsequious to the "rules," is significant only in Dryden, and even there the empirical methods of English criticism are energetically and, in their variousness, sometimes annoyingly at play. This criticism, although prescriptive, distinctly avoids the vanity of dogmatizing. "To circumscribe poetry by a definition will only shew the narrowness of the definer," concludes Johnson in the *Life of Pope*. It addresses itself, not to academicians or fellow-critics, but to the community of intelligent readers. And if in its method it is opposed to the French "regular" criticism on the one hand, on the other it aligns itself against the sentimentalist school presided over in England by the Earl of Shaftesbury. This aesthetics, far from emulating the French, disdained principles as repressive and referred critical judgments to an innate and ineffable taste.

Criticism was thus threatened by the one extreme with paralysis, and by the other with dissolution.

In one of his most illuminating definitions of the term, Johnson says:

> Next to the excursions of fancy are the disquisitions of criticism, which, in my opinion, is only to be ranked among the subordinate and instrumental arts. Arbitrary decision and general exclamation I have carefully avoided, by asserting nothing without a reason, and establishing all my principles of judgment on unalterable and evident truth. [*Rambler* no. 208]

As a subordinate and instrumental art, criticism cannot claim an a priori precision or certitude, but yet it is more than sentiment and has a connection with permanent truth. On this understanding of the function of criticism Johnson dilates in the *Preface to Shakespeare* (see pp. 139–40): criticism is comparative and empirical in its manner, and must consider such irrational factors as the test of time and consensus. Yet as the rest of that *Preface* so admirably exemplifies, it cannot carelessly acquiesce in popular decision or seek an illusory refuge in mere impressionism. It must find and apply those principles which, however tentative, seem useful and valid.

"A man skilled in the art of judging literature; a man able to distinguish the faults and beauties of writing": such is Johnson's lexical definition of *critick*. Judicial criticism, a deliberate weighing of merits and defects, is his one unvarying practice, and his one aversion is indiscriminate enthusiasm, whether eulogistic or denunciatory. To identify in his criticism any other consistent methods is less easy. Sometimes he will discuss a piece generally, and sometimes criticize its structure and language with more rigor. He regularly examines the relationship of the author's life to his work, and more occasionally that of the work to its genre. But most consistently he considers the effect produced by a work on the reader. More than Dryden or Pope, more even than Addison, he is a psychological critic. This emphasis, together with his unrelenting empiricism, most distinguishes him from the other neoclassicists. In writers he desires above all that mental animation and energy, the *vivida vis animi,* without which there can be neither originality nor vigor of expression. But though this originality and vigor are requisite to important literature, Johnson venerates neither. Originality, degenerating into an obsession, yields the showy but trifling conceits of metaphysical poetry (see pp. 208–9) and even the vehement and versatile genius of Shakespeare, undisciplined or misdirected, may slide into puerility and bombast (pp. 149–51). Johnson places some value on sincerity (e.g., *Lycidas,* p. 211), but never on the cult of sincerity. That a work express universal themes is more essential than that it should expose the private, but not necessarily interesting or important, thoughts and feelings of the poet. He commonly dismisses inspirational theories of poetic creation, and chastises Shakespeare for failing to labor more assiduously at his craft. He exhibits a formidable ingenuity in analyzing images and figures of speech, although he seldom scrutinizes whole patterns of imagery or attends to symbolism; of Johnson's limitations, this is perhaps the most serious. Like all neoclassicists, but less sequaciously than some, he observes in his criticism the principles of propriety and decorum: the language or expression must be suited to the writer's subject and to his rhetorical intention. But in no critic, not even Pope, does pedantry less obtrude: Johnson is always prepared to allow, as he affirms in the *Preface to Shakespeare,* an appeal from theoretical criticism to empirical nature. His view of his own profession is indeed not exorbitant. Surely no irritable poet has ever had a more satisfactory fling at his enemy the critic than has Johnson himself when exposing the sententious fatuity of "Dick Minim" (see pp. 15–22).

For Johnson, the greatest English poets were Shakespeare, Milton, Pope, and Dryden. And as Jean H. Hagstrum has shown so persuasively, each of these poets but the last exemplifies one of the three types of poetry most favored by Johnson: the beautiful, the sublime, and the pathetic. Since these are terms frequently iterated in his criticism, they must be considered briefly. To commend a poet as beautiful may at first seem insipid, but Johnson signifies by the word a cluster of important and related rhetorical qualities—harmony, balance, elegance, gracefulness

—which can be manifested only in literature of a highly civilized order. Of this species Pope is the most sedulous cultivator and *The Rape of the Lock* its most exquisite blossom. By the sublime Johnson means the exalted style, nobility of thought, and magnificence of language. A sublime effect proceeds from a skillful representation of the vast, the general, the great, "that comprehension and expanse of thought which at once fills the whole mind, and of which the first effect is sudden astonishment, and the second rational admiration. Sublimity is produced by aggregation, and littleness by dispersion. Great thoughts are always general, and consist in positions not limited by exceptions, and in descriptions not descending to minuteness" (p. 209). As such, the sublime contrasts sharply with the beautiful, which, as in Pope's *Lock*, can comprehend the elegant and small. Milton's *Paradise Lost* is naturally the supreme specimen of this type. But one must not too rigorously impose the distinction or segregate skillful writers into separate camps: there is beauty in *L'Allegro* and *Il Penseroso*, and sublimity at the close of *The Dunciad*. As Imlac says in *Rasselas* (p. 132), the universal poet ought to master all that is awfully (i.e., awesomely) vast and elegantly little. Finally, there is the pathetic: that poetry capable of moving the deepest but yet the most common human emotions. This effect *The Rape of the Lock*, with its miniature and shivery beauty, cannot achieve. But neither, despite its sublimity, can *Paradise Lost*: that poem, says Johnson, treats mainly of prelapsarian or paradisaical man, and "human passions did not enter the world before the Fall." Shakespeare, representing postlapsarian humanity in all its profusion and tumult, is the poet of the pathetic.

Howsoever we may regard these discriminations—and they do not seem notably less useful or comprehensive than more recent aesthetic schemes—they are the nearest to formal principles of any in Johnson's informal criticism; and he applies them, or refuses them, to many other poets besides these three: Dryden is denied the pathetic and Rowe credited with it, while the unfortunate Cowley has no claim on the sublime or pathetic, and but very little on the beautiful. To succeed in any of these several poetic species the writer must observe nature, both human and physical, with attention; he must stock his mind with images (a favorite phrase of Johnson's) that from this store he may select those images most appropriate for the effect he intends. In Johnson's poetics, therefore, the senses play an indispensable role. A poet, unlike God, does not create *ex nihilo*, nor does some amiable afflatus infuse him with ideas and language. Genius or wit he must have, to be sure, for without that there can be in his works no justness, vivacity, and grace, but he must acquire the store through diligence. To use a homely figure of which Johnson was fond, there can be no flame without fuel. Both books and first-hand observation may contribute to the poet's supply, of course. A writer like Milton, who relies extensively on books, is consequently the more artificial poet, while Shakespeare, a less erudite but more acute observer, is the more natural. Johnson is apt to prefer the second type, but can praise very generously the first.

For any species of poetry, then, a proper selection is necessary, and this selection must inexorably reflect moral and universal truth. No poet, not even the beautiful poet, can be content with mere description. Johson says in the *Life of Milton*: "Poetry is the art of uniting pleasure with truth, by calling imagination to the help of reason." And he elsewhere maintains: "The only end of writing is to enable the readers better to enjoy life, or better to endure it." Like all neoclassicists, Johnson is strongly in the tradition of *miscere utile dulci* ramifying from Horace and Quintilian: the poet should both please and instruct; and indeed the poet himself must have integrity and wisdom as well as verbal skill. The *ars gratia artis* school, under its sprightly headmaster Oscar Wilde, ridiculed as bourgeois, or for them what is worse, tiresome, this obsession with ethics, as do a few contemporary commentators who start up righteously at any intrusion, however deferential, of morality into aesthetics. Some modern readers may find Johnson's didacticism a clog and a vexation, but modernism, after all, will one day be obsolete, and meanwhile Johnson's robust and realistic morality has an attraction lacking in the vacant relativism and superficial neutrality of some subsequent critics. It is not priggish, insensitive, or simple-minded. He advocates no pollyanna conclusion to every tragedy, and he is perpetually vigilant to detect pretentious and hypocritical moralizing. For any gross misrepresentation of life he has a profound aversion. Writing to his friend Bennet Langton he reflects: "Whether to see life as it is will give us much comfort I know not, but the consolation which is drawn from truth, if any there be, is solid and durable, that which may be derived from errour must be like its original fallacious and fugitive." Yet he is no prophet of nineteenth-century naturalism. He says in *Rambler* no. 4: "If the world be promiscuously described, I cannot see of what use it can be to read the account; or why it may not be as safe to turn the eye immediately upon mankind, as upon a mirror which shows all that presents itself without discrimination."

In discussing the catastrophe of *King Lear*, a work that had always strongly affected him, he penetrates the problem most deeply (see p. 189): a play failing to observe poetic justice may be good, for it has duly represented human life; yet since we are reasonable beings, we "naturally love justice" (as Johnson had said in the *Preface to Shakespeare*, "he that thinks reasonably must think morally"). And is a poet, then, to be barred from representing this facet of nature, this sense of ulterior if ineffable justice that is scored so ineradicably on the human consciousness? Modern, hedonistic criticism, in defining all experience as moral (though in its more candid moments it will employ the term *vital* or *healthy*) has evacuated the word of significance; nor is such criticism faithful to human behavior. All men, whether carpenters, professors, poets, or critics, and regardless of the ethical scheme to which they adhere, submit their experience every day to moral scrutiny and judgment. Furthermore, no writer can escape trenching on morality or adumbrating a pattern of values; for words have meaning, and even a Wilde or a Swinburne, as he writes, will inevitably let slip ideas. These ideas are seldom morally neutral—and that the poet or commentator should be so who expresses them is for Johnson neither possible nor to be desired. That artist or critic who blinks morality, in the interests of "pure" art or "pure" criticism, has sequestered himself from reality; and in such a retreat neither Johnson's empiricism nor his religion could acquiesce.

In style, too, Johnson's criticism is not detached from life. Though it is stately, it is not in fact difficult. Johnson favors the direct, declarative sentence which, by virtue of its balances, antitheses, and emphatic rhythms, is easily followed, compact, and clear—though not, perhaps, an ideal subject for speed-reading. And even with the lapse of two centuries his vocabulary is neither obscurely technical nor seriously obsolete. Such terms as *wit, genius, imagination, invention, pathetic,* require only an occasional gloss, for the context usually carries the sense. That this is true of modern criticism cannot safely be affirmed. Place next to any passage from Johnson the following asseveration from a recent critic: "The effective meaning of . . . sentences arises from the placement within the cognitive force field of the generic structure in which they are embedded and not atomistically and additively from any inherently literary character of their own." His point, as I apprehend it, is sound: that we should read what a poet writes in the context of the entire work and in light of whatever generic tradition it shares. Yet his meaning is baffled by a jargon plundered from the sciences and pseudo-sciences, and by a structure highly inharmonious (note the -y endings straggling lamely along). This is not English but a dialect thereof, to be understood and valued only by those whose fatality it is to share it. It is an aesthetic sundered effectively from the common language and hence violating a capital principle of Johnson's own. In the face of such proliferating and ungainly criticism, the relevance of Johnson requires no very ample demonstration.

A Note on the Selections and the Text

To assemble in one convenient volume the essential criticism of Johnson has been my aim. I have therefore confined myself to those works upon which, in his own time and since, his critical reputation has chiefly stood. His epistolary and colloquial criticism, his miscellaneous and fugitive book reviews, prefaces, etc., have necessarily been ignored. With the obvious exception of *The Lives of the Poets*, the major selections are printed entire. No true Johnsonian will much relish the *Lives* in the eviscerated form they have assumed here, but total exclusion was the only alternative, and what volume could call itself *Johnson's Literary Criticism* and yet lack his extended comments on Milton, Dryden, Pope, Gray, or on the metaphysical poets in *Cowley*? Throughout, I have preferred general or theoretical criticism to closer scrutinies of poems, language, etc., although I have presented enough of these in his periodical essays, his notes to Shakespeare, and the *Lives* to exemplify his capacity for precise if occasionally perverse analysis. I have also excluded that criticism in which morality or philosophy preponderates over aesthetics: hence the incisive review of Soame Jenyns, readily available in many anthologies, will not be found here. Except for the internal organization of the periodical matter, the selections are arranged chronologically.

The standard edition of Johnson is at present being published by the Yale University Press. However, the text of this edition is constructed upon such controversial principles that it seemed best to return, for each work, to the most authoritative eighteenth-century edition. Except for correcting obvious misprints, modernizing obsolete typography, and, very timidly, clarifying ambiguous punctuation, I have presented these texts in their original state. Orthography is by Johnson's time sufficiently modern to be no hindrance; and to meddle unduly with the eighteenth-century punctuation, although it is heavier than that now favored, is often to obscure the proper cadence of a Johnsonian period. Where Johnson fails to provide his own or another's translation or paraphrase of a foreign passage, I have supplied one in brackets immediately following the original; unless otherwise identified, they are my own. For the substance of my notes I can claim little originality, but must instead record my obligation to a number of antecedent and indefatigable annotators, of whom the most indispensable have been W. J. Bate and Albrecht B. Strauss, G. B. Hill, and Arthur Sherbo.

R. D. STOCK

University of Nebraska

SAMUEL JOHNSON'S
LITERARY CRITICISM

From the Periodical Criticism (1750–59)

Johnson's reputation as critic hangs finally upon the two great prefaces to the *Dictionary* and the edition of Shakespeare, his notes to the Shakespeare, and the *Lives of the Poets*. His published criticism assumes three additional forms, however: the essays in the *Rambler*, *Adventurer*, and *Idler*, the book reviews and biographies executed for the *Literary Magazine* and kindred periodicals, and the various prefaces and dedications commissioned for other people's books. Much of this work was performed in the 1750s—when Johnson, despite his acquiring a substantial reputation, was still a laborer in grubstreet—and it has limited interest for the general reader. In the book reviews and minor biographies, the "fugitive pieces" Johnson would call them, scholars have lately been finding permanent merit; but to Johnson himself they were largely the productions of financial necessity, and no academic rehabilitation, howsoever assiduous or artful, can raise them, as a body, to the eminence of his major criticism.

But the *Rambler*, though not immediately popular, was in its collected editions to win Johnson considerable fame. Appearing twice weekly from March 1750 to March 1752, and running ultimately to 208 issues, it is his first sustained attempt in prose. Although the essays were composed hastily, he revised them for subsequent editions and seems to have hoped for them, what he dared not anticipate for his other journalism, the benedictions of posterity. In these papers, together with his contributions to the *Adventurer* (1753–54) and his weekly *Idler* (1758–60) is Johnson's most enduring periodical criticism. He is consciously emulating Addison, who, forty years before in the *Spectator*, was the first to aim literary

1

criticism at a truly general audience. Like Addison's criticism too, his is strongly psychological in its emphasis, although in tone the two could scarcely be more dissimilar: in the *Rambler* Addisonian sprightliness is replaced with a more sententious gravity.

Remembering Johnson's scorn of all pretentious or obfuscating systems, I have sought to reduce these miscellaneous essays into some simple and reasonable scheme, placing first those dealing mainly with the nature and function of criticism. *Rambler* no. 3 delineates the goddess Criticism in her ideal form—severe yet just; but with Astraea she is now retiring to heaven, fatigued by her unremitting critical exertions, and literary judgment is abandoned to the caprices of Prejudice and False-Taste, Flattery and Malevolence. From this relaxation have proceeded the discouraging conditions portrayed in *Rambler* no. 176, where the poet and critic are seen indeed to be natural enemies, and where modern criticism shows no trace of its ancient deity. It is either precise to the point of aridity, obsessed with the trivial, and astringent in spirit, or it expands itself in aesthetic *O Altitudo*s, imagining recondite allusions and arcane meanings, expatiating in improbable and nebulous conjectures. Neither extreme is capable of apprehending the truly significant elements in a work, and, it may be added, no exceptional sophistication is required to discern in their twentieth-century guise the same perversions. In Dick Minim (*Idler* nos. 60, 61) this inferior criticism, heretofore abstractly considered, is made palpable. Conning such critics as Dryden and Pope with an unreflective and indiscriminating docility, Minim has memorized the neoclassical commonplaces and can rehearse them with all the ostentation of original discovery. They are by no means patently ridiculous: Johnson "reiterates" in the *Preface to Shakespeare* Minim's opinion of Addison's *Cato* and his complaint against the predominance of dramatic love. But here the notions, so platitudinized, fall hollow and trite. When in a venturesome moment Minim *does* wander away from accepted opinion, as in his comments on Milton's verse in no. 61, he flounders into absurdity. In dispensing with ancillary criticism and endeavoring to engage a work directly, he exhibits no sound insight. Now to rail against the fatuousness of contemporary criticism is perhaps as perennial as to lament the barbarism of the latest generation. Yet such railings and lamentations are sometimes salubrious, and in their reactionary vehemence may suppose an active ideal. For Johnson, as for Pope in the *Essay on Criticism* or Swift in the *Battle of the Books*, the critical virtues are impartiality, intelligence, independence but yet modesty of mind, and a will to scrutinize in a work its most important facets.

The next group is concerned with authors. *Adventurer* no. 138 presents a disillusioned and typically Johnsonian view of the psychology of composition, after which it meditates on the ways by which literary merit will finally be determined. Johnson believes the public, in the long run, will decide, but he is no sanguine democrat: few of the public have good taste or independence of judgment. Moreover, many factors quite unrelated to a work's real value may throw it into obscurity. This last point has been represented as contradicting Johnson's later assertion, in the *Preface to Shakespeare*, that the ultimate criteria of literary worth are length of duration and continuance of esteem (i.e., the test of time, the *consensus gentium*); however, he is there contending, not that *all* excellent works are by this means assured of survival, but that those which *do* satisfy this test are probably valuable. The remaining essays in this group touch on the relationship of the poet to the past and tradition. Johnson emphasizes, though it can hardly be said that he exaggerates, the impediments to originality, and he rebukes those who, in their obsecration of that virtue, ignore or despise traditional wisdom. (The opening of *Rambler* no. 154 calls Swift to mind, who with more gusto if less gravity withered such insolent and barbarian individualists in the fable of the spider and the bee.) "Most truths are too important to be new," said Johnson in another context; wherefore to unite truth with originality is no common achievement. But withal he concedes in these papers that some value is indeed to be had from presenting the old ideas anew—either in a more organized and intelligible way than has hitherto been done, or in some manner specially adapted to the requirements of the present age.

We have next a sampling of Johnson's generic criticism. It must be asserted first that he is never fond of applying theoretical, generic prescriptions to specific works. The psychological effect of a piece on the reader or audience is invariably for him a more pertinent question. Nevertheless, save possibly for his defense of tragicomedy in *Rambler* no. 156, Johnson accepts and employs the generic distinctions: various types of literature meditate various effects, and hence to categorize them may be useful. The first two essays take up two relatively new forms, the novel (called by Johnson the comedy of romance—*novel* not quite having acquired its modern sense) and biography. Both genres, it will be noted, draw on the techniques of realism, a fact of which Johnson is most aware. This realism in no way exempts the novelist or biographer from his duty to select: a novelist will perforce exhibit evil, but he should show it only in its loathsomeness; and he should also portray an attractive but attainable virtue. So too the biographer must not mindlessly encumber us with facts, howsoever tedious or impertinent, but neither should he suppress those points, even the trivial, that may elucidate his subject or render it more instructive: "nothing is too little for so little a creature as man," and from the domestic and quotidian happenings of a life we may extract valuable lessons. Just as the novelist should not so far idealize virtue as to discourage emulation, so the biographer ought never to sink into mere panegyric: he must present the man himself. It bears stressing that Johnson, enamored as he was with the "grandeur of generality," and resentful as he was of the welter of clogging details, can recognize and appreciate the realism of these new genres: those details, judiciously selected, are appropriate to these forms.

The pastoral (*Rambler* nos. 36, 37), a far more conventional and yet factitious genre than the novel or biography, demands a much more exclusive selection. Johnson pursues here a temperate course, rejecting those critics on the one hand who affirmed that the pastoral should delineate a paradisaical golden age, and repudiating on the other those who argued that it should be contemporary, realistic, and rustic in its style, and that it should admit of vigorous, topical satire. Johnson thus tolerates more realism than could any rigorous, genre critic, but he recognizes that, except for some selective supervision, useful generic distinctions would lapse into desuetude. The desirable tone is an elevated simplicity. It is interesting that although Johnson remarks correctly on the limited range of human experience available to the pastoral, there is nothing of that contempt for the form evinced years later in his famous critique of *Lycidas* (see pp. 210–12).

The psychological emphasis of Johnson's criticism is well exemplified in the final three selections of this group, all concerned with the drama. In *Rambler* no. 125 he recommends that tragedy and comedy be defined "only by their effects upon the mind"; he then reprehends farcical elements in tragedy, not from the strictly generic standpoint (i.e., tragedies by definition cannot admit humor), but because they counteract the proper tragic response. In *Rambler* no. 156 he distinguishes between those rules derived from nature and reason, and those that are engendered by accident or expedient, and preserved by superstition. He then impeaches the unity of time as a rule of the latter order, and undermines it by appealing to experience. On the same grounds he defends tragicomedy: we sense in our daily lives the mixture of serious and trivial, pathetic and joyful; why then can we not endure a similar mélange on the stage? This position is not inconsistent with *Rambler* no. 125: after all, a dramatist may produce a mishmash more easily than a mixture. Johnson criticizes Shakespeare's comic scenes in this paper even as, in *Rambler* 125, he censures the farce in Dryden's serious plays. He says, moreover, that Shakespeare's triumph in tragicomedy does not so much vindicate that form as it does the fecundity of Shakespeare's own genius, for he has excelled where failure is more frequent than success. *Rambler* no. 168 condemns inappropriate language in tragedy, and again the appeal is not to generic prescription, but to psychology. By association, Johnson says, some words acquire low or ridiculous connotations and should therefore be ejected from scenes whose aim is to excite repugnance or terror. Johnson can "scarce check his risibility" at some of Shakespeare's alleged lapses, and we may have difficulty, as we contemplate his examples, in repressing our own—at the commentator, however, not the dramatist. Why *knife*, even in the more fastidious eighteenth century, should necessarily summon up the odors of the kitchen or the shambles, or why the phrase "peeping through a blanket" (actually used by Lady Macbeth) should so provoke his hilarity—these are questions neither easily answered nor perhaps worth asking. Even conceding, for argument, the domestic connotations of *knife*, one might contend that these intensify our horror at Macbeth's atrocious violation of the laws of hospitality. But if Johnson's criticism lacks conviction, that is not because he has shifted his principles: the argument is not drawn from prescriptive rules but from experience, though in this instance, it may be, from an experience more idiosyncratic than Johnson supposed.

The final group is devoted to specific criticism. In the

three essays concerned with Milton's versification, Johnson several times confesses the difficulty of rendering
such subjects interesting. The present reader may assent
to the difficulty and pass over these papers with deliberate speed. But in these *Ramblers*, more fully than elsewhere in his criticism, Johnson addresses the important
subject of prosody. The series was intended, as he tells us,
to supplement Addison's essays on Milton in the *Spectator*,
which, otherwise comprehensive, scanted this problem.
Johnson's theory of meter is traditionally accentual-
syllabic. His practical applications, though they are also
conventional, are diligent and enlightening. He prefers
the variety of the mixed measure to the tedium of the
pure, approves of initial but not always of medial inversions of accent, is concerned with the harmonious deploy-
ing of vowels and consonants, and with where the
caesurae ought properly to fall. His use of Milton to
illustrate or exemplify these various problems is, if not
exciting, at least precise. The essays on *Samson Agonistes*
take up first its structure, which Johnson finds in need of
a middle, though sufficiently provided with a beginning
and end, and then its sentiments. We are more apt to
concur with the second essay than with the first, for
there Johnson exhibits his fine ability to scrutinize images
and metaphors acutely; and his complaints against inde-
corously ornate expressions, improper verbal conceits,
etc.—censures appealing not to rules but experience
—have plausibility. But as to whether or not the play is
indeed deficient in a middle, that will be left to the determination of more resourceful commentators. *Adventurer* no. 92 on Virgil's pastorals combines general survey
with some detailed analysis. There Johnson commends
above all the naturalness and felicity with which Virgil
describes the human emotions; and if we put next to this
Johnson's condemnation of topical satire and praise of
metrical simplicity in *Rambler* 37, we may begin to understand, if not to forgive, his subsequent depreciation of

Lycidas. No other specimen of the genre comes to mind so exquisitely offensive to the taste here engaged.

To compare this earlier criticism with the later is to discover more consistency and development than contradiction or unexpected sinuosities of thought. The didacticism, the psychological emphasis, the empiricism, the alert common sense, persist. These essays are spoiled occasionally by a convolution or pomposity of phrase and sometimes as well by a perversity of judgment, from which the later criticism, and especially the *Lives of the Poets*, is by comparison immune. Yet had Johnson ceased to write when he completed the *Rambler* in March 1752, he would have left a residue of neoclassical criticism which might challenge, without hazarding certain humiliation, that of Dryden, Addison, and Pope.

The text of the *Rambler* is from the fourth edition (1756); of the *Idler*, the third (1767); and of the *Adventurer*, the edition of 1754.

RAMBLER no. 3. Tuesday, March 27, 1750

Virtus, repulsae nescia sordidae,
Intaminatis fulget honoribus,
　　Nec sumit aut ponit secures
　　Arbitrio popularis aurae.　　Hor.[1]

Undisappointed in designs,
With native honours virtue shines;
Nor takes up pow'r, nor lays it down,
As giddy rabbles smile or frown.　　Elphinston.

The task of an author is, either to teach what is not known, or to recommend known truths, by his manner of adorning them; either to let new light in upon the mind, and open new scenes to the prospect, or to vary the dress and situation of common objects, so as to give them fresh grace and more powerful attractions, to spread such flowers over the regions through which the intellect has already made its progress, as may tempt it to return, and take a second view of things hastily passed over, or negligently regarded.

Either of these labours is very difficult, because, that they may not be fruitless, men must not only be persuaded of their errors, but reconciled to their guide; they must not only confess their ignorance, but, what is still less pleasing, must allow that he from whom they are to learn is more knowing than themselves.

It might be imagined that such an employment was in itself sufficiently irksome and hazardous; that none would be found so malevolent as wantonly to add weight to the stone of Sisyphus; and that few endeavours would be used to obstruct those advances to reputation, which must be made at such an expense of time and thought, with so great hazard in the miscarriage, and with so little advantage from the success.

Yet there is a certain race of men, that either imagine it their duty, or make it their amusement, to hinder the reception of every work of learning or genius, who stand as centinels in the avenues of fame, and value themselves upon giving IGNORANCE and ENVY the first notice of a prey.

To these men, who distinguish themselves by the appellation of CRITICKS, it is necessary for a new author to find some means of recommendation. It is probable, that the most malignant of these persecutors might be somewhat softened, and prevailed on, for a short time, to remit their fury. Having for this purpose considered many expedients, I find in the records of ancient times, that ARGUS was lulled by music, and CERBERUS quieted with a sop; and am, therefore, inclined to believe that modern criticks, who, if they have not the eyes, have the watchfulness of ARGUS, and can bark as loud as CERBERUS, though, perhaps, they cannot bite with equal force, might be subdued by methods of the same kind. I have heard how some have been pacified with claret and a supper, and others laid asleep by the soft notes of flattery.

Though the nature of my undertaking gives me sufficient reason to dread the united attacks of this virulent generation, yet I have not hitherto persuaded myself to take any measures for flight or treaty. For I am in doubt, whether they can act against me by lawful authority, and suspect that they have presumed upon a forged commission, stiled themselves the ministers of CRITICISM, without any authentic evidence of delegation, and uttered their own determinations as the decrees of a higher judicature.

CRITICISM, from whom they derive their claim to decide the fate of writers, was the eldest daughter of LABOUR and of TRUTH: she was, at her birth, committed to the care of JUSTICE, and brought up by her in the palace of WISDOM. Being soon distinquished by the celestials, for her uncommon qualities, she was appointed the governess of FANCY, and impowered to beat time to the chorus of the MUSES, when they sung before the throne of JUPITER.

When the MUSES condescended to visit this lower world, they came accompanied by CRITICISM, to whom, upon her descent from her native regions, JUSTICE gave a scepter, to be carried aloft in her right hand, one end of which was tinctured with ambrosia, and inwreathed with a golden foliage of amaranths and bays; the other end was incircled with cypress and poppies, and dipped in the waters of oblivion. In her left hand, she bore an unextinguishable torch, manufactured by LABOUR, and lighted by TRUTH, of which it was the particular quality immediately to shew every thing in its true form, however it might be disguised to common eyes. Whatever ART could complicate, or FOLLY could confound, was, upon the first gleam of the torch of TRUTH, exhibited in its distinct parts and original simplicity; it darted through the labyrinths of sophistry, and shewed at once all the absurdities to which they served for refuge; it pierced through the robes, which rhetorick often sold to falshood, and detected the disproportion of parts, which artificial veils had been contrived to cover.

Thus furnished for the execution of her office, CRITICISM came down to survey the performances of those who professed themselves the votaries of the MUSES. Whatever was brought before her, she beheld by the steady light of the torch of TRUTH, and when her examination had convinced her, that the laws of just writing had been observed, she touched it with the amaranthine end of the scepter, and consigned it over to immortality.

But it more frequently happened, that in the works, which

required her inspection, there was some imposture attempted; that false colours were laboriously laid; that some secret inequality was found between the words and sentiments, or some dissimilitude of the ideas and the original objects; that incongruities were linked together, or that some parts were of no use but to enlarge the appearance of the whole, without contributing to its beauty, solidity, or usefulness.

Wherever such discoveries were made, and they were made whenever these faults were committed, CRITICISM refused the touch which conferred the sanction of immortality, and, when the errors were frequent and gross, reversed the scepter, and let drops of lethe distil from the poppies and cypress, a fatal mildew, which immediately began to waste the work away, till it was at last totally destroyed.

There were some compositions brought to the test, in which, when the strongest light was thrown upon them, their beauties and faults appeared so equally mingled, that CRITICISM stood with her scepter poised in her hand, in doubt whether to shed lethe, or ambrosia, upon them. These at last increased to so great a number, that she was weary of attending such doubtful claims, and, for fear of using improperly the scepter of JUSTICE, referred the cause to be considered by TIME.[2]

The proceedings of TIME, though very dilatory, were, some few caprices excepted, conformable to justice: and many, who thought themselves secure by a short forbearance, have sunk under his scythe, as they were posting down with their volumes in triumph to futurity. It was observable that some were destroyed by little and little, and others crushed for ever by a single blow.

CRITICISM having long kept her eye fixed steadily upon TIME, was at last so well satisfied with his conduct, that she withdrew from the earth with her patroness ASTREA, and left PREJUDICE and FALSE-TASTE to ravage at large as the associates of FRAUD and MISCHIEF; contenting herself thenceforth to shed her influence from afar upon some select minds, fitted for its reception by learning and by virtue.

Before her departure, she broke her scepter, of which the shivers, that formed the ambrosial end, were caught up by

FLATTERY, and those that had been infected with the waters of lethe were, with equal haste, seized by MALEVOLENCE. The followers of FLATTERY, to whom she distributed her part of the scepter, neither had nor desired light, but touched indiscriminately whatever POWER or INTEREST happened to exhibit. The companions of MALEVOLENCE were supplied by the FURIES with a torch, which had this quality peculiar to infernal lustre, that its light fell only upon faults.

> *No light, but rather darkness visible*
> *Serv'd only to discover sights of woe.*[3]

With these fragments of authority, the slaves of FLATTERY and MALEVOLENCE marched out, at the command of their mistresses, to confer immortality, or condemn to oblivion. But the scepter had now lost its power; and TIME passes his sentence at leisure, without any regard to their determinations.

RAMBLER NO. 176. SATURDAY, NOV. 23, 1751

—Naso suspendere adunco.   HOR.[4]

On me you turn the nose—

There are many vexatious accidents and uneasy situations which raise little compassion for the sufferer, and which no man but those whom they immediately distress, can regard with seriousness. Petty mischiefs, that have no influence on futurity, nor extend their effects to the rest of life, are always seen with a kind of malicious pleasure. A mistake or embarrasment, which for the present moment fills the face with blushes, and the mind with confusion, will have no other effect upon those who observe it than that of convulsing them with irresistible laughter. Some circumstances of misery are so powerfully ridiculous, that neither kindness nor duty can withstand them; they bear down love, interest, and reverence, and force the friend, the dependent, or the child, to give way to instantaneous motions of merriment.

Among the principal of comick calamities, may be reckoned the pain which an author, not yet hardened into insensibility, feels at the onset of a furious critick, whose age, rank or fortune gives him confidence to speak without reserve; who heaps one objection upon another, and obtrudes his remarks, and enforces his corrections without tenderness or awe.

The author, full of the importance of his work, and anxious for the justification of every syllable, starts and kindles at the slightest attack; the critick, eager to establish his superiority, triumphing in every discovery of failure, and zealous to impress the cogency of his arguments, pursues him from line to line without cessation or remorse. The critick, who hazards little, proceeds with vehemence, impetuosity and fearlessness; the author, whose quiet and fame, and life and immortality are involved in the controversy, tries every art of subterfuge and defence; maintains modestly what he resolves never to yield, and yields unwillingly what cannot be maintained. The critick's purpose is to conquer, the author only hopes to escape; the critick therefore knits his brow, and raises his voice, and rejoices whenever he perceives any tokens of pain excited by the pressure of his assertions, or the point of his sarcasms. The author, whose endeavour is at once to mollify and elude his persecutor, composes his features, and softens his accent, breaks the force of assault by retreat, and rather steps aside than flies or advances.

As it very seldom happens that the rage of extemporary criticism inflicts fatal or lasting wounds, I know not that the laws of benevolence entitle this distress to much sympathy. The diversion of baiting an author has the sanction of all ages and nations, and is more lawful than the sport of teizing other animals, because for the most part he comes voluntarily to the stake, furnished, as he imagines, by the patron powers of literature, with resistless weapons, and impenetrable armour, with the mail of the boar of *Erymanth,* and the paws of the lion of *Nemea.*[5]

But the works of genius are sometimes produced by other motives than vanity; and he whom necessity or duty enforces to write, is not always so well satisfied with himself, as not to be discouraged by censorious impudence. It may therefore be necessary to consider how they whom publication lays open to the insults of such as their obscurity secures against reprisals, may extricate themselves from unexpected encounters.

Vida, a man of considerable skill in the politicks of literature, directs his pupil wholly to abandon his defence, and even when he can irrefragably refute all objections, to suffer tamely the exultations of his antagonist.[6]

This rule may perhaps be just, when advice is asked, and severity solicited, because no man tells his opinion so freely as when he imagines it received with implicit veneration; and critics ought never to be consulted but while errors may yet be rectified or insipidity suppressed. But when the book has once been dismissed into the world, and can be no more retouched, I know not whether a very different conduct should be prescribed, and whether firmness and spirit may not sometimes be of use to overpower arrogance and repel brutality. Softness, dissidence and moderation will often be mistaken for imbecility and dejection; they lure cowardice to the attack by the hopes of easy victory, and it will soon be found that he whom every man thinks he can conquer, shall never be at peace.

The animadversions of criticks are commonly such as may easily provoke the sedatest writer to some quickness of resentment and asperity of reply. A man who by long consideration has familiarised a subject to his own mind, carefully surveyed the series of his thoughts, and planned all the parts of his composition into a regular dependance on each other, will often start at the sinistrous interpretations, or absurd remarks of haste and ignorance, and wonder by what infatuation they have been led away from the obvious sense, and upon what peculiar principles of judgment they decide against him.

The eye of the intellect, like that of the body, is not equally perfect in all, nor equally adapted in any to all objects; the end of criticism is to supply its defects; rules are the instruments of mental vision, which may indeed assist our faculties when properly used, but produce confusion and obscurity by unskilful application.

Some seem always to read with the microscope of criticism, and employ their whole attention upon minute elegance, or faults scarcely visible to common observation. The dissonance of a syllable, the recurrence of the same sound, the repetition of a

particle, the smallest deviation from propriety, the slightest defect in construction or arrangement, swell before their eyes into
enormities. As they discern with great exactness, they comprehend but a narrow compass, and know nothing of the justness
of the design, the general spirit of the performance, the artifice of
connection, or the harmony of the parts; they never conceive how
small a proportion that which they are busy in contemplating
bears to the whole, or how the petty inaccuracies with which they
are offended, are absorbed and lost in general excellence.

Others are furnished by criticism with a telescope. They see
with great clearness whatever is too remote to be discovered by
the rest of mankind, but are totally blind to all that lies immediately before them. They discover in every passage some
secret meaning, some remote allusion, some artful allegory, or
some occult imitation which no other reader ever suspected; but
they have no perception of the cogency of arguments, the force of
pathetick sentiments, the various colours of diction, or the flowery embellishments of fancy; of all that engages the attention of
others, they are totally insensible, while they pry into worlds of
conjecture, and amuse themselves with phantoms in the clouds.

In criticism, as in every other art, we fail sometimes by our
weakness, but more frequently by our fault. We are sometimes
bewildered by ignorance, and sometimes by prejudice, but we
seldom deviate far from the right, but when we deliver ourselves
up to the direction of vanity.

IDLER no. 60. Saturday, June 9, 1759

Criticism is a study by which men grow important and formidable at a very small expence. The power of invention has been
conferred by Nature upon few, and the labour of learning those
sciences which may, by mere labour, be obtained, is too great to be
willingly endured; but every man can exert such judgment as he
has upon the works of others; and he whom Nature has made
weak, and Idleness keeps ignorant, may yet support his vanity by
the name of a Critick.

I hope it will give comfort to great numbers who are passing thro' the world in obscurity, when I inform them how easily distinction may be obtained. All the other powers of literature are coy and haughty, they must be long courted, and at last are not always gained; but Criticism is a goddess easy of access and forward of advance, who will meet the slow and encourage the timorous; the want of meaning she supplies with words, and the want of spirit she recompenses with malignity.

This profession has one recommendation peculiar to itself, that it gives vent to malignity without real mischief. No genius was ever blasted by the breath of Criticks. The poison which if confined, would have burst the heart, fumes away in empty hisses, and malice is set at ease with very little danger to merit. The Critick is the only man whose triumph is without another's pain, and whose greatness does not rise upon another's ruin.

To a study at once so easy and so reputable, so malicious and so harmless, it cannot be necessary to invite my readers by a long or laboured exhortation; it is sufficient, since all would be Criticks if they could, to shew by one eminent example that all can be Criticks if they will.

Dick Minim, after the common course of puerile studies, in which he was no great proficient, was put apprentice to a Brewer, with whom he had lived two years, when his uncle died in the city, and left him a large fortune in the stocks. *Dick* had for six months before used the company of the lower players, of whom he had learned to scorn a trade, and being now at liberty to follow his genius, he resolved to be a man of wit and humour. That he might be properly initiated in his new character, he frequented the coffee-houses near the theatres, where he listened very diligently, day after day, to those who talked of language and sentiments, and unities and catastrophes, till by slow degrees he began to think that he understood something of the Stage, and hoped in time to talk himself.

But he did not trust so much to natural sagacity, as wholly to neglect the help of books. When the Theatres were shut, he retired to *Richmond* with a few select writers, whose opinions he impressed upon his memory by unwearied diligence; and when he returned with other wits to the town, was able to tell, in very proper phrases, that the chief business of art is to copy nature; that a perfect writer is not to be expected, because genius decays as judgment increases; that the great art is the art of blotting; and that according to the rule of *Horace*, every piece should be kept nine years.[7]

Of the great Authors he now began to display the Characters, laying down as an universal position, that all had beauties and defects. His opinion was, that *Shakespear*, committing himself wholly to the impulse of Nature, wanted that correctness which learning would have given him; and that *Jonson*, trusting to learning, did not sufficiently cast his eye on Nature. He blamed the *Stanza* of *Spenser*, and could not bear the *Hexameters* of *Sidney*. *Denham* and *Waller* he held the first reformers of *English* Numbers, and thought that if *Waller* could have obtained the strength of *Denham*, or *Denham* the sweetness of *Waller*, there had been nothing wanting to complete a Poet. He often expressed his commiseration of *Dryden*'s poverty, and his indignation at the age which suffered him to write for bread; he repeated with rapture the first lines of *All for Love*, but wondered at the corruption of taste which could bear any thing so unnatural as rhyming tragedies. In *Otway* he found uncommon powers of moving the passions, but was disgusted by his general negligence, and blamed him for making a Conspirator his Hero; and never concluded his disquisition, without remarking how happily the sound of the clock is made to alarm the audience. *Southern* would have been his favourite, but that he mixes comick with tragick scenes, intercepts the natural course of the passions, and fills the mind with a wild confusion of mirth and melancholy. The versification of *Rowe* he thought too melodious for the stage, and too little varied in different passions. He made it the great fault of *Congreve*, that all his persons were wits, and that he always wrote with more art than nature. He considered *Cato* rather as a poem than a play, and allowed *Addison* to be the complete master of Allegory and grave humour, but paid no great deference to him as a Critick. He thought the chief merit of *Prior* was in his easy tales and lighter poems, tho' he allowed that his *Solomon* had many noble sentiments elegantly expressed. In *Swift* he discovered an inimitable vein of irony, and an easiness which all would hope and few would attain. *Pope* he was inclined to degrade from a Poet to a Versifier, and thought his numbers rather luscious than sweet. He often lamented the neglect of *Phaedra and Hippolytus,* and wished to see the stage under better regulations.[8]

These assertions passed commonly uncontradicted; and if now and then an opponent started up, he was quickly repressed by the suffrages of the company, and *Minim* went away from every dispute with elation of heart and increase of confidence.

He now grew conscious of his abilities, and began to talk of the present state of dramatick Poetry; wondered what was become of the comick genius which supplied our ancestors with wit and pleasantry, and why no writer could be found that durst now venture beyond a Farce. He saw no reason for thinking that the vein of humour was exhausted, since we live in a country where liberty suffers every character to spread itself to its utmost bulk, and which therefore produces more originals than all the rest of the world together. Of Tragedy he concluded business to be the soul, and yet often hinted that love predominates too much upon the modern stage.

He was now an acknowledged Critick, and had his own seat in a coffee-house, and headed a party in the pit. *Minim* has more vanity than ill-nature, and seldom desires to do much mischief; he will perhaps murmur a little in the ear of him that sits next him, but endeavours to influence the audience to favour, by clapping when an actor exclaims *ye Gods,* or laments the misery of his country.

By degrees he was admitted to Rehearsals, and many of his friends are of opinion, that our present Poets are indebted to him for their happiest thoughts; by his contrivance the bell was rung twice in *Barbarossa,* and by his persuasion the author of *Cleone* concluded his Play without a couplet;[9] for what can be more absurd, said *Minim,* than that part of a play should be rhymed, and part written in blank verse? and by what acquisition of faculties is the Speaker who never could find rhymes before, enabled to rhyme at the conclusion of an Act?

He is the great investigator of hidden beauties, and is particu-

larly delighted when he finds *the Sound an Echo to the Sense*.[10] He
has read all our Poets with particular attention to this delicacy of
Versification, and wonders at the supineness with which their
Works have been hitherto perused, so that no man has found
the sound of a Drum in his distich,

> When Pulpit, Drum ecclesiastic,
> Was beat with fist instead of a stick;

and that the wonderful lines upon Honour and a Bubble have
hitherto passed without notice,

> Honour is like the glassy Bubble,
> Which costs Philosophers such trouble;
> Where one part crack'd, the whole does fly,
> And Wits are crack'd to find out why.[11]

In these Verses, says *Minim*, we have two striking accommoda-
tions of the Sound to the Sense. It is impossible to utter the two
lines emphatically without an act like that which they describe;
Bubble and *Trouble* causing a momentary inflation of the Cheeks
by the retention of the breath, which is afterwards forcibly emit-
ted, as in the practice of *blowing bubbles*. But the greatest excellence is in the third line, which is *crack'd* in the middle to express a
crack, and then shivers into monosyllables. Yet has this diamond
lain neglected with common stones, and among the innumerable
admirers of *Hudibras* the observation of this superlative passage
has been reserved for the sagacity of *Minim*.

IDLER NO. 61. SATURDAY, JUNE 16, 1759

Mr. Minim had now advanced himself to the zenith of critical
reputation; when he was in the Pit, every eye in the Boxes was
fixed upon him; when he entered his Coffee-house, he was sur-
rounded by circles of candidates, who passed their noviciate of
literature under his tuition; his opinion was asked by all who had
no opinion of their own, and yet loved to debate and decide; and
no composition was supposed to pass in safety to posterity, till it
had been secured by *Minim*'s approbation.

Minim professes great admiration of the wisdom and munificence by which the Academies of the continent were raised, and often wishes for some standard of taste, for some tribunal, to which merit may appeal from caprice, prejudice, and malignity. He has formed a plan for an Academy of Criticism, where every work of Imagination may be read before it is printed, and which shall authoritatively direct the Theatres what pieces to receive or reject, to exclude or to revive.

Such an institution would, in *Dick*'s opinion, spread the fame of *English* Literature over *Europe*, and make *London* the metropolis of elegance and politeness, the place to which the learned and ingenious of all countries would repair for instruction and improvement, and where nothing would any longer be applauded or endured that was not conformed to the nicest rules, and finished with the highest elegance.

Till some happy conjunction of the planets shall dispose our Princes or Ministers to make themselves immortal by such an Academy, *Minim* contents himself to preside four nights in a week in a Critical Society selected by himself, where he is heard without contradiction, and whence his judgment is disseminated through the great vulgar and the small.

When he is placed in the chair of Criticism, he declares loudly for the noble simplicity of our ancestors, in opposition to the petty refinements, and ornamental luxuriance. Sometimes he is sunk in despair, and perceives false delicacy daily gaining ground, and sometimes brightens his countenance with a gleam of hope, and predicts the revival of the true sublime. He then fulminates his loudest censures against the monkish barbarity of rhyme; wonders how beings that pretend to reason can be pleased with one line always ending like another; tells how unjustly and unnaturally sense is sacrificed to sound; how often the best thoughts are mangled by the necessity of confining or extending them to the dimensions of a couplet; and rejoices that genius has, in our days shaken off the shackles which had encumbered it so long. Yet he allows that rhyme may sometimes be borne, if the lines be often broken, and the pauses judiciously diversified.

From Blank Verse he makes an easy transition to *Milton*, whom he produces as an example of the slow advance of lasting reputation. *Milton* is the only writer whose books *Minim* can read for ever without weariness. What cause it is that exempts this pleasure from satiety he has long and diligently enquired, and believes it to consist in the perpetual variation of the numbers, by which the ear is gratified and the attention awakened. The lines that are commonly thought rugged and unmusical, he conceives to have been written to temper the melodious luxury of the rest, or to express things by a proper cadence: for he scarcely finds a verse that has not this favourite beauty; he declares that he could shiver in a hot-house when he reads that

> the ground
> Burns frore, and cold performs th' effect of fire;

and that when *Milton* bewails his blindness, the verse

> So thick a drop serene has quench'd these orbs,[12]

has, he knows not how, something that strikes him with an obscure sensation like that which he fancies would be felt from the sound of Darkness.

Minim is not so confident of his rules of Judgment as not very eagerly to catch new light from the name of the author. He is commonly so prudent as to spare those whom he cannot resist, unless, as will sometimes happen, he finds the publick combined against them. But a fresh pretender to fame he is strongly inclined to censure, 'till his own honour requires that he commend him. 'Till he knows the success of a composition, he intrenches himself in general terms; there are some new thoughts and beautiful passages, but there is likewise much which he would have advised the author to expunge. He has several favourite epithets, of which he has never settled the meaning, but which are very commodiously applied to books which he has not read, or cannot understand. One is *manly*, another is *dry*, another *stiff*, and another *flimzy*; sometimes he discovers delicacy of style, and sometimes meets with *strange expressions*.

He is never so great, or so happy, as when a youth of promising parts is brought to receive his directions for the prosecution of his studies. He then puts on a very serious air; he advises the pupil to read none but the best Authors, and, when he finds one congenial to his own mind, to study his beauties, but avoid his faults, and, when he sits down to write, to consider how his favorite Author would think at the present time on the present occasion. He exhorts him to catch those moments when he finds his thoughts expanded and his genius exalted, but to take care lest imagination hurry him beyond the bounds of Nature. He holds Diligence the mother of Success, yet enjoins him, with great earnestness, not to read more than he can digest, and not to confuse his mind by pursuing studies of contrary tendencies. He tells him, that every man has his genius, and that *Cicero* could never be a Poet. The boy retires illuminated, resolves to follow his genius, and to think how *Milton* would have thought; and *Minim* feasts upon his own beneficence till another day brings another Pupil.

ADVENTURER no. 138. SATURDAY, MARCH 2, 1754

Quid purè tranquillet? honos, an dulce lucellum,
An secretum iter et fallentis semita vitae?   HOR.[13]

Whether the tranquil mind and pure,
Honours or wealth our bliss insure;
Or down through life unknown to stray,
Where lonely leads the silent way.   FRANCIS.

Having considered the importance of authors to the welfare of the public, I am led by a natural train of thought, to reflect on their condition with regard to themselves; and to enquire, what degree of happiness or vexation is annexed to the difficult and laborious employment, of providing instruction or entertainment for mankind.

In estimating the pain or pleasure of any particular state, every man, indeed, draws his decisions from his own breast, and cannot with certainty determine, whether other minds are affected by the same causes in the same manner. Yet by this criterion we must be content to judge, because no other can be obtained; and, indeed, we have no reason to think it very fallacious, for excepting here and there an anomalous mind, which either does not feel like others, or dissembles its sensibility, we find men unanimously concur in attributing happiness or misery to particular conditions, as they agree in acknowledging the cold of winter and the heat of autumn.

If we apply to authors themselves for an account of their state, it will appear very little to deserve envy; for they have in all ages been addicted to complaint. The neglect of learning, the ingratitude of the present age, and the absurd preference by which ignorance and dullness often obtain favour and rewards, have been from age to age topics of invective; and few have left their names to posterity, without some appeal to future candour from the perverseness and malice of their own times.

I have, nevertheless, been often inclined to doubt, whether authors, however querulous, are in reality more miserable than their fellow mortals. The present life is to all a state of infelicity; every man, like an author, believes himself to merit more than he obtains, and solaces the present with the prospect of the future; others, indeed, suffer those disappointments in silence, of which the writer complains, to shew how well he has learnt the art of lamentation.

There is at least one gleam of felicity, of which few writers have missed the enjoyment: he whose hopes have so far overpowered his fears, as that he has resolved to stand forth a candidate for fame, seldom fails to amuse himself, before his appearance, with pleasing scenes of affluence or honour; while his fortune is yet under the regulation of fancy, he easily models it to his wish, suffers no thoughts of critics or rivals to intrude upon his mind, but counts over the bounties of patronage or listens to the voice of praise.

Some there are, that talk very luxuriously of the second period of an author's happiness, and tell of the tumultuous raptures of invention, when the mind riots in imagery, and the choice stands suspended between different sentiments.

These pleasures, I believe, may sometimes be indulged to those, who come to a subject of disquisition with minds full of ideas, and with fancies so vigorous, as easily to excite, select, and arrange them. To write, is, indeed, no unpleasing employment, when one sentiment readily produces another, and both ideas and expressions present themselves at the first summons: but such happiness, the greatest genius does not always obtain; and common writers know it only to such a degree, as to credit its possibility. Composition is, for the most part, an effort of slow diligence and steady perseverance, to which the mind is dragged by necessity or resolution, and from which the attention is every moment starting to more delightful amusements.

It frequently happens, that a design which, when considered at a distance, gave flattering hopes of facility, mocks us in the execution with unexpected difficulties; the mind which, while it considered it in the gross, imagined itself amply furnished with materials, finds sometimes an unexpected barrenness and vacuity, and wonders whither all those ideas are vanished, which a little before seemed struggling for emission.

Sometimes many thoughts present themselves; but so confused and unconnected, that they are not without difficulty reduced to method, or concatenated in a regular and dependent series: the mind falls at once into a labyrinth, of which neither the beginning nor end can be discovered, and toils and struggles without progress or extrication.

It is asserted by HORACE, that "if matter be once got together, words will be found with very little difficulty;"[14] a position which, though sufficiently plausible to be inserted in poetical precepts, is by no means strictly and philosophically true. If words were naturally and necessarily consequential to sentiments, it would always follow, that he who has most knowledge must have most eloquence, and that every man would clearly express what he fully understood: yet we find, that to think, and to discourse, are often the qualities of different persons; and many books might surely be produced, where just and noble sentiments are degraded and obscured by unsuitable diction.

Words, therefore, as well as things, claim the care of an author. Indeed, of many authors, and those not useless or contemptible, words are almost the only care: many make it their study, not so much to strike out new sentiments, as to recommend those which are already known to more favourable notice by fairer decorations; but every man, whether he copies or invents, whether he delivers his own thoughts or those of another, has often found himself deficient in the power of expression, big with ideas which he could not utter, obliged to ransack his memory for terms adequate to his conceptions, and at last unable to impress upon his reader the image existing in his own mind.

It is one of the common distresses of a writer to be within a word of a happy period, to want only a single epithet to give amplification its full force, to require only a correspondent term in order to finish a paragraph with elegance and make one of its members answer to the other: but these deficiencies cannot always be supplied; and after long study and vexation, the passage is turned anew, and the web unwoven that was so nearly finished.

But when thoughts and words are collected and adjusted, and the whole composition at last concluded, it seldom gratifies the author, when he comes coolly and deliberately to review it, with the hopes which had been excited in the fury of the performance: novelty always captivates the mind; as our thoughts rise fresh upon us, we readily believe them just and original, which, when the pleasure of production is over, we find to be mean and common, or borrowed from the works of others, and supplied by memory rather than invention.

But though it should happen, that the writer finds no such faults in his performance, he is still to remember, that he looks upon it with partial eyes; and when he considers, how much men who could judge of others with great exactness, have often failed in judging of themselves, he will be afraid of deciding too hastily in his own favour, or of allowing himself to contemplate with too much complacence, treasure that has not yet been brought to the test, nor passed the only trial that can stamp its value.

From the public, and only from the public, is he to await a confirmation of his claim, and a final justification of self esteem; but the public is not easily persuaded to favour an author. If mankind were left to judge for themselves, it is reasonable to imagine, that of such writings, at least, as describe the movements of the human passions, and of which every man carries the arche-type within him, a just opinion would be formed; but whoever has remarked the fate of books, must have found it governed by other causes, than general consent arising from general conviction. If a new performance happens not to fall into the hands of some, who have courage to tell, and authority to propagate their opinion, it often remains long in obscurity, and perhaps perishes unknown and unexamined. A few, a very few, commonly constitute the taste of the time; the judgment which they have once pronounced, some are too lazy to discuss, and some too timorous to contradict: it may, however, be I think observed that their power is greater to depress than exalt, as mankind are more credulous of censure than of praise.

This perversion of the public judgment, is not to be rashly numbered amongst the miseries of an author; since it commonly serves, after miscarriage, to reconcile him to himself. Because the world has sometimes passed an unjust sentence, he readily concludes the sentence unjust by which his performance is condemned; because some have been exalted above their merits by partiality, he is sure to ascribe the success of a rival, not to the merit of his work, but the zeal of his patrons. Upon the whole, as the author seems to share all the common miseries of life, he appears to partake likewise of its lenitives and abatements.

RAMBLER no. 121. Tuesday, May 14, 1751

O imitatores, servum pecus!   Hor.[15]

Away, ye imitators, servile herd!   Elphinston.

I have been informed by a letter, from one of the universities, that among the youth from whom the next swarm of reasoners is to learn philosophy, and the next flight of beauties to hear elegies and sonnets, there are many, who, instead of endeavouring by books and meditation to form their own opinions, content themselves with the secondary knowledge, which a convenient bench in a coffee-house can supply; and, without any examinations or distinction, adopt the criticisms and remarks, which happen to drop from those, who have risen, by merit or fortune, to reputation and authority.

These humble retailers of knowledge my correspondent stigmatizes with the name of *Echoes*; and seems desirous, that they should be made ashamed of lazy submission, and animated to attempts after new discoveries, and original sentiments.

It is very natural for young men to be vehement, acrimonious, and severe. For, as they seldom comprehend at once all the consequences of a position, or perceive the difficulties by which cooler and more experienced reasoners are restrained from confidence, they form their conclusions with great precipitance. Seeing nothing that can darken or embarrass the question, they expect to find their own opinion universally prevalent, and are inclined to impute uncertainty and hesitation to want of honesty, rather than of knowledge. I may, perhaps, therefore be reproached by my lively correspondent, when it shall be found, that I have no inclination to persecute these collectors of fortuitous knowledge with the severity required; yet, as I am now too old to be much pained by hasty censure, I shall not be afraid of taking into protection those whom I think condemned without a sufficient knowledge of their cause.

He that adopts the sentiments of another, whom he has reason to believe wiser than himself, is only to be blamed, when he claims the honours which are not due but to the author, and endeavours to deceive the world into praise and veneration; for, to learn, is the proper business of youth; and whether we encrease our knowledge by books, or by conversation, we are equally indebted to foreign assistance.

The greater part of students are not born with abilities to construct systems, or advance knowledge; nor can have any hope beyond that of becoming intelligent hearers in the schools of art, of being able to comprehend what others discover, and to remember what others teach. Even those to whom Providence has allotted greater strength of understanding, can expect only to improve a single science. In every other part of learning, they must be content to follow opinions, which they are not able to examine; and, even in that which they claim as peculiarly their own, can seldom add more than some small particle of knowledge, to the hereditary stock devolved to them from ancient times, the collective labour of a thousand intellects.

In science, which being fixed and limited, admits of no other variety than such as arises from new methods of distribution, or new arts of illustration, the necessity of following the traces of our predecessors is indisputably evident; but there appears no reason, why imagination should be subject to the same restraint. It might be conceived, that of those who profess to forsake the narrow paths of truth every one may deviate towards a different point, since though rectitude is uniform and fixed, obliquity may be infinitely diversified. The roads of science are narrow, so that they who travel them, must either follow or meet one another; but in the boundless regions of possibility, which fiction claims for her dominion, there are surely a thousand recesses unexplored, a thousand flowers unplucked, a thousand fountains unexhausted, combinations of imagery yet unobserved, and races of ideal inhabitants not hitherto described.

Yet, whatever hope may persuade, or reason evince, experience can boast of very few additions to ancient fable. The wars of *Troy*, and the travels of *Ulysses*, have furnished almost all succeeding poets with incidents, characters, and sentiments.[16] The *Romans* are confessed to have attempted little more than to display in their own tongue the inventions of the *Greeks*. There is, in all their writings, such a perpetual recurrence of allusions to the tales of the fabulous age, that they must be confessed often to want that power of giving pleasure which novelty supplies; nor can we wonder, that they excelled so much in the graces of diction, when we consider how rarely they were employed in search of new thoughts.

The warmest admirers of the great *Mantuan* poet[17] can extol him for little more than the skill with which he has, by making his hero both a traveller and a warrior, united the beauties of the *Iliad* and *Odyssey* in one composition: yet his judgment was perhaps sometimes overborn by his avarice of the *Homeric* treasures; and, for fear of suffering a sparkling ornament to be lost, he has inserted it where it cannot shine with its original splendor.

When *Ulysses* visited the infernal regions, he found, among the heroes that perished at *Troy*, his competitor *Ajax*, who, when the arms of *Achilles* were adjudged to *Ulysses*, died by his own hand in the madness of disappointment. He still appeared to resent, as on earth, his loss and disgrace. *Ulysses* endeavoured to pacify him with praises and submission; but *Ajax* walked away without reply. This passage has always been considered as eminently beautiful; because *Ajax*, the haughty chief, the unlettered soldier, of unshaken courage, of immoveable constancy, but without the power of recommending his own virtues by eloquence, or enforcing his assertions by any other argument than the sword, had no way of making his anger known, but by gloomy sullenness, and dumb ferocity. His hatred of a man whom he conceived to have defeated him only by volubility of tongue, was therefore naturally shewn by silence more contemptuous and piercing than any words that so rude an orator could have found, and by which he gave his enemy no opportunity of exerting the only power in which he was superior.

When *Aeneas* is sent by *Virgil* to the shades, he meets *Dido* the queen of *Carthage*, whom his perfidy had hurried to the grave; he accosts her with tenderness and excuses; but the lady turns away like *Ajax* in mute disdain. She turns away like *Ajax*, but she resembles him in none of those qualities which give either dignity or propriety to silence. She might, without any departure from the tenour of her conduct, have burst out like other injured women into clamour, reproach, and denunciation; but *Virgil* had his imagination full of *Ajax*, and therefore could not prevail on himself to teach *Dido* any other mode of resentment.

If *Virgil* could be thus seduced by imitation, there will be little hope, that common wits should escape; and accordingly we find, that besides the universal and acknowledged practice of copying the ancients, there has prevailed in every age a particular species of fiction. At one time all truth was conveyed in allegory; at another, nothing was seen but in a vision; at one period, all the poets followed sheep, and every event produced a pastoral; at another they busied themselves wholly in giving directions to a painter.

It is indeed easy to conceive why any fashion should become popular, by which idleness is favoured, and imbecillity assisted; but surely no man of genius can much applaud himself for repeating a tale with which the audience is already tired, and which could bring no honour to any but its inventor.

There are, I think, two schemes of writing, on which the laborious wits of the present time employ their faculties. One is the adaptation of sense to all the rhymes which our language can supply to some word, that makes the burden of the stanza; but this, as it has been only used in a kind of amorous burlesque, can scarcely be censured with much acrimony. The other is the imitation of *Spenser*, which, by the influence of some men of learning and genius, seems likely to gain upon the age, and therefore deserves to be more attentively considered.

To imitate the fictions and sentiments of *Spenser* can incur no reproach, for allegory is perhaps one of the most pleasing vehicles of instruction. But I am very far from extending the same respect to his diction or his stanza. His stile was in his own time allowed to be vicious, so darkened with old words and peculiarities of phrase, and so remote from common use, that *Johnson* boldly pronounces him *to have written no language*.[18] His stanza is at once difficult and unpleasing; tiresome to the ear by its uniformity, and to the attention by its length. It was at first formed in imitation of the *Italian* poets, without due regard to the genius of our language. The *Italians* have little variety of termination, and were forced to contrive such a stanza as might admit the greatest number of similar rhymes; but our words end with so much diversity, that it is seldom convenient for us to bring more than two of the same sound together. If it be justly observed by *Milton*,[19] that rhyme obliges poets to express their thoughts in improper terms, these improprieties must always be mulitiplied, as the difficulty of rhyme is encreased by long concentrations.

The imitators of *Spenser* are indeed not very rigid censors of themselves, for they seem to conclude, that when they have disfigured their lines with a few obsolete syllables, they have accomplished their design, without considering that they ought not only to admit old words, but to avoid new. The laws of imitation are broken by every word introduced since the time of *Spenser*, as the character of *Hector* is violated by quoting *Aristotle* in the play.[20] It would indeed be difficult to exclude from a long poem all modern phrases, though it is easy to sprinkle it with gleanings of antiquity. Perhaps, however, the stile of *Spenser* might by long labour be justly copied; but life is surely given us for higher purposes than to gather what our ancestors have wisely thrown away, and to learn what is of no value, but because it has been forgotten.

RAMBLER NO. 154. SATURDAY, SEPT. 7, 1751

—Tibi res antiquae laudis & artis
Aggredior, sanctos ausus recludere fontes.   VIRG.[21]

For thee my tuneful accents will I raise,
And treat of arts disclos'd in ancient days;
Once more unlock for thee the sacred spring.   DRYDEN.

The direction of *Aristotle* to those that study politicks, is, first to examine and understand what has been written by the ancients upon government; then to cast their eyes round upon the world, and consider by what causes the prosperity of communities is visibly influenced, and why some are worse, and others better administered.[22]

The same method must be pursued by him who hopes to become eminent in any other part of knowledge. The first task is to search books, the next to contemplate nature. He must first possess himself of the intellectual treasures which the diligence of former ages has accumulated, and then endeavour to encrease them by his own collections.

The mental disease of the present generation, is impatience of study, contempt of the great masters of ancient wisdom, and a disposition to rely wholly upon unassisted genius and natural sagacity. The wits of these happy days have discovered a way to fame, which the dull caution of our laborious ancestors durst never attempt; they cut the knots of sophistry which it was formerly the business of years to untie, solve difficulties by sudden irradiations of intelligence, and comprehend long processes of argument by immediate intuition.

Men who have flattered themselves into this opinion of their own abilities, look down on all who waste their lives over books, as a race of inferior beings condemned by nature to perpetual pupillage, and fruitlessly endeavouring to remedy their barrenness by incessant cultivation, or succour their feebleness by subsidiary strength. They presume that none would be more industrious than they, if they were not more sensible of deficiencies, and readily conclude, that he who places no confidence in his own powers, owes his modesty only to his weakness.

It is however certain that no estimate is more in danger of erroneous calculations than those by which a man computes the force of his own genius. It generally happens at our entrance into the world, that by the natural attraction of similitude, we associate with men like ourselves young, sprightly, and ignorant, and rate our accomplishments by comparison with theirs; when we have once obtained an acknowledged superiority over our acquaintances, imagination and desire easily extend it over the rest of mankind, and if no accident forces us into new emulations, we grow old, and die in admiration of ourselves.

Vanity, thus confirmed in her dominion, readily listens to the voice of idleness, and sooths the slumber of life with continual dreams of excellence and greatness. A man elated by confidence in his natural vigor of fancy and sagacity of conjecture, soon concludes that he already possesses whatever toil and enquiry can confer. He then listens with eagerness to the wild objections which folly has raised against the common means of improvement; talks of the dark chaos of indigested knowledge; describes the mischievous effects of heterogeneous sciences fermenting in the mind; relates the blunders of lettered ignorance; expatiates on the heroick merit of those who deviate from prescription, or shake off authority; and gives vent to the inflations of his heart by declaring that he owes nothing to pedants and universities.

All these pretensions, however confident, are very often vain. The laurels which superficial acuteness gains in triumphs over ignorance unsupported by vivacity, are observed by *Locke*[23] to be lost whenever real learning and rational diligence appear against her; the sallies of gaiety are soon repressed by calm confidence, and the artifices of subtilty are readily detected by those who having carefully studied the question, are not easily confounded or surprised.

But though the contemner of books had neither been deceived by others nor himself, and was really born with a genius surpassing the ordinary abilities of mankind; yet surely such gifts of providence may be more properly urged as incitements to labour, than encouragements to negligence. He that neglects the culture of ground, naturally fertile, is more shamefully culpable than he whose field would scarcely recompence his husbandry.

CICERO remarks, that not to know what has been transacted in former times is to continue always as a child. [24] If no use is made of the labours of past ages, the world must remain always in the infancy of knowledge. The discoveries of every man must terminate in his own advantage, and the studies of every age be employed on questions which the past generation had discussed and determined. We may with as little reproach borrow science as manufactures from our ancestors; and it is as rational to live in caves till our own hands have erected a palace, as to reject all knowledge of architecture, which our understandings will not supply.

To the strongest and quickest mind it is far easier to learn than to invent. The principles of arithmetick and geometry may be comprehended by a close attention in a few days; yet who can flatter himself that the study of a long life would have enabled him to discover them, when he sees them yet unknown to so many nations, whom he cannot suppose less liberally endowed with natural reason,.than the *Grecians* or *Egyptians*?

Every science was thus far advanced towards perfection, by the emulous diligence of contemporary students, and the gradual discoveries of one age improving on another. Sometimes unexpected flashes of instruction were struck out by the fortuitous collision of happy incidents, or an involuntary concurrence of ideas, in which the philosopher to whom they happened had no other merit than that of knowing their value, and transmitting unclouded to posterity that light which had been kindled by causes out of his power. The happiness of these casual illuminations no man can promise to himself, because no endeavours can procure them; and therefore, whatever be our abilities or application, we must submit to learn from others what perhaps would have lain hid for ever from human penetration, had not some remote enquiry brought it to view; as treasures are thrown up by the ploughman and the digger in the rude exercise of their common occupations.

The man whose genius qualifies him for great undertakings, must at least be content to learn from books the present state of human knowledge; that he may not ascribe to himself the invention of arts generally known; weary his attention with experiments of which the event has been long registered; and waste, in attempts which have already succeeded or miscarried, that time which might have been spent with usefulness and honour upon new undertakings.

But though the study of books is necessary, it is not sufficient to constitute literary eminence. He that wishes to be counted among the benefactors of posterity, must add by his own toil to the acquisitions of his ancestors, and secure his memory from neglect by some valuable improvement. This can only be effected by looking out upon the wastes of the intellectual world, and extending the power of learning over regions yet undisciplined and barbarous; or by surveying more exactly her antient dominions, and driving ignorance from the fortresses and retreats where she skulks undetected and undisturbed. Every science has its difficulties which yet call for solution before we attempt new systems of knowledge; as every country has its forests and marshes, which it would be wise to cultivate and drain, before distant colonies are projected as a necessary discharge of the exuberance of inhabitants.

No man ever yet became great by imitation. Whatever hopes for the veneration of mankind must have invention in the design or execution; either the effect must itself be new, or the means by which it is produced. Either truths hitherto unknown must be discovered, or those which are already known enforced by stronger evidence, facilitated by clearer method, or ellucidated by brighter illustrations.

Fame cannot spread wide or endure long that is not rooted in nature, and manured by art. That which hopes to resist the blast of malignity, and stand firm against the attacks of time, must contain in itself some original principle of growth. The reputation which arises from the detail or transposition of borrowed sentiments, may spread for a while, like ivy on the rind of antiquity, but will be torn away by accident or contempt, and suffered to rot unheeded on the ground.

RAMBLER no. 4. SATURDAY, MARCH 31, 1750

Simul et jucunda et idonea dicere Vitae. ' HOR.[25]

And join both profit and delight in one.   CREECH.

The works of fiction, with which the present generation seems more particularly delighted, are such as exhibit life in its true state, diversified only be accidents that daily happen in the world, and influenced by passions and qualities which are really to be found in conversing with mankind.

This kind of writing may be termed not improperly the comedy of romance, and is to be conducted nearly by the rules of comic poetry. Its province is to bring about natural events by easy means, and to keep up curiosity without the help of wonder: it is therefore precluded from the machines and expedients of the heroic romance, and can neither employ giants to snatch away a lady from the nuptial rites, nor knights to bring her back from captivity; it can neither bewilder its personages in desarts, nor lodge them in imaginary castles.

I remember a remark made by Scaliger upon Pontanus, that all his writings are filled with the same images; and that if you take from him his lillies and his roses, his satyrs and his dryads, he will have nothing left that can be called poetry. In like manner, almost all the fictions of the last age will vanish, if you deprive them of a hermit and a wood, a battle and a shipwreck.

Why this wild strain of imagination found reception so long, in polite and learned ages, it is not easy to conceive; but we cannot wonder that, while readers could be procured, the authors were willing to continue it: for when a man had by practice gained some fluency of language, he had no further care than to retire to his closet, let loose his invention, and heat his mind with incredibilities; a book was thus produced without fear of criticism, without the toil of study, without knowledge of nature, or acquaintance with life.

The task of our present writers is very different; it requires, together with that learning which is to be gained from books, that experience which can never be attained by solitary diligence, but must arise from general converse, and accurate observation of the living world. Their performances have, as Horace expresses it, *plus oneris quantum veniae minus*, little indulgence, and therefore more difficulty.[26] They are engaged in portraits of which every one knows the original, and can detect any deviation from exactness of resemblance. Other writings are safe, except from the malice of learning, but these are in danger from every common reader; as the the slipper ill executed was censured by a shoemaker who happened to stop in his way at the Venus of Apelles.[27]

But the fear of not being approved as just copyers of human manners, is not the most important concern that an author of this sort ought to have before him. These books are written chiefly to the young, the ignorant, and the idle, to whom they serve as lectures of conduct, and introductions into life. They are the entertainment of minds unfurnished with ideas, and therefore easily susceptible of impressions; not fixed by principles, and therefore easily following the current of fancy; not informed by experience, and consequently open to every false suggestion and partial account.

That the highest degree of reverence should be paid to youth, and that nothing indecent should be suffered to approach their eyes or ears; are precepts extorted by sense and virtue from an ancient writer, by no means eminent for chasity of thought.[28] The same kind, tho' not the same degree of caution, is required to everything which is laid before them, to secure them from unjust prejudices, perverse opinions, and incongruous combinations of images.

In the romances formerly written, every transaction and sentiment was so remote from all that passes among men, that the reader was in very little danger of making any applications to himself; the virtues and crimes were equally beyond his sphere of activity; and he amused himself with heroes and with traitors, deliverers and persecutors, as with beings of another species, whose actions were regulated upon motives of their own, and who had neither faults nor excellencies in common with himself.

But when an adventurer is levelled with the rest of the world, and acts in such scenes of the universal drama, as may be the lot of any other man; young spectators fix their eyes upon him with closer attention, and hope by observing his behaviour and success to regulate their own practices, when they shall be engaged in the like part.

For this reason these familiar histories may perhaps be made of greater use than the solemnities of professed morality, and convey the knowledge of vice and virtue with more efficacy than axioms and definitions. But if the power of example is so great, as to take possession of the memory by a kind of violence, and produce effects almost without the intervention of the will, care ought to be taken that, when the choice is unrestrained, the best examples only should be exhibited; and that which is likely to operate so strongly, should not be mischievous or uncertain in its effects.

The chief advantage which these fictions have over real life is, that their authors are at liberty, tho' not to invent, yet to select objects, and to cull from the mass of mankind, those individuals upon which the attention ought most to be employ'd; as a diamond, though it cannot be made, may be polished by art, and placed in such a situation, as to display that lustre which before was buried among common stones.

It is justly considered as the greatest excellency of art, to imitate nature; but it is necessary to distinguish those parts of nature, which are most proper for imitation: greater care is still required in representing life, which is so often discoloured by passion, or deformed by wickedness. If the world be promiscuously described, I cannot see of what use it can be to read the account; or why it may not be as safe to turn the eye immediately upon mankind, as upon a mirror which shows all that presents itself without discrimination.[29]

It is therefore not a sufficient vindication of a character, that it is drawn as it appears, for many characters ought never to be drawn; nor of a narrative, that the train of events is agreeable to observation and experience, for that observation which is called knowledge of the world, will be found much more frequently to make men cunning than good. The purpose of these writings is surely not only to show mankind, but to provide that they may be seen hereafter with less hazard; to teach the means of avoiding the snares which are laid by TREACHERY for INNOCENCE, without infusing any wish for that superiority with which the betrayer flatters his vanity; to give the power of counteracting fraud, without the temptation to practise it; to initiate youth by mock encounters in the art of necessary defence, and to increase prudence without impairing virtue.

Many writers, for the sake of following nature, so mingle good and bad qualities in their principal personages, that they are both equally conspicuous; and as we accompany them through their adventures with delight, and are led by degrees to interest ourselves in their favour, we lose the abhorrence of their faults, because they do not hinder our pleasure, or, perhaps, regard them with some kindness for being united with so much merit.

There have been men indeed splendidly wicked, whose endowments threw a brightness on their crimes, and whom scarce any villainy made perfectly detestable, because they never could be wholly divested of their excellencies; but such have been in all ages the great corrupters of the world, and their resemblance ought no more to be preserved, than the art of murdering without pain.

Some have advanced, without due attention to the consequences of this notion, that certain virtues have their correspondent faults, and therefore that to exhibit either apart is to deviate from probability. Thus men are observed by Swift to be "grateful in the same degree as they are resentful." This principle, with others of the same kind, supposes man to act from a brute impulse, and persue a certain degree of inclination, without any choice of the object; for, otherwise, though it should be allowed that gratitude and resentment arise from the same constitution of the passions, it follows not that they will be equally indulged when reason is consulted; yet unless that consequence be admitted, this sagacious maxim becomes an empty sound, without any relation to practice or to life.

Nor is it evident, that even the first motions to these effects are always in the same proportion. For pride, which produces quickness of resentment, will obstruct gratitude, by unwillingness to admit that inferiority which obligation implies; and it is very unlikely, that he who cannot think he receives a favour will acknowledge or repay it.

It is of the utmost importance to mankind, that positions of this tendency should be laid open and confuted; for while men consider good and evil as springing from the same root, they will spare the one for the sake of the other, and in judging, if not of others at least of themselves, will be apt to estimate their virtues by their vices. To this fatal error all those will contribute, who confound the colours of right and, wrong, and instead of helping to settle their boundaries, mix them with so much art, that no common mind is able to disunite them.

In narratives, where historical veracity has no place, I cannot discover why there should not be exhibited the most perfect idea of virtue; of virtue not angelical, nor above probability, for what we cannot credit we shall never imitate, but the highest and purest that humanity can reach, which, exercised in such trials as the various revolutions of things shall bring upon it, may, by conquering some calamities, and enduring others, teach us what we may hope, and what we can perform. Vice, for vice is necessary to be shewn, should always disgust; nor should the graces of gaiety, or the dignity of courage, be so united with it, as to reconcile it to the mind. Wherever it appears, it should raise hatred by the malignity of its practices, and contempt by the meanness of its stratagems; for while it is supported by either parts or spirit, it will be seldom heartily abhorred. The Roman tyrant was content to be hated, if he was but feared,[30] and there are thousands of the readers of romances willing to be thought wicked, if they may be allowed to be wits. It is therefore to be steadily inculcated, that virtue is the highest proof of understanding, and the only solid basis of greatness; and that vice is the natural consequence of narrow thoughts, that it begins in mistake, and ends in ignominy.

RAMBLER NO. 60. SATURDAY, OCTOBER 13, 1750

—Quid sit pulchrum, quid turpe, quid utile, quid non,
Plenius et melius Chrysippo et Crantore dicit.   HOR.[31]

Whose works the beautiful and base contain;
Of vice and virtue more instructive rules,
Than all the sober sages of the schools.   FRANCIS.

All joy or sorrow for the happiness or calamities of others is produced by an act of the imagination, that realises the event however fictitious, or approximates it however remote, by placing us, for a time, in the condition of him whose fortune we contemplate; so that we feel, while the deception lasts, whatever motions would be excited by the same good or evil happening to ourselves.

Our passions are therefore more strongly moved, in proportion as we can more readily adopt the pains or pleasure proposed to our minds, by recognizing them as once our own, or considering them as naturally incident to our state of life. It is not easy for the most artful writer to give us an interest in happiness or misery, which we think ourselves never likely to feel, and with which we have never yet been made acquainted. Histories of the downfal of kingdoms, and revolutions of empires, are read with great tranquillity; the imperial tragedy pleases common auditors only by its pomp of ornament, and grandeur of ideas; and the man whose faculties have been engrossed by business, and whose heart never fluttered but at the rise or fall of stocks, wonders how the attention can be seized, or the affection agitated by a tale of love.

Those parallel circumstances, and kindred images, to which we readily conform our minds, are, above all other writings, to be found in narratives of the lives of particular persons; and therefore no species of writing seems more worthy of cultivation than biography, since none can be more delightful or more useful, none can more certainly enchain the heart by irresistible interest, or more widely diffuse instruction to every diversity of condition.

The general and rapid narratives of history, which involve a

thousand fortunes in the business of a day, and complicate innumerable incidents in one great transaction, afford few lessons
applicable to private life, which derives its comforts and its
wretchedness from the right or wrong management of things
which nothing but their frequency makes considerable, *Parva, si
non fiant quotidie* [Slight things, were they not daily],[32] says Pliny,
and which can have no place in those relations which never
descend below the consultation of senates, the motions of armies,
and the schemes of conspirators.

I have often thought that there has rarely passed a life of which
a judicious and faithful narrative would not be useful. For, not
only every man has, in the mighty mass of the world, great
numbers in the same condition with himself, to whom his mistakes and miscarriages, escapes and expedients, would be of
immediate and apparent use; but there is such an uniformity in
the state of man, considered apart from adventitious and separ-
able decorations and disguises, that there is scarce any possibility
of good or ill, but is common to human kind. A great part of the
time of those who are placed at the greatest distance by fortune,
or by temper, must unavoidably pass in the same manner; and
though, when the claims of nature are satisfied, caprice, and
vanity, and accident, begin to produce discriminations and
peculiarities, yet the eye is not very heedful, or quick, which
cannot discover the same causes still terminating their influence
in the same effects, though sometimes accelerated, sometimes
retarded, or perplexed by multiplied combinations. We are all
prompted by the same motives, all deceived by the same fallacies,
all animated by hope, obstructed by danger, entangled by desire,
and seduced by pleasure.

It is frequently objected to relations of particular lives, that they
are not distinguished by any striking or wonderful vicissitudes.
The scholar who passed his life among his books, the merchant
who conducted only his own affairs, the priest, whose sphere of
action was not extended beyond that of his duty, are considered
as no proper objects of publick regard, however they might have
excelled in their several stations, whatever might have been their
learning, integrity, and piety. But this notion arises from false

measures of excellence and dignity, and must be eradicated by considering, that, in the esteem of uncorrupted reason, what is of most use is of most value.

It is, indeed, not improper to take honest advantages of prejudice, and to gain attention by a celebrated name; but the business of the biographer is often to pass slightly over those performances and incidents, which produce vulgar greatness, to lead the thoughts into domestick privacies, and display the minute details of daily life, where exterior appendages are cast aside, and men excel each other only by prudence and by virtue. The account of Thuanus is, with great propriety, said by its author to have been written, that it might lay open to posterity the private and familiar character of that man, *cujus ingenium et candorem ex ipsius scriptis sunt olim semper miraturi,* whose candour and genius will to the end of time be by his writings preserved in admiration.[33]

There are many invisible circumstances which, whether we read as enquirers[34] after natural or moral knowledge, whether we intend to enlarge our science, or increase our virtue, are more important than publick occurrences. Thus Salust, the great master of nature, has not forgot, in his account of Catiline, to remark that *his walk was now quick, and again slow,* as an indication of a mind revolving something with violent commotion. Thus the story of Melancthon affords a striking lecture on the value of time, by informing us, that when he made an appointment, he expected not only the hour, but the minute to be fixed, that the day might not run out in the idleness of suspense; and all the plans and enterprizes of De Wit are now of less importance to the world, than that part of his personal character which represents him as *careful of his health, and negligent of his life.*[35]

But biography has often been allotted to writers who seem very little acquainted with the nature of their talk, or very negligent about the performance. They rarely afford any other account than might be collected from publick papers, but imagine themselves writing a life when they exhibit a chronological series of actions or preferments; and so little regard the manners or behaviour of their heroes, that more knowledge may be gained of a man's real character, by a short conversation with one of his servants, than from a formal and studied narrative, begun with his pedigree, and ended with his funeral.

If now and then they condescend to inform the world of particular facts, they are not always so happy as to select the most important. I know not well what advantage posterity can receive from the only circumstance by which Tickell has distinguished Addison from the rest of mankind, *the irregularity of his pulse:* nor can I think myself overpaid for the time spent in reading the life of Malherb, by being enabled to relate, after the learned biographer, that Malherb had two predominant opinions; one, that the looseness of a single woman might destroy all her boast of ancient descent; the other, that the French beggars made use very improperly and barbarously of the phrase *noble Gentlemen*, because either word included the sense of both.[36]

There are, indeed, some natural reasons why these narratives are often written by such as were not likely to give much instruction or delight, and why most accounts of particular persons are barren and useless. If a life be delayed till interest and envy are at an end, we may hope for impartiality, but must expect little intelligence; for the incidents which give excellence to biography are of a volatile and evanescent kind, such as soon escape the memory, and are rarely transmitted by tradition. We know how few can portray a living acquaintance, except by his most prominent and observable particularities, and the grosser features of his mind; and it may be easily imagined how much of this little knowledge may be lost in imparting it, and how soon a succession of copies will lose all resemblance of the original.

If the biographer writes from personal knowledge, and makes haste to gratify the publick curiosity, there is danger lest his interest, his fear, his gratitude, or his tenderness, overpower his fidelity, and tempt him to conceal, if not to invent. There are many who think it an act of piety to hide the faults or failings of their friends, even when they can no longer suffer by their detection; we therefore see whole ranks of characters adorned with uniform panegyrick, and not to be known from one another, but by extrinsick and casual circumstances. "Let me remember," says

Hale, "when I find myself inclined to pity a criminal, that there is likewise a pity due to the country."[37] If we owe regard to the memory of the dead, there is yet more respect to be paid to knowledge, to virtue, and to truth.

RAMBLER no. 36.   SATURDAY, JULY 21, 1750

ʹΑμ' ἕποντο νομῆες
Τερπόμενοι σύριγξι· δόλον δ' οὔτι προνόησαν.   HOMER.[38]

—Piping on their reeds, the shepherds go,
Nor fear an ambush, nor suspect a foe.   POPE.

There is scarcely any species of poetry, that has allured more readers, or excited more writers, than the pastoral. It is generally pleasing, because it entertains the mind with representations of scenes familiar to almost every imagination, and of which all can equally judge whether they are well described. It exhibits a life, to which we have been always accustomed to associate peace, and leisure, and innocence: and therefore we readily set open the heart, for the admission of its images, which contribute to drive away cares and perturbations, and suffer ourselves, without resistance, to be transported to elysian regions, where we are to meet with nothing but joy, and plenty, and contentment; where every gale whispers pleasure; and every shade promises repose.

It has been maintained by some, who love to talk of what they do not know, that pastoral is the most antient poetry; and, indeed, since it is probable, that poetry is nearly of the same antiquity with rational nature, and since the life of the first men was certainly rural, we may reasonably conjecture, that, as their ideas would necessarily be borrowed from those objects with which they were acquainted, their composures, being filled chiefly with such thoughts on the visible creation as must occur to the first observers, were pastoral hymns like those which *Milton* introduces the original pair singing, in the day of innocence, to the praise of their Maker.[39]

For the same reason that pastoral poetry was the first employment of the human imagination, it is generally the first literary amusement of our minds. We have seen fields, and meadows, and groves from the time that our eyes opened upon life; and are pleased with birds, and brooks, and breezes, much earlier than we engage among the actions and passions of mankind. We are therefore delighted with rural pictures, because we know the original at an age when our curiosity can be very little awakened, by descriptions of courts which we never beheld, or representations of passion which we never felt.

The satisfaction received from this kind of writing not only begins early, but lasts long; we do not, as we advance into the intellectual world, throw it away among other childish amusements and pastimes, but willingly return to it in any hour of indolence and relaxation. The images of true pastoral have always the power of exciting delight, because the works of nature, from which they are drawn, have always the same order and beauty, and continue to force themselves upon our thoughts, being at once obvious to the most careless regard, and more than adequate to the strongest reason, and severest contemplation. Our inclination to stillness and tranquillity is seldom much lessened by long knowledge of the busy and tumultuary part of the world. In childhood we turn our thoughts to the country, as to the region of pleasure, we recur to it in old age as a port of rest, and perhaps with that secondary and adventitious gladness, which every man feels on reviewing those places, or recollecting those occurrences, that contributed to his youthful enjoyments, and bring him back to the prime of life, when the world was gay with the bloom of novelty, when mirth wantoned at his side, and hope sparkled before him.

The sense of this universal pleasure has invited *numbers without number* to try their skill in pastoral performances, in which they have generally succeeded after the manner of other imitators, transmitting the same images in the same combination from one to another, till he that reads the title of a poem, may guess at the whole series of the composition; nor will a man, after the perusal of thousands of these performances, find his knowledge enlarged with a single view of nature not produced before, or his imagination amused with any new application of those views to moral purposes.

The range of pastoral is indeed narrow, for though nature itself, philosophically considered, be inexhaustible, yet its general effects on the eye and on the ear are uniform, and incapable of much variety of description. Poetry cannot dwell upon the minuter distinctions, by which one species differs from another, without departing from that simplicity of grandeur which fills the imagination; nor dissect the latent qualities of things, without losing its general power of gratifying every mind by recalling its conceptions. However, as each age makes some discoveries, and those discoveries are by degrees generally known, as new plants or modes of culture are introduced, and by little and little become common, pastoral might receive, from time to time, small augmentations, and exhibit once in a century a scene somewhat varied.

But pastoral subjects have been often, like others, taken into the hands of those that were not qualified to adorn them, men to whom the face of nature was so little known, that they have drawn it only after their own imagination, and changed or distorted her features, that their portraits might appear something more than servile copies from their predecessors.

Not only the images of rural life, but the occasions on which they can be properly produced, are few and general. The state of a man confined to the employments and pleasures of the country, is so little diversified, and exposed to so few of those accidents which produce perplexities, terrors and surprises, in more complicated transactions, that he can be shewn but seldom in such circumstances as attract curiosity. His ambition is without policy, and his love without intrigue. He has no complaints to make of his rival, but that he is richer than himself; nor any disasters to lament, but a cruel mistress, or a bad harvest.

The conviction of the necessity of some new source of pleasure induced *Sannazarius* to remove the scene from the fields to the sea, to substitute fishermen for shepherds, and derive his sentiments from the piscatory life;[40] for which he has been censured by succeeding critics, because the sea is an object of terrour, and by no means proper to amuse the mind, and lay the passions asleep. Against this objection he might be defended by the established maxim, that the poet has a right to select his images, and is no more obliged to shew the sea in a storm, than the land under an inundation; but may display all the pleasures, and conceal the dangers of the water, as he may lay his shepherd under a shady beech, without giving him an ague, or letting a wild beast loose upon him.

There are however two defects in the piscatory eclogue, which perhaps cannot be supplied. The sea, though in hot countries it is considered by those who live, like *Sannazarius,* upon the coast, as a place of pleasure and diversion, has notwithstanding much less variety than the land, and therefore will be sooner exhausted by a descriptive writer. When he has once shewn the sun rising or setting upon it, curled its waters with the vernal breeze, rolled the waves in gentle succession to the shore, and enumerated the fish sporting in the shallows, he has nothing remaining but what is common to all other poetry, the complaint of a nymph for a drowned lover, or the indignation of a fisher that his oysters are refused, and Mycon's accepted.

Another obstacle to the general reception of this kind of poetry, is the ignorance of maritime pleasures, in which the greater part of mankind must always live. To all the inland inhabitants of every region, the sea is only known as an immense diffusion of waters, over which men pass from one country to another, and in which life is frequently lost. They have, therefore, no opportunity of tracing, in their own thoughts, the descriptions of winding shores, and calm bays, nor can look on the poem in which they are mentioned, with other sensations, than on a sea-chart, or the metrical geography of *Dionysius*.

This defect *Sannazarius* was hindered from perceiving, by writing in a learned language to readers generally acquainted with the works of nature; but if he had made his attempt in any vulgar tongue, he would soon have discovered how vainly he had endeavoured to make that loved, which was not understood.

I am afraid it will not be found easy to improve the pastorals of antiquity, by any great additions or diversifications. Our descriptions may indeed differ from those of Virgil, as an English from an Italian summer, and, in some respects, as modern from ancient life; but as nature is in both countries nearly the same, and as poetry has to do rather with the passions of men, which are uniform, than their customs, which are changeable, the varieties, which time or place can furnish, will be inconsiderable: and I shall endeavour to shew, in the next paper, how little the latter ages have contributed to the improvement of the rustick muse.

RAMBLER NO. 37. TUESDAY, JULY 24, 1750

Canto quae solitus, si quando armenta vocabat,
Amphion Dircaeus.   VIRG.[41]

Such strains I sing as once *Amphion* play'd,
When list'ning flocks the pow'rful call obey'd.   ELPHINSTON.

In writing or judging of pastoral poetry, neither the authors nor criticks of latter times seem to have paid sufficient regard to the originals left us by antiquity, but have entangled themselves with unnecessary difficulties, by advancing principles, which, having no foundation in the nature of things, are wholly to be rejected from a species of composition in which, above all others, mere nature is to be regarded.

It is, therefore, necessary to enquire after some more distinct and exact idea of this kind of writing. This may, I think, be easily found in the pastorals of Virgil, from whose opinion it will not appear very safe to depart, if we consider that every advantage of nature, and of fortune, concurred to complete his productions; that he was born with great accuracy and severity of judgment, enlightened with all the learning of one of the brightest ages, and embellished with the elegance of the Roman court; that he employed his powers rather in improving, than inventing, and therefore must have endeavoured to recompense the want of novelty by exactness; that taking Theocritus for his original, he found pastoral far advanced towards perfection, and that having so great a rival, he must have proceeded with uncommon caution.

If we search the writings of Virgil, for the true definition of a pastoral, it will be found *a poem in which any action or passion is represented by its effects upon a country life.* Whatsoever therefore may, according to the common course of things, happen in the country, may afford a subject for a pastoral poet.

In this definition, it will immediately occur to those who are versed in the writings of the modern criticks, that there is no mention of the golden age. I cannot indeed easily discover why it is thought necessary to refer descriptions of a rural state to remote times, nor can I perceive that any writer has consistently preserved the Arcadian manners and sentiments. The only reason, that I have read, on which this rule has been founded, is, that, according to the customs of modern life, it is improbable that shepherds should be capable of harmonious numbers, or delicate sentiments; and therefore the reader must exalt his ideas of the pastoral character, by carrying his thoughts back to the age in which the care of herds and flocks was the employment of the wisest and greatest men.

These reasoners seem to have been led into their hypothesis, by considering pastoral, not in general, as a representation of rural nature, and consequently as exhibiting the ideas and sentiments of those, whoever they are, to whom the country affords pleasure or employment, but simply as a dialogue, or narrative of men actually tending sheep, and busied in the lowest and most laborious offices; from whence they very readily concluded, since characters must necessarily be preserved, that either the sentiments must sink to the level of the speakers, or the speakers must be raised to the height of the sentiments.

In consequence of these original errors, a thousand precepts have been given, which have only contributed to perplex and to confound. Some have thought it necessary that the imaginary manners of the golden age should be universally preserved, and have therefore believed, that nothing more could be admitted in pastoral, than lilies and roses, and rocks and streams, among which are heard the gentle whispers of chaste fondness, or the soft complaints of amorous impatience. In pastoral, as in other writings, chastity of sentiment ought doubtless to be observed, and purity of manners to be represented; not because the poet is confined to the images of the golden age, but because, having the subject in his own choice, he ought always to consult the interest of virtue.

These advocates for the golden age lay down other principles, not very consistent with their general plan; for they tell us, that, to support the character of the shepherd, it is proper that all re-finement should be avoided, and that some slight instances of ignorance should be interspersed. Thus the shepherd in Virgil is supposed to have forgot the name of Anaximander, and in Pope the term Zodiack is too hard for a rustick apprehension. But if we place our shepherds in their primitive condition, we may give them learning among their other qualifications; and if we suffer them to allude at all to things of later existence, which, perhaps, cannot with any great propriety be allowed, there can be no danger of making them speak with too much accuracy, since they conversed with divinities, and transmitted to succeeding ages the arts of life.

Other writers, having the mean and despicable condition of a shepherd always before them, conceive it necessary to degrade the language of pastoral, by obsolete terms and rustick words, which they very learnedly call Dorick, without reflecting, that they thus become authors of a mingled dialect, which no human being ever could have spoken, that they may as well refine the speech as the sentiments of their personages, and that none of the inconsistencies which they endeavour to avoid, is greater than that of joining elegance of thought with coarseness of diction. Spenser begins one of his pastorals with studied barbarity:

> Diggon Davie, *I bid her good-day:*
> *Or,* Diggon *her is, or I missay.*
> Dig. *Her was her while it was day-light,*
> *But now her is a most wretched wight.*[42]

What will the reader imagine to be the subject on which speakers like these exercise their eloquence? Will he not be somewhat disappointed, when he finds them met together to condemn the corruptions of the church of Rome? Surely, at the same time that a shepherd learns theology, he may gain some acquaintance with his native language.

Pastoral admits of all ranks of persons, because persons of all ranks inhabit the country. It excludes not, therefore, on account of the characters necessary to be introduced, any elevation or delicacy of sentiment; those ideas only are improper, which, not owing their original to rural objects, are not pastoral. Such is the exclamation in Virgil:

> *Nunc scio quid sit Amor, duris in cautibus illum*
> *Ismarus, aut Rhodope, aut extremi Garamantes,*
> *Nec generis nostri puerum nec sanguinis, edunt;*[43]

> I know thee, love, in desarts thou wert bred,
> And at the dugs of savage tygers fed:
> Alien of birth, usurper of the plains.   DRYDEN.

which Pope endeavouring to copy, was carried to still greater impropriety.

> *I know thee, Love, wild as the raging main,*
> *More fierce than tigers on the Libyan plain;*
> *Thou wert from Aetna's burning entrails torn,*
> *Begot in tempests, and in thunders born!*[44]

Sentiments like these, as they have no ground in nature, are indeed of little value in any poem, but in pastoral they are particularly liable to censure, because it wants that exaltation above common life, which in tragick or heroick writings often reconciles us to bold flights and daring figures.

Pastoral being the *representation of an action or passion, by its effects upon a country life,* has nothing peculiar but its confinement to rural imagery, without which it ceases to be pastoral. This is its true characteristick, and this it cannot lose by any dignity of sentiment, or beauty of diction. The Pollio of Virgil,[45] with all its elevation, is a composition truly bucolic, though rejected by the criticks; for all the images are either taken from the country, or from the religion of the age common to all parts of the empire.

The Silenus[46] is indeed of a more disputable kind, because though the scene lies in the country, the song being religious and historical, had been no less adapted to any other audience or place. Neither can it well be defended as a fiction, for the introduction of a god seems to imply the golden age, and yet he alludes to many subsequent transactions, and mentions Gallus the poet's contemporary.

It seems necessary, to the perfection of this poem, that the occasion which is supposed to produce it, be at least not inconsistent with a country life, or less likely to interest those who have retired into places of solitude and quiet, than the more busy part of mankind. It is therefore improper to give the title of a pastoral to verses, in which the speakers, after the slight mention of their flocks, fall to complaints of errors in the church, and corruptions in the government, or to lamentations of the death of some illustrious person, whom when once the poet has called a shepherd, he has no longer any labour upon his hands, but can make the clouds weep, and lilies wither, and the sheep hang their heads, without art or learning, genius or study.[47]

It is part of Claudian's character of his rustick, that he computes his time not by the succession of consuls, but of harvests. Those who pass their days in retreats distant from the theatres of business, are always least likely to hurry their imagination with publick affairs.

The facility of treating actions or events in the pastoral stile, has incited many writers, from whom more judgment might have been expected, to put the sorrow or the joy which the occasion required into the mouth of Daphne or of Thyrsis, and as one absurdity must naturally be expected to make way for another, they have written with an utter disregard both of life and nature, and filled their productions with mythological allusions, with incredible fictions, and with sentiments which neither passion nor reason could have dictated, since the change which religion has made in the whole system of the world.

RAMBLER no. 125. Tuesday, May 28, 1751

Descriptas servare vices, operumque colores,
Cur ego, si nequeo ignoroque, poeta salutor?   Hor.[48]

But if, through weakness, or my want of art,
I can't to every different style impart
The proper strokes and colours it may claim,
Why am I honour'd with a poet's name?   Francis.

It is one of the maxims of the civil law, that *definitions are hazardous*. Things modified by human understandings, subject to varieties of complication, and changeable as experience advances knowledge, or accident influences caprice, are scarcely to be included in any standing form of expression, because they are always suffering some alteration of their state. Definition is, indeed, not the province of man; every thing is set above or below our faculties. The works and operations of nature are too great in their extent, or too much diffused in their relations, and the performances of art too inconstant and uncertain, to be reduced to any determinate idea. It is impossible to impress upon our minds an adequate and just representation of an object so great that we can never take it into our view, or so mutable that it is always changing under our eye, and has already lost its form while we are labouring to conceive it.

Definitions have been no less difficult or uncertain in criticisms than in law. Imagination, a licentious and vagrant faculty, unsusceptible of limitations, and impatient of restraint, has always endeavoured to baffle the logician, to perplex the confines of distinction, and burst the inclosures of regularity. There is therefore scarcely any species of writing, of which we can tell what is its essence, and what are its constituents; every new genius produces some innovation, which, when invented and approved, subverts the rules which the practice of foregoing authors had established.

Comedy has been particularly unpropitious to definers; for though perhaps they might properly have contented themselves, with declaring it to be *such a dramatic representation of human life, as may excite mirth*, they have embarrassed their definition with the means by which the comic writers attain their end, without considering that the various methods of exhilarating their audience, not being limited by nature, cannot be comprised in precept. Thus, some make comedy a representation of mean, and others of bad men; some think that its essence consists in the unimportance, others in the fictitiousness, of the transaction. But any man's reflections will inform him, that every dramatick composition which raises mirth is comick; and that, to raise mirth, it is by no means universally necessary, that the personages should be either mean or corrupt; nor always requisite, that the action should be trivial, nor ever, that it should be fictitious.

If the two kinds of dramatick poetry had been defined only by their effects upon the mind, some absurdities might have been prevented, with which the compositions of our greatest poets are disgraced, who, for want of some settled ideas and accurate distinctions, have unhappily confounded tragick with comick sentiments. They seem to have thought, that as the meanness of personages constituted comedy, their greatness was sufficient to form a tragedy; and that nothing was necessary but that they should croud the scene with monarchs, and generals, and guards; and make them talk, at certain intervals, of the downfal of kingdoms, and the rout of armies. They have not considered, that thoughts or incidents in themselves ridiculous, grow still more grotesque by the solemnity of such characters; that reason and nature are uniform and inflexible; and that what is despicable and absurd, will not, by any association with splendid titles, become rational or great; that the most important affairs, by an intermixture of an unseasonable levity, may be made contemptible; and that the robes of royalty can give no dignity to nonsense or to folly.

"Comedy," says *Horace*, "sometimes raises her voice;"[49] and tragedy may likewise on proper occasions abate her dignity; but as the comick personages can only depart from their familiarity of stile, when the more violent passions are put in motion, the heroes and queens of tragedy should never descend to trifle, but in the hours of ease, and intermissions of danger. Yet in the tragedy of *Don Sebastian*,[50] when the king of *Portugal* is in the hands of his enemy, and having just drawn the lot, by which he is condemned to die, breaks out into a wild boast that his dust shall take possession of *Africk*, the dialogue proceeds thus between the captive and his conqueror:

> *Muley Moluch.* What shall I do to conquer thee?
> *Seb.* Impossible!
> Souls know no conquerors.
> *M. Mol.* I'll shew thee for a monster thro' my *Africk*.
> *Seb.* No, thou canst only shew me for a man:
> *Africk* is stor'd with monsters; man's a prodigy
> Thy subjects have not seen.
> *M. Mol.* Thou talk'st as if

Still at the head of battle.
   Seb. Thou mistak'st,
For there I would not talk.
   Benducar, the Minister. Sure he would sleep.

This conversation, with the sly remark of the minister, can only be found not to be comick, because it wants the probability necessary to representations of common life, and degenerates too much towards buffoonry and farce.

The same play affords a smart return of the general to the emperor, who, enforcing his orders for the death of *Sebastian*, vents his impatience in this abrupt threat:

> —No more replies,
> But see thou do'st it: Or—

To which *Dorax* answers,

> Choak in that threat: I can say Or as loud.

A thousand instances of such impropriety might be produced, were not one scene in *Aureng-Zebe* sufficient to exemplify it. *Indamora*, a captive queen, having *Aureng-Zebe* for her lover, employs *Arimant*, to whose charge she had been intrusted, and whom she had made sensible of her charms, to carry a message to his rival.

> ARIMANT, *with a letter in his hand:* INDAMORA.
>   *Arim.* And I the messenger to him from you?
> Your empire you to tyranny pursue:
> You lay commands, both cruel and unjust,
> To serve my rival, and betray my trust.
>   *Ind.* You first betray'd your trust in loving me:
> And should not I my own advantage see?
> Serving my love, you may my friendship gain:
> You know the rest of your pretences vain.
> You must, my *Arimant*, you must be kind:
> 'Tis in your nature, and your noble mind.
>   *Arim.* I'll to the king, and strait my trust resign.
>   *Ind.* His trust you may, but you shall never mine.
> Heav'n made you love me for no other end,
> But to become my confident and friend:

As such, I keep no secret from your sight,
And therefore make you judge how ill I write:
Read it, and tell me freely then your mind,
If 'tis indited, as I meant it, kind.
 Arim. *I ask not heav'n my freedom to restore,*

             [Reading.

But only for your sake—I'll read no more.
And yet I must—
Less for my own, than for your sorrow sad—[Reading.
Another line, like this, would make me mad—
Heav'n! she goes on—yet more—and yet more kind!

           [*As Reading.*

Each sentence is a dagger to my mind.
See me this night—

             [Reading.

Thank fortune, who did such a friend provide;
For faithful Arimant *shall be your guide.*
Not only to be made an instrument,
But pre-engag'd without my own consent!
 Ind. Unknown t'engage you, still augments my score,
And gives you scope of meriting the more.
 Arim. The best of men
Some int'rest in their actions must confess;
None merit, but in hope they may possess,
The fatal paper rather let me tear,
Than, like *Bellerophon,* my own sentence bear.
 Ind. You may; but 'twill not be your best advice:
'Twill only give me pains of writing twice.
You know you must obey me, soon or late:
Why should you vainly struggle with your fate?
 Arim. I thank thee, heav'n! thou hast been wond'rous kind!
Why am I thus to slavery design'd,
And yet am cheated with a freeborn mind?
Or make thy orders with my reason suit,
Or let me live by sense, a glorious brute—

           [*She frowns.*

You frown, and I obey with speed, before
That dreadful sentence comes, *See me no more.*[51]

In this scene, every circumstance concurs to turn tragedy to farce. The wild absurdity of the expedient; the contemptible subjection of the lover; the folly of obliging him to read the letter only because it ought to have been concealed from him; the frequent interruptions of amorous impatience; the faint expostulations of a voluntary slave; the imperious haughtiness of a tyrant without power; the deep reflection of the yielding rebel upon fate and freewill; and his wise wish to lose his reason as soon as he finds himself about to do what he cannot persuade his reason to approve, are surely sufficent to awaken the most torpid risibility.

There is scarce a tragedy of the last century which has not debased its most important incidents, and polluted its most serious interlocutions with buffoonry and meanness; but though perhaps it cannot be pretended that the present age has added much to the force and efficacy of the drama, it has at least been able to escape many faults, which either ignorance had overlooked, or indulgence had licensed. The later tragedies indeed have faults of another kind, perhaps more destructive to delight, though less open to censure. That perpetual tumour of phrase with which every thought is now expressed by every personage, the paucity of adventures which regularity admits, and the unvaried equality of flowing dialogue, has taken away from our present writers almost all that dominion over the passions which was the boast of their predecessors. Yet they may at least claim this commendation, that they avoid gross faults, and that if they cannot often move terror or pity, they are always careful not to provoke laughter.

RAMBLER no. 156. SATURDAY, SEPTEMBER 14, 1751

Nunquam aliud natura, aliud sapientia dicit. Juv.[52]

For wisdom ever echoes nature's voice.

Every government, say the politicians, is perpetually degenerating towards corruption, from which it must be rescued at certain periods by the resuscitation of its first principles, and the re-establishment of its original constitution. Every animal body, according to the methodick physicians, is, by the predominance of some exuberant quality, continually declining towards disease and death, which must be obviated by a seasonable reduction of the peccant humour to the just equipoise which health requires.

In the same manner the studies of mankind, all at least which, not being subject to rigorous demonstration, admit the influence of fancy and caprice, are perpetually tending to error and confusion. Of the great principles of truth which the first speculatists discovered, the simplicity is embarrassed by ambitious additions, or the evidence obscured by inaccurate argumentation; and as they descend from one succession of writers to another, like light transmitted from room to room, they lose their strength and splendour, and fade at last in total evanescence.

The systems of learning therefore must be sometimes reviewed, complications analised into principles, and knowledge disentangled from opinion. It is not always possible, without a close inspection, to separate the genuine shoots of consequential reasoning, which grow out of some radical postulate, from the branches which art has engrafted on it. The accidental prescriptions of authority, when time has procured them veneration, are often confounded with the laws of nature, and those rules are supposed coeval with reason, of which the first rise cannot be discovered.

Criticism has sometimes permitted fancy to dictate the laws by which fancy ought to be restrained, and fallacy to perplex the principles by which fallacy is to be detected; her superintendance of others has betrayed her to negligence of herself; and, like the antient *Scythians*,[53] by extending her conquests over distant regions, she has left her throne vacant to her slaves.

Among the laws of which the desire of extending authority, or ardour of promoting knowledge has prompted the prescription, all which writers have received, had not the same original right to our regard. Some are to be considered as fundamental and indispensable, others only as useful and convenient; some as dictated by reason and necessity, others as enacted by despotick antiquity; none as invincibly supported by their conformity to the order of nature and operations of the intellect; others as formed by accident, or instituted by example, and therefore always liable to dispute and alteration.

That many rules have been advanced without consulting nature or reason, we cannot but suspect, when we find it peremptorily decreed by the antient masters, that *only three speaking personages should appear at once upon the stage*;[54] a law which, as the variety and intricacy of modern plays has made it impossible to be observed, we now violate without scruple, and, as experience proves, without inconvenience.

The original of this precept was merely accidental. Tragedy was a monody or solitary song in honour of *Bacchus*, improved afterwards into a dialogue by the addition of another speaker; but the antients, remembering that the tragedy was at first pronounced only by one, durst not for some time venture beyond two; at last when custom and impunity had made them daring, they extended their liberty to the admission of three, but restrained themselves by a critical edict from further exorbitance.

By what accident the number of acts was limited to five, I know not that any author has informed us; but certainly it is not determined by any necessity arising either from the nature of action or propriety of exhibition. An act is only the representation of such a part of the business of the play as proceeds in an unbroken tenor, or without any intermediate pause. Nothing is more evident than that of every real, and by consequence of every dramatick action, the intervals may be more or fewer than five; and indeed the rule is upon the *English* stage every day broken in effect, without any other mischief than that which arises from an absurd endeavour to observe it in appearance. Whenever the scene is shifted the act ceases, since some time is necessarily supposed to elapse while the personages of the drama change their place.

With no greater right to our obedience have the criticks confined the dramatic action to a certain number of hours. Probability requires that the time of action should approach somewhat nearly to that of exhibition, and those plays will always be thought most happily conducted which croud the greatest variety into the least space. But since it will frequently happen that some delusion must be admitted, I know not where the limits of imagination can be fixed.[55] It is rarely observed that minds not prepossessed by mechanical criticism feel any offence from the extension of the intervals between the acts; nor can I conceive it absurd or impossible, that he who can multiply three hours into twelve or twenty-four, might image with equal ease a greater number.

I know not whether he that professes to regard no other laws than those of nature, will not be inclined to receive tragi-comedy to his protection, whom, however generally condemned, her own laurels have hitherto shaded from the fulminations of criticism. For what is there in the mingled drama which impartial reason can condemn? The connexion of important with trivial incidents, since it is not only common but perpetual in the world, may surely be allowed upon the stage, which pretends only to be the mirrour of life. The impropriety of suppressing passions before we have raised them to the intended agitation, and of diverting the expectation from an event which we keep suspended only to raise it, may be speciously urged. But will not experience shew this objection to be rather subtle than just? is it not certain that the tragic and comic affections have been moved alternately with equal force, and that no plays have oftner filled the eye with tears, and the breast with palpitation, than those which are variegated with interludes of mirth?

I do not however think it safe to judge of works of genius merely by the event. These resistless vicissitudes of the heart, this alternate prevalence of merriment and solemnity, may sometimes be more properly ascribed to the vigour of the writer than the justness of the design: and instead of vindicating tragi-comedy by the success of *Shakespear*, we ought perhaps to pay new honours to that transcendent and unbounded genius that could preside over the passions in sport; who, to actuate the affections, needed not the slow gradation of common means, but could fill the heart with instantaneous jollity or sorrow, and vary our disposition as he changed his scenes. Perhaps the effects even of *Shakespeare*'s poetry might have been yet greater, had he not counter-acted himself; and we might have been more interested in the distresses of his heros had we not been so frequently diverted by the jokes of his buffoons.[56]

There are other rules more fixed and obligatory. It is necessary that of every play the chief action should be single; for since a play represents some transaction, through its regular maturation to its final event, two actions equally important must evidently constitute two plays.[57]

As the design of tragedy is to instruct by moving the passions, it must always have a hero, a personage apparently and incontestably superior to the rest, upon whom the attention may be fixed, and the anxiety suspended. For though of two persons opposing each other with equal abilities and equal virtue, the auditor will inevitably in time choose his favourite, yet as that choice must be without any cogency of conviction, the hopes or fears which it raises will be faint and languid. Of two heroes acting in confederacy against a common enemy, the virtues or dangers will give little emotion, because each claims our concern with the same right, and the heart lies at rest between equal motives.

It ought to be the first endeavour of a writer to distinguish nature from custom, or that which is established because it is right, from that which is right only because it is established; that he may neither violate essential principles by a desire of novelty, nor debar himself from the attainment of beauties within his view by a needless fear of breaking rules which no literary dictator had authority to enact.

RAMBLER no. 168. Saturday, October 26, 1751

—— —— —— *Decipit*
Frons prima multos, rara mens intelligit
Quod interiore condidit cura angulo.　　PHAEDRUS.[58]

The tinsel glitter, and the specious mein,
Delude the most; few pry behind the scene.

It has been observed by *Boileau*, that "a mean or common thought expressed in pompous diction, generally pleases more than a new or noble sentiment delivered in low and vulgar language; because the number is greater of those whom custom has enabled to judge of words, than whom study has qualified to examine things."[59]

This solution might satisfy, if such only were offended with meanness of expression as are unable to distinguish propriety of thought, and to separate propositions or images from the vehicles by which they are conveyed to the understanding. But this kind of disgust is by no means confined to the ignorant or superficial; it operates uniformly and universally upon readers of all classes; every man, however profound or abstracted, perceives himself irresistibly alienated by low terms; they who profess the most zealous adherence to truth are forced to admit that she owes part of her charms to her ornaments, and loses much of her power over the soul, when she appears disgraced by a dress uncouth or ill-adjusted.

We are all offended by low terms, but are not disgusted alike by the same compositions, because we do not all agree to censure the same terms as low. No word is naturally or intrinsically meaner than another; our opinion therefore of words, as of other things arbitrarily and capriciously established, depends wholly upon accident and custom. The cottager thinks those apartments splendid and spacious, which an inhabitant of palaces will despise for their inelegance;[60] and to him who has passed most of his hours with the delicate and polite, many expressions will seem sordid, which another, equally acute, may hear without offence; but a mean term never fails to displease him to whom it appears mean, as poverty is certainly and invariably despised, though he who is poor in the eyes of some, may by others be envied for his wealth.

Words become low by the occasions to which they are applied, or the general character of them who use them; and the disgust which they produce, arises from the revival of those images with which they are commonly united. Thus if, in the most solemn discourse, a phrase happens to occur which has been successfully employed in some ludicrous narrative, the gravest auditor finds it difficult to refrain from laughter, when they who are not pre-possessed by the same accidental association, are utterly unable to guess the reason of his merriment. Words which convey ideas of dignity in one age, are banished from elegant writing or conversation in another, because they are in time debased by vulgar mouths, and can be no longer heard without the involuntary recollection of unpleasing images.

When *Mackbeth* is confirming himself in the horrid purpose of stabbing his king, he breaks out amidst his emotions into a wish natural to a murderer,

> —— —— Come, thick night!
> And pall thee in the dunnest smoke of hell,
> That my keen knife see not the wound it makes;
> Nor heav'n peep through the blanket of the dark,
> To cry, hold, hold! —— ——[61]

In this passage is exerted all the force of poetry, that force which calls new powers into being, which embodies sentiment, and animates matter; yet perhaps scarce any man now peruses it without some disturbance of his attention from the counteraction of the words to the ideas. What can be more dreadful than to implore the presence of night, invested not in common obscurity, but in the smoke of hell? Yet the efficacy of this invocation is destroyed by the insertion of an epithet now seldom heard but in the stable, and *dun* night may come or go without any other notice than contempt.

If we start into raptures when some hero of the Iliad tells us that δόρυ μάινεται, his lance rages with eagerness to destroy; if we are alarmed at the terror of the soldiers commanded by *Caesar* to hew down the sacred grove, who dreaded, says *Lucan*, lest the axe aimed at the oak should fly back upon the striker,

> —*Si robora sacra ferirent,*
> *In sua credebant redituras membra secures,*[62]

> None dares with impious steel the grove to rend,
> Lest on himself the destin'd stroke descend.

we cannot surely but sympathise with the horrors of a wretch about to murder his master, his friend, his benefactor, who suspects that the weapon will refuse its office, and start back from the breast which he is preparing to violate. Yet this sentiment is weakened by the name of an instrument used by butchers and cooks in the meanest employments; we do not immediately conceive that any crime of importance is to be committed with a *knife*; or who does not, at last, from the long habit of connecting a knife with sordid offices, feel aversion rather than terror?

Mackbeth proceeds to wish, in the madness of guilt, that the inspection of heaven may be intercepted, and that he may in the involutions of infernal darkness escape the eye of providence. This is the utmost extravagance of determined wickedness; yet this is so debased by two unfortunate words, that while I endeavour to impress on my reader the energy of the sentiment, I can scarce check my risibility, when the expression forces itself upon my mind; for who, without some relaxation of his gravity, can hear of the avengers of guilt *peeping through a blanket?*

These imperfections of diction are less obvious to the reader, as he is less acquainted with common usages; they are therefore wholly imperceptible to a foreigner, who learns our language from books, and will strike a solitary academick less forcibly than a modish lady.

Among the numerous requisites that must concur to complete an author, few are of more importance than an early entrance into the living world. The seeds of knowledge may be planted in solitude, but must be cultivated in publick. Argumentation may be taught in colleges, and theories formed in retirement, but the artifice of embellishment, and the powers of attraction, can be gained only by general converse.

An acquaintance with prevailing customs and fashionable elegance is necessary likewise for other purposes. The injury that grand imagery suffers from unsuitable language, personal merit may fear from rudeness and indelicacy. When the success of *Aeneas* depended on the favour of the queen upon whose coasts he was driven, his celestial protectress thought him not sufficiently secured against rejection by his piety or bravery, but decorated him for the interview with preternatural beauty.[63] Whoever desires, for his writings or himself, what none can reasonably contemn, the favour of mankind, must add grace to strength, and make his thoughts agreeable as well as useful. Many complain of neglect who never tried to attract regard. It cannot be expected that the patrons of science or virtue should be solicitous to discover excellencies which they who possess them shade and disguise. Few have abilities so much needed by the rest of the world as to be caressed on their own terms; and he that will not condescend to recommend himself by external embellishments, must submit to the fate of just sentiments meanly expressed, and be ridiculed and forgotten before he is understood.

RAMBLER no. 86. SATURDAY, JAN. 12, 1751

Legitimumque sonum Digitis callemus et Aure.   HOR.[64]
By fingers, or by ear, we numbers scan.   ELPHINSTON.

One of the ancients has observed, that the burthen of government is encreased upon princes by the virtues of their immediate predecessors. It is, indeed, always dangerous to be placed in a state of unavoidable comparison with excellence, and the danger is still greater when that excellence is consecrated by death, when envy and interest cease to act against it, and those passions by which it was at first vilified and opposed, now stand in its defence, and turn their vehemence against honest emulation.

He that succeeds a celebrated writer, has the same difficulties to encounter; he stands under the shade of exalted merit, and is hindered from rising to his natural height, by the interception of those beams which should invigorate and quicken him. He applies to that attention which is already engaged, and unwilling to be drawn off from certain satisfaction; or perhaps to an attention already wearied, and not to be recalled to the same object. One of the old poets[65] congratulates himself that he has the untrodden regions of *Parnassus* before him, and that his garland will be gathered from plantations which no writer had yet culled. But the imitator treads a beaten walk, and with all his diligence can only hope to find a few flowers or branches untouched by his predecessor, the refuse of contempt, or the omissions of negligence. The *Macedonian* conqueror,[66] when he was once invited to hear a man that sung like a nightingale, replied with contempt, "that he had heard the nightingale herself;" and the same treatment must every man expect, whose praise is, that he imitates another.

Yet, in the midst of these discouraging reflexions, I am about to offer to my reader some observations upon *Paradise Lost*, and hope, that, however I may fall below the illustrious writer who has so long dictated to the commonwealth of learning, my attempt may not be wholly useless. There are in every age, new errors to be rectify'd, and new prejudices to be opposed. False taste is always busy to mislead those that are entering upon the regions of learning; and the traveller, uncertain of his way, and forsaken by the sun, will be pleased to see a fainter orb arise on the horizon, that may rescue him from total darkness, though with weak and borrowed lustre.

Addison, though he has considered this poem under most of the general topicks of criticism, has barely touched upon the versification; not probably because he thought the art of numbers unworthy of his notice, for he knew with how minute attention the ancient criticks considered the disposition of syllables, and had himself given hopes of some metrical observations upon the great *Roman* poet; but being the first who undertook to display the beauties, and point out the defects of *Milton*, he had many objects at once before him, and passed willingly over those which were most barren of ideas, and required labour, rather than genius.[67]

Yet versification, or the art of modulating his numbers, is indispensably necessary to a poet. Every other power by which the understanding is enlightened, or the imagination enchanted, may be exercised in prose. But the poet has this peculiar superiority, that to all the powers which the perfection of every other composition can require, he adds the faculty of joining musick with reason, and of acting at once upon the senses and the passions. I suppose there are few who do not feel themselves touched by poetical melody, and who will not confess that they are more or less moved by the same thoughts, as they are conveyed by different sounds, and more affected by the same words in one order, than in another. The perception of harmony is indeed conferred upon men in degrees very unequal, but there are none who do not perceive it, or to whom a regular series of proportionate sounds cannot give delight.

In treating on the versification of *Milton* I am desirous to be generally understood, and shall therefore studiously decline the dialect of grammarians; though, indeed, it is always difficult and sometimes scarcely possible to deliver the precepts of an art without the terms by which the peculiar ideas of that art are expressed, and which had not been invented but because the language already in use, was insufficient. If therefore I shall sometimes seem obscure, may it be imputed to this voluntary interdiction, and to a desire of avoiding that offence which is always given by unusual words.

The heroic measure of the *English* language may be properly considered as pure or mixed. It is pure when the accent rests upon every second syllable through the whole line.

> Courage uncertain dangers may abate
> But whó can beár th' appróach of cértain fáte.   DRYDEN.[68]

> Here love his golden shafts employs, here lights
> His cónstant lámp, and wáves his púrple wíngs,
> Reigns here, and revels; not in the bought smile
> Of hárlots, lóveless, jóyless, únendéar'd.   MILTON.[69]

The accent may be observed, in the second line of *Dryden*, and the second and fourth of *Milton*, to repose upon every second syllable.

The repetition of this sound or percussion at equal times, is the most complete harmony of which a single verse is capable, and should therefore be exactly kept in distichs, and generally in the last line of a paragraph, that the ear may rest without any sense of imperfection.

But, to preserve the series of sounds untransposed in a long composition, is not only very difficult but tiresome and disgusting; for we are soon wearied with the perpetual recurrence of the same cadence. Necessity has therefore enforced the mixed measure, in which some variation of the accents is allowed; this, tho' it always injures the harmony of the line considered by itself, yet compensates the loss by relieving us from the continual tyranny of the same sound, and makes us more sensible of the harmony of the pure measure.

Of these mixed numbers every poet affords us innumerable instances, and *Milton* seldom has two pure lines together, as will

appear if any of his paragraphs be read with attention merely to
the musick.

> Thus at their shady lodge arriv'd, both stood,
> Both turn'd, and under open sky ador'd
> The God that made both sky, air, earth, and heav'n,
> Which they beheld; the moon's resplendent globe,
> *And starry pole: thou also mad'st the night,*
> Maker omnipotent! and thou the day,
> Which we in our appointed work employ'd
> Have finish'd, happy in our mutual help,
> *And mutual love, the crown of all our bliss*
> Ordain'd by thee; and this delicious place,
> For us too large; where thy abundance wants
> Partakers, and uncrop'd falls to the ground,
> But thou hast promis'd from us two a race
> To fill the earth, who shall with us extol
> Thy goodness infinite, both when we wake,
> And when we seek, as now, thy gift of sleep.
>   [*Paradise Lost*, 4.   720–35]

In this passage it will be at first observed, that all the lines are
not equally harmonious, and upon a nearer examination it will be
found that only the fifth and ninth lines are regular, and the rest
are more or less licentious with respect to the accent. In some the
accent is equally upon two syllables together, and in both strong.
As

> Thus at their shady lodge arriv'd, *both stood,*
> *Both turn'd,* and under open sky ador'd
> The God that made both sky, *air, earth,* and heav'n.

In others the accent is equally upon two syllables, but upon both
weak.

> ——— ——— ——— a race
> To fill the earth, who shall with us extol
> Thy goodness in*finite,* both when we wake,
> *And when* we seek, as now, thy gift of sleep.

In the first pair of syllables the accent may deviate from the rigour
of exactness, without any unpleasing diminution of harmony, as

may be observed in the lines already cited, and more remarkably in this:

> —— Thou also mad'st the night,
> *Maker* omnipotent! and thou the day.

But, excepting in the first pair of syllables, which may be considered as arbitrary, a poet who, not having the invention or knowledge of *Milton,* has more need to allure his audience by musical cadences, should seldom suffer more than one aberration from the rule in any single verse.

There are two lines in this passage more remarkably unharmonious.

> —— —— This delicious place,
> For us too large; *where thy* abundance wants
> Partakers, and uncrop'd *falls to* the ground.

Here the third pair of syllables in the first, and fourth pair in the second verse, have their accents retrograde or inverted; the first syllable being strong or acute, and the second weak. The detriment which the measure suffers by this inversion of the accents is sometimes less perceptible, when the verses are carried one into another, but is remarkably striking in this place, where the vicious verse concludes a period; and is yet more offensive in rhyme, when we regularly attend to the flow of every single line. This will appear by reading a couplet in which *Cowley,* an author not sufficiently studious of harmony, has committed the same fault.

> —— His harmless life
> Does with substantial blessedness abound,
> And the soft wings of peace *cover* him round.[70]

In these the law of metre is very grossly violated by mingling combinations of sound directly opposite to each other, as *Milton* expresses it in his sonnet, by *committing short and long,*[71] and setting one part of the measure at variance with the rest. The ancients, who had a language more capable of variety than ours, had two kinds of verse, the *Iambick,* consisting of short and long syllables alternately, from which our heroic measure is derived, and the *Trochaick,* consisting in a like alternation of long and short. These were considered as opposites, and conveyed the contrary images of speed and slowness; to confound them, therefore, as in these lines, is to deviate from the established practice. But where the senses are to judge, authority is not necessary, the ear is sufficient to detect dissonance, nor should I have sought auxiliaries on such an occasion against any name but that of *Milton*.

RAMBLER NO. 88. SATURDAY, JAN. 19, 1751

Cum Tabulis animum censoris sumet honesti,
Audebit quaecunque minus splendoris habebunt,
Aut sine pondere erunt, et honore indigna ferentur
Verba movere loco, quamvis invita recedant
Et versentur adhuc intra penetralia Vestae.   HOR.[72]

But he that hath a curious piece design'd,
When he begins must take a censor's mind,
Severe and honest; and what words appear
Too light and trivial, or too weak to bear
The weighty sense, nor worth the reader's care,
Shake off; tho' stubborn, they are loth to move,
And tho' we fancy, dearly tho' we love.   CREECH.

"There is no reputation for genius," says *Quintilian*, "to be gained by writing on things, which, however necessary, have little splendor or shew. The height of a building attracts the eye, but the foundations lie without regard. Yet since there is not any way to the top of science, but from the lowest parts, I shall think nothing unconnected with the art of oratory, which he that wants cannot be an orator."[73]

Confirmed and animated by this illustrious precedent, I shall continue my inquiries into *Milton*'s art of versification. Since, however minute the employment may appear, of analysing lines into syllables, and whatever ridicule may be incurred by a solemn deliberation upon accents and pauses, it is certain that without this petty knowledge no man can be a poet; and that from the proper disposition of single sounds results that harmony that adds force to reason, and gives grace to sublimity; that shackles attention, and governs passion.

That verse may be melodious and pleasing, it is necessary, not only that the words be so ranged as that the accent may fall on its proper place, but that the syllables themselves be so chosen as to flow smoothly into one another. This is to be effected by a proportionate mixture of vowels and consonants, and by tempering the mute consonants with liquids and semivowels. The *Hebrew* grammarians have observ'd, that it is impossible to pronounce two consonants without the intervention of a vowel, or without some emission of the breath between one and the other; this is longer and more perceptible, as the sounds of the consonants are less harmonically conjoined, and, by consequence, the flow of the verse is longer interrupted.

It is pronounced by *Dryden*, that a line of monosyllables is almost always harsh. This, with regard to our language, is evidently true, not because monosyllables cannot compose harmony, but, because our monosyllables being of *Teutonic* original, or formed by contraction, commonly begin and end with consonants, as

——— Every lower faculty
Of sense, whereby they hear, see, smell, touch, taste.
[*Paradise Lost*, 5. 410–11]

The difference of harmony arising principally from the collocation of vowels and consonants, will be sufficiently conceived by attending to the following passages.

Immortal *Amarant*—there grows
And flow'rs aloft, shading the fount of life,
And where the river of bliss thro' midst of heav'n
Rolls o'er Elysian flow'rs her amber stream;
With these that never fade, the spirits elect
Bind their resplendent locks inwreath'd with beams.   [3. 353, 356–61]

The same comparison that I propose to be made between the fourth and sixth verses of this passage, may be repeated between the last lines of the following quotations.

Under foot the violet,
Crocus, and hyacinth, with rich in-lay

> *Broider'd the ground, more colour'd than with stone,*
> Of costliest emblem.   [4. 700–03]
>   Here in close recess,
> With flowers, garlands, and sweet-smelling herbs,
> Espoused *Eve* first deck'd her nuptial bed:
> *And heav'nly choirs the hymenean sung.*   [4. 708–11]

Milton, whose ear had been accustomed, not only to the musick of the antient tongues, which, however vitiated by our pronunciation, excel all that are now in use, but to the softness of the *Italian,* the most mellifluous of all modern poetry, seems fully convinced of the unfitness of our language for smooth versification, and is therefore pleased with an opportunity of calling in a softer word to his assistance; for this reason, and I believe for this only, he sometimes indulges himself in a long series of proper names, and introduces them where they add little but musick to his poem.

>   ——— The richer seat
> Of *Atabalipa,* and yet unspoil'd
> *Guiana,* whose great city *Gerion's* sons
> Call *El Dorado,* ———   [11. 408–11]

>   The Moon—The *Tuscan* artist views
> At evening, from the top of *Fesole*
> Or in *Valdarno,* to descry new lands.—   [1. 288–90]

He has indeed, been more attentive to his syllables than to his accents, and does not often offend by collisions of consonants, or openings of vowels upon each other, at least not more often than other writers who have had less important or complicated subjects to take off their care from the cadence of their lines.

The great peculiarity of *Milton's* versification, compared with that of later poets, is the elision of one vowel before another, or the suppression of the last syllable of a word ending with a vowel, when a vowel begins the following word. As

>   Knowledge—
> Oppresses else with surfeit, and soon turns
> Wisdom to folly, as nourishment to wind.   [7. 126, 129–30]

This licence, though now disused in *English* poetry, was practised by our old writers, and is allowed in many other languages antient and modern, and therefore the critics on *Paradise Lost* have, without much deliberation, commended *Milton* for continuing it. But one language cannot communicate its rules to another. We have already tried and rejected the hexameter of the antients, the double close of the *Italians,* and the alexandrine of the *French*; and the elision of vowels, however graceful it may seem to other nations, may be very unsuitable to the genius of the *English* Tongue.

There is reason to believe that we have negligently lost part of our vowels, and that the silent *e* which our ancestors added to most of our monosyllables, was once vocal. By this detruncation of our syllables, our language is overstocked with consonants, and it is more necessary to add vowels to the beginning of words, than to cut them off from the end.

Milton therefore seems to have somewhat mistaken the nature of our language, of which the chief defect is ruggedness and asperity, and has left our harsh cadences yet harsher. But his elisions are not all equally to be censured; in some syllables they may be allowed, and perhaps in a few may be safely imitated. The abscision of a vowel is undoubtedly vicious when it is strongly sounded, and makes, with its associate consonant, a full and audible syllable.

—— What he gives,
Spiritual, may to purest spirits be found
No ingrateful food, and food alike these pure
Intelligential substances require.   [5. 404, 406–8]

Fruits,—*Hesperian* fables true,
If true, here *only,* and of delicious taste.   [4. 250–51]

—— Evening now approach'd
For we have *also* our evening and our morn.   [5. 627–28]

Of guests he makes them slaves
Inhospit*ably*, and kills their infant males.   [12. 167–68]

And vital Vir*tue* infus'd, and vital warmth
Throughout the fluid mass.—   [7. 236–37]

God made *thee* of choice his own, and of his own
To serve him.   [10. 766–67]

I believe every reader will agree that in all these passages, though not equally in all, the music is injured, and in some the meaning obscured. There are other lines in which the vowel is cut off, but it is so faintly pronounced in common speech, that the loss of it in poetry is scarcely perceived; and therefore such compliance with the measure may be allowed.

> Nature breeds
> Perverse, all monstrous, all prodigious things,
> Abomina*ble*, inuttera*ble*; and worse
> Than fables yet have feign'd—   [2. 624–27]
>   —From the shore
> They view'd the vast immensura*ble* abyss.   [7. 210–11]
>
> Impenetra*ble*, impal'd with circling fire.   [2. 647]
>
> To none communica*ble* in earth or heav'n.   [7. 124]

Yet even these contractions encrease the roughness of a language too rough already; and though in long Poems they may be sometimes suffered, it never can be faulty to forbear them.

Milton frequently uses in his poems the hypermetrical or redundant line of eleven syllables.

> —Thus it shall befall
> Him who to worth in woman over-trust*ing*
> Lets her will rule.—   [9. 1182–84]
>
> I also err'd in over-much admi*ring*.   [9. 1178]

Verses of this kind occur almost in every page; but though they are not unpleasing or dissonant, they ought not to be admitted into heroic poetry, since the narrow limits of our language allow us no other distinction of epic and tragic measures, than is afforded by the liberty of changing at will the terminations of the dramatic lines, and bringing them by that relaxation of metrical rigour nearer to prose.

RAMBLER ǹ. 90. Saturday, Jan. 26, 1751

In tenui labor.   Virg.[74]
What toil in slender things!

It is very difficult to write on the minuter parts of literature without failing either to please or instruct. Too much nicety of detail disgusts the greatest part of readers, and to throw a multitude of particulars under general heads, and lay down rules of extensive comprehension, is to common understandings of little use. They who undertake these subjects are therefore always in danger, as one or other inconvenience arises to their imagination, of frighting us with rugged science, or amusing us with empty sound.

In criticising the work of *Milton*, there is, indeed, opportunity to intersperse passages that can hardly fail to relieve the languors of attention; and since, in examining the variety and choice of the pauses with which he has diversified his numbers, it will be necessary to exhibit the lines in which they are to be found, perhaps the remarks may be well compensated by the examples, and the irksomeness of grammatical disquisitions somewhat alleviated.

Milton formed his scheme of versification by the poets of *Greece* and *Rome,* whom he proposed to himself for his models so far as the difference of his language from theirs would permit the imitation. There are indeed many inconveniencies inseparable from our heroick measure compared with that of *Homer* and *Virgil*; inconveniencies, which it is no reproach to *Milton* not to have overcome, because they are in their own nature insuperable; but against which he has struggled with so much art and diligence, that he may at least be said to have deserved success.

The hexameter of the ancients may be considered as consisting of fifteen syllables, so melodiously disposed, that, as every one knows who has examined the poetical authors, very pleasing and sonorous lyrick measures are formed from the fragments of the heroick. It is, indeed, scarce possible to break them in such a manner but that *invenias etiam disjecti membra poetae* [you'll still find the scattered members of the poet],[75] some harmony will still remain, and the due proportions of sound will always be discovered. This measure therefore allowed great variety of pauses, and great liberties of connecting one verse with another, because wherever the line was interrupted, either part singly was musical. But the ancients seem to have confined this privilege to hexameters; for in their other measures, though longer than the *English* heroick, those who wrote after the refinements of versification venture so seldom to change their pauses, that every variation may be supposed rather a compliance with necessity than the choice of judgment.

Milton was constrained within the narrow limits of a measure not very harmonious in the utmost perfection; the single parts, therefore, into which it was to be sometimes broken by pauses, were in danger of losing the very form of verse. This has, perhaps, notwithstanding all his care, sometimes happened.

As harmony is the end of poetical measures, no part of a verse ought to be so separated from the rest as not to remain still more harmonious than prose, or to shew, by the disposition of the tones, that it is part of a verse. This rule in the old hexameter might be easily observed, but in *English* will very frequently be in danger of violation; for the order and regularity of accents cannot well be perceived in a succession of fewer than three syllables, which will confine the English poet to only five pauses; it being supposed, that, when he connects one line with another, he should never make a full pause at less distance than that of three syllables from the beginning or end of a verse.

That this rule should be universally and indispensably established, perhaps cannot be granted; something may be allowed to variety, and something to the adaptation of the numbers to the subject; but it will be found generally necessary, and the ear will seldom fail to suffer by its neglect.

Thus when a single syllable is cut off from the rest, it must either be united to the line with which the sense connects it, or be sounded alone. If it be united to the other line, it corrupts its harmony; if disjoined, it must stand alone and with regard to musick, be superfluous; for there is no harmony in a single sound, because it has no proportion to another.

> Hypocrites austerely talk,
> Defaming as impure what God declares
> *Pure*; and commands to some, leaves free to all.
> [4. 744, 746–47]

When two syllables likewise are abscinded from the rest, they evidently want some associate sounds to make them harmonious.

> — Eyes——
> —more wakeful than to drouze,
> Charm'd with arcadian pipe, the past'ral reed
> Of *Hermes*, or his opiate rod. *Meanwhile*
> To re-salute the world with sacred light
> *Leucothea* wak'd.   [11. 130, 131–35]

> He ended, and the Son gave signal high
> To the bright minister that watch'd: *he blew*
> His trumpet   [11. 72–74]

> First in his east the glorious lamp was seen,
> Regent of day; and all th' horizon round
> Invested with bright rays, jocund to run
> His longitude through heav'n's high road; *the gray*
> Dawn, and the pleiades, before him danc'd,
> Shedding sweet influence.   [7. 370–75]

The same defect is perceived in the following lines, where the pause is at the second syllable from the beginning.

> The race
> Of that wild rout that tore the *Thracian* bard
> In *Rhodope*, where woods and rocks had ears,
> To rapture, 'till the savage clamour drown'd
> Both harp and voice; nor could the muse defend
> *Her son.* So fail not thou, who thee implores.   [7. 33–38]

When the pause falls upon the third syllable or the seventh, the harmony is better preserved; but as the third and seventh are weak syllables, the period leaves the ear unsatisfied, and in expectation of the remaining part of the verse.

> He, with his horrid crew,
> Lay vanquish'd, rolling in the fiery gulph,
> Confounded though immor*tal*. But his doom
> Reserv'd him to more wrath; for now the thought
> Both of lost happiness and lasting pain
> Torments *him*.   [1. 51–56]

> God,—with frequent intercourse,
> Thither will send his winged messengers
> On errands of supernal grace. So sung
> The glorious train ascend*ing*.   [7. 569, 571–74]

It may be, I think, established as a rule, that a pause which concludes a period should be made for the most part upon a strong syllable, as the fourth and sixth; but those pauses which only suspend the sense may be placed upon the weaker. Thus the rest in the third line of the first passage satisfies the ear better than in the fourth, and the close of the second quotation better than of the third.

> The evil soon
> Drawn back, redounded (as a flood) on those
> From whom it *sprung*; impossible to mix
> With *blessedness*.   [7. 56–59]

> —What we by day
> Lop overgrown, or prune, or prop, or bind
> One night or two with wanton growth derides,
> Tending to *wild*.   [9. 209–12]

> The paths and bow'rs doubt not but our joint hands
> Will keep from wilderness with ease as wide
> As we need walk, till younger hands ere long
> Assist *us*.   [9. 244–47]

The rest in the fifth place has the same inconvenience as in the seventh and third, that the syllable is weak.

> Beast now with beast 'gan war, and fowl with fowl,
> And fish with fish, to graze the herb all leaving,
> Devour'd each *other:* Nor stood much in awe
> Of man, but fled *him*, or with countenance grim,
> Glar'd on him pass*ing*.   [10. 710–14]

The noblest and most majestic pauses which our versification admits, are upon the fourth and sixth syllables, which are both strongly sounded in a pure and regular verse, and at either of which the line is so divided, that both members participate of harmony.

> But now at last the sacred influence
> Of light *appears*, and from the walls of heav'n
> Shoots far into the bosom of dim night
> A glimmering *dawn:* here nature first begins
> Her farthest verge, and chaos to retire.   [2. 1034–38]

But far above all others, if I can give any credit to my own ear, is the rest upon the sixth syllable, which taking in a complete compass of sound, such as is sufficient to constitute one of our lyrick measures, makes a full and solemn close. Some passages which conclude at this stop, I could never read without some strong emotions of delight or admiration.

> Before the hills appear'd, or fountain flow'd,
> Thou with the eternal wisdom didst converse,
> Wisdom thy sister; and with her didst play
> In presence of the almighty father, pleas'd
> With thy celestial *song*.   [7. 8–12]

> Or other worlds they seem'd, or happy isles,
> Like those *Hesperian* gardens fam'd of old,
> Fortunate fields, and groves, and flow'ry vales,
> Thrice happy isles! But who dwelt happy there,
> He staid not to in*quire*.   [3. 567–71]

>   He blew
> His trumpet, heard in *Oreb* since, perhaps
> When GOD descended; and, perhaps, once more
> To sound at general *doom*.   [11. 74–76]

If the poetry of *Milton* be examined, with regard to the pauses and flow of his verses into each other, it will appear, that he has performed all that our language would admit; and the comparison of his numbers with those who have cultivated the same manner of writing, will show that he excelled as much in the lower as the higher parts of his art, and that his skill in harmony was not less than his invention or his learning.

RAMBLER NO. 139. TUESDAY , JULY 16, 1751

—Sit quod vis simplex duntaxat et unum.   HOR.[76]

Let ev'ry piece be simple and be one.

It is required by *Aristotle* to the perfection of a tragedy, and is equally necessary to every other species of regular composition, that it should have a beginning, a middle, and an end. "The beginning," says he, "is that which has nothing necessarily previous, but to which that which follows is naturally consequent; the end, on the contrary, is that which by necessity, or at least according to the common course of things, succeeds something else, but which implies nothing consequent to itself; the middle is connected on one side to something that naturally goes before, and on the other to something that naturally follows it."[77]

Such is the rule laid down by this great critick, for the disposition of the different parts of a well constituted fable. It must begin, where it may be made intelligible without introduction; and end, where the mind is left in repose, without expectation of any farther event. The intermediate passages must join the last effect to the first cause, by a regular and unbroken concatenation; nothing must be therefore inserted which does not apparently arise from something foregoing, and properly make way for something that succeeds it.

This precept is to be understood in its rigour, only with respect to great and essential events, and cannot be extended in the same force to minuter circumstances and arbitrary decorations, which yet are more happy as they contribute more to the main design; for it is always a proof of extensive thought and accurate circumspection, to promote various purposes by the same act; and the idea of an ornament admits use, though it seems to exclude necessity.

Whoever purposes, as it is expressed by *Milton, to build the lofty rhyme*,[78] must acquaint himself with this law of poetical architecture, and take care that his edifice be solid as well as beautiful; that nothing stand single or independent, so as that it may be taken away without injuring the rest; but that from the foundation to the pinnacles one part rest firm upon another.

This regular and consequential distribution, is among common authors frequently neglected; but the failures of those, whose example can have no influence, may be safely overlooked, nor is it of much use to recall obscure and unregarded names to memory for the sake of sporting with their infamy. But if there is any writer whose genius can embellish impropriety, and whose authority can make error venerable, his works are the proper objects of critical inquisition. To expunge faults where there are no excellencies, is a task equally useless with that of the chemist, who employs the arts of separation and refinement upon ore in which no precious metal is contained to reward his operations.

The tragedy of *Samson Agonistes* has been celebrated as the second work of the great author of *Paradise Lost*, and opposed with all the confidence of triumph to the dramatick performances of other nations. It contains indeed just sentiments, maxims of wisdom, and oracles of piety, and many passages written with the antient spirit of choral poetry, in which there is a just and pleasing mixture of *Seneca*'s moral declamation with the wild enthusiasm of the *Greek* writers. It is therefore worthy of examination, whether a performance thus illuminated with genius, and enriched with learning, is composed according to the indispensable laws of *Aristotelian* criticism; and, omitting at present all other considerations, whether it exhibits a beginning, a middle, and an end.

The beginning is undoubtedly beautiful and proper, opening with a graceful abruptness, and proceeding naturally to a mournful recital of facts necessary to be known.

> *Samson.* A little onward lend thy guiding hand
> To these dark steps, a little farther on;
> For yonder bank hath choice of sun and shade;
> There I am wont to sit when any chance
> Relieves me from my task of servile toil,
> Daily in the common prison else enjoin'd me.——
> —O wherefore was my birth from heav'n foretold
> Twice by an angel?——
> —Why was my breeding order'd and prescrib'd,
> As of a person separate to God,
> Design'd for great exploits; if I must die
> Betray'd, captiv'd, and both my eyes put out?
> —Whom have I to complain of but myself?
> Who this high gift of strength, committed to me,
> In what part lodg'd, how easily bereft me,
> Under the seat of silence could not keep,
> But weakly to a woman must reveal it.
>   [11. 1–6, 23–24, 30–33, 46–50]

His soliloquy is interrupted by a chorus or company of men of his own tribe, who condole his miseries, extenuate his fault, and conclude with a solemn vindication of divine justice. So that at the conclusion of the first act there is no design laid, no discovery made, nor any disposition formed towards the subsequent event.

In the second act, *Manoah*, the father of *Samson*, comes to seek his son, and, being shown him by the chorus, breaks out into lamentations of his misery, and comparisons of his present with his former state, representing to him the ignominy which his religion suffers, by the festival this day celebrated in honour of *Dagon*, to whom the idolaters ascribed his overthrow.

> —Thou bear'st
> Enough, and more, the burthen of that fault;
> Bitterly hast thou paid, and still art paying
> That rigid score. A worse thing yet remains,
> This day the *Philistines* a pop'lar feast
> Here celebrate in *Gaza*; and proclaim
> Great pomp and sacrifice, and praises loud
> To *Dagon*, as their God, who hath deliver'd
> Thee, *Samson*, bound and blind into their hands,
> Them out of thine, who slew'st them many a slain.
>   [ll. 430–39]

Samson, touched with this reproach, makes a reply equally penitential and pious, which his father considers as the effusion of prophetick confidence.

> *Samson* ——— ——— God, be sure,
> Will not connive or linger thus provok'd,
> But will arise and his great name assert:
> *Dagon* must stoop, and shall e'er long receive
> Such a discomfit, as shall quite despoil him
> Of all these boasted trophies won on me.   [ll. 465–70]
> *Manoah*. With cause this hope relieves thee, and these words
> I as a prophecy receive; for God,
> Nothing more certain, will not long defer
> To vindicate the glory of his name.   [ll. 472–75]

This part of the dialogue, as it might tend to animate or exasperate *Samson*, cannot, I think, be censured as wholly superfluous; but the succeeding dispute, in which *Samson* contends to die, and which his father breaks off, that he may go to sollicit his release, is only valuable for its own beauties, and has no tendency to introduce any thing that follows it.

The next event of the drama is the arrival of *Dalilah*, with all her graces, artifices, and allurements. This produces a dialogue, in a very high degree elegant and instructive, from which she retires, after she has exhausted her persuasions, and is no more seen or heard of; nor has her visit any effect but that of raising the character of *Samson*.

In the fourth act enters *Harapha*, the giant of *Gath*, whose name had never been mentioned before, and who has now no other motive of coming than to see the man whose strength and actions are so loudly celebrated.

> *Harapha.* ——— ——— Much I have heard
> Of thy prodigious might, and feats perform'd,
> Incredible to me; in this displeas'd,
> That I was never present in the place
> Of those encounters, where we might have tried
> Each others force in camp or listed fields:
> And now am come to see of whom such noise
> Hath walk'd about, and each limb to survey,
> If thy appearance answer loud report.   [11. 1082–90]

Samson challenges him to the combat; and, after an interchange of reproaches, elevated by repeated defiance on one side, and imbittered by contemptuous insults on the other, *Harapha* retires; we then hear it determined, by *Samson* and the chorus, that no consequence good or bad will proceed from their interview.

> *Chorus.* He will directly to the lords, I fear,
> And with malicious counsel stir them up
> Some way or other farther to afflict thee.
>
> *Samson.* He must allege some cause, and offer'd fight
> Will not dare mention, lest a question rise,
> Whether he durst accept the offer or not;
> And that he durst not, plain enough appear'd.   [11. 1250–56]

At last, in the fifth act, appears a messenger from the lords assembled at the festival of *Dagon*, with a summons, by which

Samson is required to come and entertain them with some proof of his strength. *Samson*, after a short expostulation, dismisses him with a firm and resolute refusal; but during the absence of the messenger, having a while defended the propriety of his conduct, he at last declares himself moved by a secret impulse to comply, and utters some dark presages of a great event to be brought to pass by his agency, under the direction of providence.

> *Samson.* Be of good courage; I begin to feel
> Some rousing motions in me, which dispose
> To something extraordinary my thoughts.
> I with this messenger will go along,
> Nothing to do, be sure, that may dishonour
> Our law, or stain my vow of Nazarite.
> If there be ought of presage in the mind,
> This day will be remarkable in my life
> By some great act, or of my days the last.   [ll. 1381–89]

While *Samson* is conducted off by the messenger, his father returns with hopes of success in his solicitation, upon which he confers with the chorus till their dialogue is interrupted, first by a shout of triumph, and afterwards by screams of horror and agony. As they stand deliberating where they shall be secure, a man who had been present at the show enters, and relates how *Samson* having prevailed on his guide to suffer him to lean against the main pillars of the theatrical edifice, tore down the roof upon the spectators and himself.

> ——— Those two massy pillars,
> With horrible confusion, to and fro,
> He tugg'd, he shook, till down they came, and drew
> The whole roof after them, with burst of thunder,
> Upon the heads of all who sat beneath ———
> ——— *Samson* with these immixt, inevitably
> Pull'd down the same destruction on himself.
> > [ll. 1648–52, 1657–58]

This is undoubtedly a just and regular catastrophe, and the poem, therefore, has a beginning and an end which *Aristotle* himself could not have disapproved; but it must be allowed to want a middle, since nothing passes between the first act and the last, that either hastens or delays the death of *Sampson*. The whole drama, if its superfluities were cut off, would scarcely fill a single act; yet this is the tragedy which ignorance has admired, and bigotry applauded.

RAMBLER no. 140. SATURDAY, JULY 20, 1751

—*Quis tam* Lucili *fautor inepte est,*
Ut non hoc fateaur.   HOR.[79]

What doating bigot to his faults so blind,
As not to grant me this, can *Milton* find?

It is common, says *Bacon*, to desire the end without enduring the means.[80] Every member of society feels and acknowledges the necessity of detecting crimes, yet scarce any degree of virtue or reputation is able to secure an informer from publick hatred. The learned world has always admitted the usefulness of critical disquisitions, yet he that attempts to show, however modestly, the failures of a celebrated writer, shall surely irritate his admirers, and incur the imputation of envy, captiousness, and malignity.

With this danger full in my view, I shall proceed to examine the sentiments of *Milton*'s tragedy, which, though much less liable to censure than the disposition of his plan, are, like those of other writers, sometimes exposed to just exception for want of care, or want of discernment.

Sentiments are proper and improper as they consist more or less with the character and circumstances of the person to whom they are attributed, with the rules of the composition in which they are found, or with the settled and unalterable nature of things.[81]

It is common among the tragick poets to introduce their persons alluding to events or opinions, of which they could not possibly have any knowledge. The barbarians of remote or newly discovered regions often display their skill in *European* learning. The god of love is mentioned in *Tamerlane* with all the familiarity of a *Roman* epigrammatist; and a late writer has put *Harvey*'s doctrine of the circulation of the blood into the mouth of a *Turkish* statesman, who lived near two centuries before it was known even to philosophers or anatomists.[82]

Milton's learning, which acquainted him with the manners of the antient eastern nations, and his invention, which required no assistance from the common cant of poetry, have preserved him from frequent outrages of local or chronological propriety. Yet he has mentioned *Chalybean Steel*, of which it is not very likely that his chorus should have heard, and has made *Alp* the general name of a mountain, in a region where the *Alps* could scarcely be known.

> No medicinal liquor can asswage,
> Nor breath of cooling air from snowy *Alp*.   [11. 627–28]

He has taught *Samson* the tales of *Circe* and the *Syrens*, at which he apparently hints in his colloquy with *Dalilah*.

> I know thy trains,
> Tho' dearly to my cost, thy gins and toils;
> Thy fair *enchanted cup*, and *warbling charms*
> No more on me have pow'r.   [11. 932–35]

But the grossest error of this kind is the solemn introduction of the phoenix in the last scene; which is faulty, not only as it is incongruous to the personage to whom it is ascribed, but as it is so evidently contrary to reason and nature, that it ought never to be mentioned but as a fable in any serious poem.

> —— Virtue giv'n for lost
> Deprest, and overthrown, as seem'd,
> Like that self-begotten bird
> In the *Arabian* woods embost
> That no second knows, nor third,
> And lay e'er while a holocaust;
> From out her ashy womb now teem'd
> Revives, reflourishes, then vigorous most
> When most unactive deem'd,
> And tho' her body die, her fame survives,
> A secular bird ages of lives.   [11. 1697–1707]

Another species of impropriety is the unsuitableness of thoughts to the general character of the poem. The seriousness and solemnity of tragedy necessarily rejects all pointed or epigrammatical expressions, all remote conceits and opposition of ideas. *Samson's* complaint is therefore too elaborate to be natural.

> As in the land of darkness, yet in light,
> To live a life half dead, a living death,
> And bury'd; but O yet more miserable!
> Myself my sepulchre, a moving grave!
> Bury'd, yet not exempt,
> By privilege of death and burial,
> From worst of other evils, pains and wrongs.   [11. 99–105]

All allusions to low and trivial objects, with which contempt is usually associated, are doubtless unsuitable to a species of composition which ought to be always awful, though not always magnificent.[83] The remark therefore of the chorus on good and bad news, seems to want elevation.

> *Manoah.* A little stay will bring some notice hither.
> *Chor.* Of good or bad so great, of bad the sooner;
> For evil news *rides post*, while good news *baits*.   [11. 1536–38]

But of all meanness, that has least to plead which is produced by mere verbal conceits, which depending only upon sounds, lose their existence by the change of a syllable. Of this kind is the following dialogue.

> *Chor.* But had we best retire? I see a *storm*.
> *Sams.* Fair days have oft contracted wind and rain.
> *Chor.* But this another kind of tempest brings.
> *Sams.* Be less abstruse, my ridling days are past.
> *Chor.* Look now for no inchanting voice, nor fear
> The bait of honied words; a rougher tongue
> Draws hitherward, and I know him by his stride,
> The Giant *Harapha* ———   [11. 1061–68]

And yet more despicable are the lines in which *Manoah's* paternal kindness is commended by the chorus.

> Fathers are wont to *lay up* for their sons,
> Thou for thy son art bent to *lay out* all; ——   [ll. 1485–86]

Samson's complaint of the inconveniencies of imprisonment is not wholly without verbal quaintness.

> —— I a prisoner chain'd, scarce freely draw
> The air imprison'd also, close and damp.   [ll. 7–8]

From the sentiments we may properly descend to the consideration of the language, which, in imitation of the antients, is through the whole dialogue remarkably simple and unadorned, seldom heightened by epithets, or varied by figures; yet sometimes metaphors find admission, even where their consistency is not accurately preserved. Thus *Samson* confounds loquacity with a shipwreck.

> How could I once look up, or heave the head,
> Who, like a foolish *pilot*, have *shipwreck'd*
> My *vessel* trusted to me from above,
> Gloriously *rigg'd*; and for a word, a tear,
> Fool, have *divulg'd* the *secret gift* of God
> To a deceitful woman? ——   [ll. 197–202]

And the chorus talks of adding fuel to flame in a report.

> He's gone, and who knows how he may *report*
> Thy *words*, by *adding fuel to the flame*?   [ll. 1350–51]

The versification is in the dialogue much more smooth and harmonious than in the parts allotted to the chorus, which are often so harsh and dissonant, as scarce to preserve, whether the lines end with or without rhymes, any appearance of metrical regularity.

> Or do my eyes misrepresent? Can this be he,
> That heroic, that renown'd,
> Irresistible *Samson*; whom unarm'd
> No strength of man, or fiercest wild beast, could withstand;
> Who tore the lion, as the lion tears the kid ——   [ll. 124–28]

Since I have thus pointed out the faults of *Milton*, critical integrity requires that I should endeavour to display his excellencies, tho' they will not easily be discovered in short quotations, because they consist in the justness of diffuse reasonings, or in the contexture and method of continued dialogues; this play having none of those descriptions, similes, or splendid sentences, with which other tragedies are so lavishly adorned.

Yet some passages may be selected which seem to deserve particular notice, either as containing sentiments of passion, representations of life, precepts of conduct, or sallies of imagination. It is not easy to give a stronger representation of the weariness of despondency than in the words of *Samson* to his father.

> —— I feel my genial spirits droop,
> My hopes all flat; nature within me seems
> In all her functions weary of herself;
> My race of glory run, and race of shame,
> And I shall shortly be with them that rest.   [11. 594–98]

The reply of *Samson* to the flattering *Dalilah* affords a just and striking description of the stratagems and allurements of feminine hypocrisy.

> —— These are thy wonted arts,
> And arts of ev'ry woman false like thee,
> To break all faith, all vows, deceive, betray,
> Then as repentent to submit, beseech,
> And reconcilement move with feign'd remorse,
> Confess, and promise wonders in her change;
> Not truly penitent, but chief to try
> Her husband, how far urg'd his patience bears,
> His virtue or weakness which way to assail:
> Then with more cautious and instructed skill
> Again transgresses, and again submits.   [11. 748–58]

When *Samson* has refused to make himself a spectacle at the feast of *Dagon*, he first justifies his behaviour to the chorus, who charge him with having served the *Philistines*, by a very just distinction; and then destroys the common excuse of cowardice and servility, which always confound temptation with compulsion.

> *Chor.* Yet with thy strength thou serv'st the *Philistines*.
> *Sams.* Not in their idol worship, but by labour

Honest and lawful to deserve my food
Of those who have me in their civil power.
Chor. Where the heart joins not, outward acts defile not.
Sams. Where outward force constrains, the sentence holds,
But who constrains me to the temple of *Dagon*,
Not dragging? The *Philistine* lords command.
Commands are no constraints. If I obey them,
I do it freely, vent'ring to displease
God for the fear of man, and man prefer
Set God behind.   [11. 1363, 1365–75]

The complaint of blindness which *Samson* pours out at the beginning of the tragedy is equally addressed to the passions and the fancy. The enumeration of his miseries is succeeded by a very pleasing train of poetical images, and concluded by such expostulations and wishes, as reason too often submits to learn from despair.

O first created beam, and thou great word
Let there be light, and light was over all;
Why am I thus bereav'd thy prime decree?
The sun to me is dark
And silent as the moon,
When she deserts the night,
Hid in her vacant interlunar cave.
Since light so necessary is to life,
And almost life itself; if it be true,
That light is in the soul,
She all in ev'ry part; why was the sight
To such a tender ball as th' eye confin'd,
So obvious and so easy to be quench'd,
And not, as feeling, thro' all parts diffus'd,
That she may look at will thro' ev'ry pore.   [11. 83–97]

Such are the faults and such the beauties of *Samson Agonistes*, which I have shown with no other purpose than to promote the knowledge of true criticism. The everlasting verdure of *Milton*'s laurels has nothing to fear from the blasts of malignity; nor can my attempt produce any other effect, than to strengthen their shoots by lopping their luxuriance.

ADVENTURER no. 92. September 22, 1753

Cum tabulis animum censoris sumet honesti. Hor.[84]

Bold be the critic, zealous to his trust,
Like the firm judge inexorably just.

To the Adventurer.

SIR,

In the papers of criticism which you have given to the public, I have remarked a spirit of candour and love of truth, equally remote from bigotry and captiousness; a just distribution of praise amongst the antients and the moderns; a sober deference to reputation long established, without a blind adoration of antiquity; and a willingness to favour later performances, without a light or puerile fondness for novelty.

I shall, therefore, venture to lay before you, such observations as have risen to my mind in the consideration of Virgil's pastorals,[85] without any enquiry how far my sentiments deviate from established rules or common opinions.

If we survey the ten pastorals in a general view, it will be found that Virgil can derive from them very little claim to the praise of an inventor. To search into the antiquity of this kind of poetry, is not my present purpose: that it has long subsisted in the east, the Sacred Writings sufficiently inform us; and we may conjecture, with great probability, that it was sometimes the devotion, and sometimes the entertainment of the first generations of mankind. Theocritus united elegance with simplicity; and taught his shepherds to sing with so much ease and harmony, that his countrymen, despairing to excel, forbore to imitate him; and the Greeks, however vain or ambitious, left him in quiet possession of the garlands which the wood-nymphs had bestowed upon him.

Virgil, however, taking advantage of another language, ventured to copy or to rival the Sicilian Bard: he has written with greater splendour of diction, and elevation of sentiment: but as the magnificence of his performances was more, the simplicity was less; and, perhaps, where he excels Theocritus, he sometimes obtains his superiority by deviating from the pastoral character, and performing what Theocritus never attempted.

Yet, though I would willingly pay to Theocritus the honour which is always due to an original author, I am far from intending to depreciate Virgil; of whom Horace justly declares,[86] that the rural muses have appropriated to him their elegance and sweetness, and who, as he copied Theocritus in his design, has resembled him likewise in his success; for, if we except Calphurnius, an obscure author of the lower ages, I know not that a single pastoral was written after him by any poet, till the revival of literature.

But though his general merit has been universally acknowledged, I am far from thinking all the productions of his rural Thalia equally excellent: there is, indeed, in all his pastorals a strain of versification which it is vain to seek in any other poet; but if we except the first and the tenth, they seem liable either wholly or in part to considerable objections.

The second, though we should forget the great charge against it,[87] which I am afraid can never be refuted, might, I think, have perished, without any diminution of the praise of its author; for I know not that it contains one affecting sentiment or pleasing description, or one passage that strikes the imagination or awakens the passions.

The third contains a contest between two shepherds, begun with a quarrel of which some particulars might well be spared, carried on with sprightliness and elegance, and terminated at last in a reconciliation: but, surely, whether the invectives with which they attack each other be true or false, they are too much degraded from the dignity of pastoral innocence; and instead of rejoicing that they are both victorious, I should not have grieved could they have been both defeated.

The poem to Pollio is, indeed, of another kind: it is filled with images at once splendid and pleasing, and is elevated with grandeur of language worthy of the first of Roman poets; but I am not able to reconcile myself to the disproportion, between the performance and the occasion that produced it: that the golden age should return because Pollio had a son, appears so wild a fiction, that I am ready to suspect the poet of having written, for some other purpose, what he took this opportunity of producing to the public.[88]

The fifth contains a celebration of Daphnis, which has stood to all succeeding ages as the model of pastoral elegies. To deny praise to a performance which so many thousands have laboured to imitate, would be to judge with too little deference for the opinion of mankind: yet whoever shall read it with impartiality, will find that most of the images are of the mythological kind, and, therefore, easily invented; and that there are few sentiments of rational praise or natural lamentation.

In the Silenus he again rises to the dignity of philosophic sentiment and heroic poetry. The address to Varus is eminently beautiful: but since the compliment paid to GALLUS fixed the transaction to his own time, the fiction of Silenus seems injudicious; nor has any sufficient reason yet been found, to justify his choice of those fables that make the subject of the song.

The seventh exhibits another contest of the tuneful shepherds: and, surely, it is not without some reproach to his inventive power, that of ten pastorals VIRGIL has written two upon the same plan. One of the shepherds now gains an acknowledged victory, but without any apparent superiority; and the reader, when he sees the prize adjudged, is not able to discover how it was deserved.

Of the eighth pastoral, so little is properly the work of VIRGIL, that he has no claim to other praise or blame than that of a translator.

Of the ninth, it is scarce possible to discover the design or tendency: it is said, I know not upon what authority, to have been composed from fragments of other poems; and except a few lines in which the author touches upon his own misfortunes, there is nothing that seems appropriated to any time or place, or of which any other use can be discovered than to fill up the poem.

The first and the tenth pastorals, whatever be determined of the rest, are sufficient to place their author above the reach of rivalry. The complaint of Gallus disappointed in his love, is full of such sentiments as disappointed love naturally produces; his wishes are wild, his resentment is tender, and his purposes are inconstant. In the genuine language of despair, he sooths himself a-while with the pity that shall be paid him after his death;

———— *Tamen cantabitis, Arcades, inquit,*
Montibus haec vestris: soli cantare periti
Arcades. O mihi tum quam molliter ossa quiescant,
Vestra meos olim si fistula dicat amores!   [Eclogues, 10. 31–34]

———— Yet, O Arcadian swains,
Ye best artificers of soothing strains!
Tune your soft reeds, and teach your rocks my woes,
So shall my shade in sweeter rest repose.
O that your birth and business had been mine;
To feed the flock, and prune the spreading vine!   WARTON.

Discontented with his present condition, and desirous to be any thing but what he is, he wishes himself one of the shepherds. He then catches the idea of rural tranquillity; but soon discovers how much happier he should be in these happy regions, with Lycoris at his side:

Hic gelidi fontes, hic mollia prata, Lycori:
Hic nemus; hic ipso tecum consumerer aevo.
Nunc insanus amor duri me Martis in armis;
Tela inter media, atque adversos detinet hostes.
Tu procul a patria (nec sit mihi credere) tantum
Alpinas, ah dura, nives, & frigore Rheni
Me sine sola vides. Ah te ne frigora laedant!
Ah tibi ne teneras glacies secet aspera plantas!   [10. 42–49]

Here cooling fountains roll thro' flow'ry meads,
Here woods, Lycoris, lift their verdant heads;
Here could I wear my careless life away,
And in thy arms insensibly decay.
Instead of that, me frantic love detains,
'Mid foes, and dreadful darts, and bloody plains:
While you—and can my soul the tale believe,
Far from your country, lonely wand'ring leave
Me, me your lover, barbarous fugitive!
Seek the rough Alps where snows eternal shine,
And joyless borders of the frozen Rhine.
Ah! may no cold e'er blast my dearest maid,
Nor pointed ice thy tender feet invade!   WARTON.

He then turns his thoughts on every side, in quest of something

that may solace or amuse him: he proposes happiness to himself,
first in one scheme and then in another; and at last finds that
nothing will satisfy:

> *Jam neque Hamadryades rursum, nec carmina nobis*
> *Ipsa placent: ipsae rursum concedite sylvae.*
> *Non illum nostri possunt mutare labores;*
> *Nec si frigoribus mediis Hebrumque bibamus,*
> *Sithoniasque nives hyemis subeamus aquosae:*
> *Nec si, cum moriens alta liber aret in ulmo,*
> *Aethiopum versemus oves sub sidere Cancri.*
> *Omnia vincit amor; et nos cedamus amori.*   [10. 62–69]

> But now again no more the woodland maids,
> Nor pastoral songs delight—Farewell, ye shades—
> No toils of ours the cruel god can change,
> Tho' lost in frozen deserts; we should range;
> Tho' we should drink where chilling Hebrus flows,
> Endure bleak winter's blasts, and Thracian snows;
> Or on hot India's plains our flocks should feed,
> Where the parch'd elm declines his sickening head;
> Beneath fierce-glowing Cancer's fiery beams,
> Far from cool breezes and refreshing streams.
> Love over all maintains resistless sway;
> And let us love's all conquering power obey.   WARTON.

But notwithstanding the excellence of the tenth pastoral, I
cannot forbear to give the preference to the first, which is equally
natural and more diversified. The complaint of the shepherd,
who saw his old companion at ease in the shade, while himself was
driving his little flock he knew not whither, is such as, with
variation of circumstances, misery always utters at the sight of
prosperity:

> *Nos patriae fines, & dulcia linquimus arva;*
> *Nos patriam fugimus: tu, Tityre, lentus in umbra,*
> *Formosam resonare doces Amaryllida sylvas.*   [1. 3–5]

> We leave our country's bounds, our much lov'd plains;
> We from our country fly, unhappy swains!
> You, Tit'rus, in the groves at leisure laid,
> Teach Amaryllis' name to every shade.   WARTON.

His account of the difficulties of his journey gives a very tender image of pastoral distress:

> ───── *En ipse capellas*
> *Protenus aeger ago: hanc etiam vix, Tityre, duco:*
> *Hic inter densas corylos modo namque gemellos,*
> *Spemgregis, ah! silice in nuda connixa reliquit.*   [1. 12–15]

> And lo! sad part'ner of the general care,
> Weary and faint I drive my goats afar!
> While scarcely this my leading hand sustains,
> Tir'd with the way, and recent from her pains;
> For mid' yon tangled hazels as we past,
> On the bare flints her hapless twins she cast,
> The hopes and promise of my ruin'd fold!   WARTON.

The description of VIRGIL's happiness in his little farm, combines almost all the images of rural pleasure; and he, therefore, that can read it with indifference, has no sense of pastoral poetry:

> *Fortunate senex, ergo tua rura manebunt,*
> *Et tibi magna satis; quamvis lapis omnia nudus,*
> *Limosoque palus obducat pascua junco.*
> *Non insueta graves tentabunt pabula foetas,*
> *Nec mala vicini pecoris contagia laedent.*
> *Fortunate senex, hic inter flumina nota,*
> *Et fontes sacros, frigus captabis opacum.*
> *Hinc tibi, quae semper vicino ab limite sepes,*
> *Hyblaeis apibus florem depasta salicti,*
> *Saepe levi somnum suadebit inire susurro.*
> *Hinc altâ sub rupe canet frondator ad auras;*
> *Nec tamen interea raucae, tua cura, palumbes,*
> *Nec gemere aëria cessabit turtur ab ulmo.*   [1. 47–59]

> Happy old man! then still thy farms restor'd,
> Enough for thee, shall bless thy frugal board.
> What tho' rough stones the naked soil o'erspread,
> Or marshy bulrush rear its wat'ry head,
> No foreign food thy teeming ewes shall fear,
> No touch contagious spread it's influence here.
> Happy old man! here 'mid th'accustom'd streams
> And sacred springs, you'll shun the scorching beams;

While from yon willow-fence, thy pasture's bound,
The bees that suck their flowery stores around,
Shall sweetly mingle, with the whispering boughs,
Their lulling murmurs, and invite repose:
While from steep rocks the pruner's song is heard;
Nor the soft-cooing dove, thy fav'rite bird,
Mean while shall cease to breathe her melting strain,
Nor turtles from th'aerial elm to plain.   WARTON.

It may be observed, that these two poems were produced by
events that really happened; and may, therefore, be of use to
prove, that we can always feel more than we can imagine, and that
the most artful fiction must give way to truth.

I am, SIR,

Your humble Servant,

DUBIUS.

NOTES

1. Horace *Odes* 3. 2. 17–20.
2. Cf. *Preface to Shakespeare*, pp. 139–40.
3. Milton, *Paradise Lost*, 1. 63–64.
4. Horace *Satires* 1. 65.
5. These formidable creatures were destroyed by Hercules.
6. Cf. M. Hieronymus Vida *Ars poetica* 3. 469–72.
7. Horace *Ars poetica* 1. 388.
8. The opinions in this paragraph are of course all clichés and can be traced to Pope, Dryden, Addison, and others. Johnson himself expresses similar views on the Spenserian stanza (*Rambler* no. 121, pp. 30–31) and on *Cato* (*Preface to Shakespeare*, pp. 158–59).
9. These plays were by John Brown (1754) and Robert Dodsley (1758).
10. Pope, *Essay on Criticism*, 1. 365.
11. The two passages are from Butler's *Hudibras*, 1. 1. 11–12, and 2. 2. 385–88, quoted with slight inaccuracies.
12. *Paradise Lost*, 2. 594–5; 3. 25, with inaccuracies.
13. Horace *Epistles* 1. 18. 102–3.
14. *Ars poetica* 11. 40–41.
15. Horace *Epistles* 1. 19. 19.

16. Cf. *Preface to Shakespeare*, p. 140.

17. I.e., Virgil.

18. Ben Jonson in *Timber, or Discoveries*.

19. In his prefatory matter to *Paradise Lost*, Milton says rhyme has caused some modern poets "much to thir own vexation, hindrance, and constraint to express many things otherwise, and for the most part worse than else they would have exprest them."

20. Shakespeare, *Troilus and Cressida*, 2. 2. 166.

21. Virgil *Georgics* 2. 174–75.

22. *Politics* 2. 1. 1 (Bl. 1260[b] 27–36).

23. *Of the Conduct of the Understanding*, par. 38.

24. *Brutus* 34. 120

25. Horace *Ars poetica* 1. 334.

26. *Epistles* 2. 1. 170.

27. See Pliny *Naturalis historia* 35. 36. 85.

28. I.e., Juvenal, *Satire* 14.

29. See the general introduction, pp. xiii–xiv.

30. See Suetonius *Caligula* 30. 1.

31. Horace *Epistles* 1. 2. 3–4.

32. *Epistles* 3. 1. The 1756 edition prints *'fiunt.'*

33. N. Rigault's preface to J. A. de Thou's *Historiarum sui temporis*.

34. The '56 ed. reads "enquiries."

35. The references in this paragraph are to Sallust *De conjuratione Catilinae* 15. 5; J. Camerarius, *Vita Melanchthonis*; Sir William Temple, "Essay on the Cure of Gout."

36. See Thomas Tickell's preface to Addison's *Works* (1721); H. de Racan, *Oeuvres* (1857), 1: 258–59. 265.

37. Gilbert Burnet, *Life and Death of Sir Matthew Hale*.

38. *Iliad* 18. 525–26

39. *Paradise Lost*, 5. 153–208.

40. Sannazaro (1458–1530) wrote the *Eglogae piscatoriae*.

41. Virgil *Eclogues* 2. 23–24.

42. *Shepherd's Calendar*, "September," 11. 1–4.

43. *Eclogues* 8. 43–45.

44. Pope, *Pastorals*, "Autumn," 11. 89–92.

45. I.e., Virgil's fourth eclogue.

46. I.e., Virgil's sixth eclogue.

47. Johnson, as he wrote this paragraph, doubtless had in mind Milton's *Lycidas*; see p. 211.

48. Horace *Ars poetica* 11. 86–87.

49. *Ars poetica* 1. 93.

50. Dryden, *Don Sebastian* (1689); the passages quoted are from 1. 1 and 3. 1.

51. Dryden, *Aureng-Zebe,* 3. 1.

52. Juvenal *Satires* 14. 321.

53. See Herodotus, 4. 1–4.

54. Horace *Ars poetica* 1. 192.

55. On the matter of dramatic illusion, and the unities generally, cf. *Preface to Shakespeare*, pp. 151–56.

56. On tragicomedy, cf. *Preface to Shakespeare*, pp. 144–46.

57. On unity of action specifically, cf. the *Preface to Shakespeare*, pp. 151–52.

58. Phaedrus *Fabulae Aesopiae* 4. 2. 5–7.

59. *Reflection* 9.

60. In the *Preface to Shakespeare* Johnson illustrates the variety of taste in a similar manner; see pp. 140 and 156–57. The associationism here embraced lies at the heart of Johnson's theory of decorum; see his criticism of Cowley's diction, p. 210.

61. *Macbeth*, 1. 5. 48–52.

62. *Pharsalia* 3. 430–31.

63. Virgil *Aeneid* 1. 586–93.

64. Horace *Ars poetica* 1. 274.

65. Euripides *Ion* 1. 86.

66. I.e., Agesilaus. See Plutarch, *Moralia*, 191B.9 and 212F.58, who applies the anecdote to others as well.

67. Addison wrote eighteen *Spectator* papers on Milton, of which the first is no. 267 and the last no. 369.

68. *Tyrannic Love*, 4. 1.

69. *Paradise Lost*, 4. 763–66.

70. Cowley's translation of Virgil's *Georgics*, 2. 13, 15–16.

71. "To Henry Lawes," 1. 4.

72. Horace *Epistles* 2. 2. 110–14. The first line is repeated as the motto for *Adventurer* no. 92.

73. *Institutionis oratoriae* 1, Preface, 4–5.

74. Virgil *Georgics* 4. 6.

75. Horace *Satires* 1. 4. 62.

76. Horace *Ars poetica* 1. 23.

77. *Poetics* 7. 1450^b 26–27. Cf. this discussion of *Samson Agonistes* with that in the *Life of Milton*, pp. 227–28.

78. *Lycidas* 1. 11.

79. Horace *Satires* 1. 10. 2–3.

80. "Of Youth and Age." Bacon attributes this quality specifically to young men.

81. Cf. his discussion of Shakespeare's sentiments in the *Preface*, pp. 142–43.

82. See Marlowe's *Tamburlaine*, Pt. 2. 2. 1. 81–85, and for the second reference, Johnson's own *Irene*, 1. 2. 58–59.

83. On the use of low words, cf. p. 210, and on the conceits that Johnson goes on to deplore, pp. 150–51.

84. See note 72, above.

85. Cf. the account on p. 51.

86. *Satires* 1. 10. 44–45.

87. Virgil exhibits in this pastoral the unsuccessful courtship of one young man (or boy) by another.

88. Johnson is not always insensitive to the allegorical purpose of many pastorals, but he is seldom intrigued by it and invariably protests its distortion of fact; cf. his literalistic criticism of *Lycidas*, p. 211, and his discussion of the allegorical beings of *Paradise Lost*, p. 226.

Preface to

A Dictionary of the English Language (1755)

The signal merit of Johnson's *Dictionary* lies in its being
the first. Earlier works so named were not dictionaries in
the present sense, but compilations of difficult words or
technical terms. Nathaniel Bailey's *Universal Etymological
English Dictionary* (1721) and Ephraim Chambers's *Cyclopaedia* (1728) are most nearly dictionaries in the modern
acceptation. But though Johnson respected and employed
in his own work both of these, his achievement far surpasses them. His dictionary is two and a half times the compass
of Bailey's, and is the first to contain thorough definitions
(40,000) and illustrative quotations (114,000). It is also the
first directly to confront questions of usage and propriety.
Johnson is in this capacity no captious autocrat of language, but neither is he a neutral compiler; he often dis-
commends low or slang words, and he dismisses some
"fugitive cant" as too evanescent for formal definition.
The written language takes precedence for Johnson over
the "corruptions of oral utterance." He is thus a prescriptive lexicographer: not wanton or dictatorial, but judicious
and discriminating; and in this he set the style for most
subsequent dictionaries. There has since been a revolt
among some linguists in favor of a descriptive, allegedly
scientific and impartial enumeration of all words in cur-
rency, whether oral or written; and from this school has
arisen a dictionary in which the quoted usages of baseball
players mingle democratically with those of Shakespeare
and Pope. But there are signs that this experiment, like the
spelling reform movement at the turn of the century, is
otiose; at least, it has been rejected by such recent authorities as Wilson Follett's *Modern American Usage* (1966).

In any event, it may justly be said that normative dictionaries have been developments of Johnson's, not new creations, and many of his definitions remain standard. Nine years in the making, the *Dictionary* appeared in two large folio volumes in 1755, and, together with the *Rambler* essays written earlier in that decade, securely established Johnson's reputation.

Intimate in tone but yet ornate in expression, the *Preface* may startle those readers acquainted only with the impersonal sobriety of its modern successors. Its significance is twofold: it is one of the earliest comprehensive pronouncements in English on the function and nature of a dictionary, and it is one of Johnson's most carefully worked and personal essays. As a statement of lexicography it is cogent but not exceptional: many of its positions had been anticipated in Chambers's preface to his *Cyclopaedia* and in the prefaces to the great French and Italian dictionaries—with which, confident in his achievement, Johnson continually invites a comparison. He espoused, for his day, liberal principles of lexicography, though in our own they would be termed moderate or even conservative. He is supremely conscious of the ineluctable mutability of language, and upon those who urged its petrifaction under a puritanical Academy—as, for example, Swift, Defoe, and "Dick Minim" (see p. 20)—he expends an ample disdain. And yet, although he must acquiesce, he will not rejoice, in its mutability; nor will he solace himself with the delusion that all change supposes vitality or progression, and hence all change is good. He clearly views his dictionary as a force to impede, though not to arrest it, and to determine a standard of good usage. "It remains," he says, "that we retard what we cannot repel, that we palliate what we cannot cure."

But it is by its eloquence and its candor that the *Preface* lays hold on posterity. It is saturated with Johnson's characteristically stoic pessimism. He laments that English has failed to adhere more firmly to its Anglo-Saxon origins, and believes it to be in a decline from its zenith in the Renaissance, a decline now accelerated by slang, jargon, and Gallicisms. As Paul Fussell has noted, Johnson sustains a contrast throughout between his lofty but naive aspirations when commencing the *Dictionary*, and his subsequent frustration and disillusionment. The *Preface* resonates with the theme of *Rasselas* and *The Vanity of Human Wishes*. Two Johnsons are in fact deployed within it: one recalls the sophomoric student in *Human Wishes*, or Imlac in *Rasselas* when he is expatiating rapturously on the encyclopedic knowledge required of a master writer; the other Johnson is "the poet doomed at last to wake a lexicographer," whom experience has purified of his innocent expectations. The tone seems to alternate between his own justifiable pride in performing what no other individual has ever achieved, and a belief in the ultimate imperfection and even futility of all human endeavor. The sincerity of the concluding paragraphs has been put in doubt, for there is evidence that he found not uncongenial the task of compiling a dictionary, and that he was indeed curious, possibly apprehensive, about its critical reception. But sincerity aside, his peroration succeeds in an attempt rhetorically perilous: its elegiac and valetudinarian manner, less expertly sustained, might have been polluted by sentimentality. Instead, we are induced to admire Johnson's apparent stoicism even as he solicits our sympathy.

I have followed the first edition of 1755, silently introducing a few minor stylistic changes found in the fourth (1773), the last edition to be revised by Johnson.

It is the fate of those who toil at the lower employments of life, to be rather driven by the fear of evil, than attracted by the prospect of good; to be exposed to censure, without hope of praise; to be disgraced by miscarriage, or punished for neglect,

where success would have been without applause, and diligence
without reward.

Among these unhappy mortals is the writer of dictionaries;
whom mankind have considered, not as the pupil, but the slave of
science, the pionier of literature, doomed only to remove rubbish
and clear obstructions from the paths through which Learning
and Genius press forward to conquest and glory, without bestowing a smile on the humble drudge that facilitates their progress.
Every other authour may aspire to praise; the lexicographer can
only hope to escape reproach, and even this negative recompense
has been yet granted to very few.

I have, notwithstanding this discouragement, attempted a dictionary of the *English* language, which, while it was employed in
the cultivation of every species of literature, has itself been
hitherto neglected; suffered to spread, under the direction of
chance, into wild exuberance; resigned to the tyranny of time and
fashion; and exposed to the corruptions of ignorance, and caprices of innovation.

When I took the first survey of my undertaking, I found our
speech copious without order, and energetick without rules:
wherever I turned my view, there was perplexity to be disentangled, and confusion to be regulated; choice was to be made out of
boundless variety, without any established principle of selection;
adulterations were to be detected, without a settled test of purity;
and modes of expression to be rejected or received, without the
suffrages of any writers of classical reputation or acknowledged
authority.

Having therefore no assistance but from general grammar, I
applied myself to the perusal of our writers; and noting whatever
might be of use to ascertain or illustrate any word or phrase,
accumulated in time the materials of a dictionary, which, by
degrees, I reduced to method, establishing to myself, in the
progress of the work, such rules as experience and analogy suggested to me; experience, which practice and observation were
continually increasing; and analogy, which, though in some
words obscure, was evident in others.

In adjusting the ORTHOGRAPHY, which has been to this time

unsettled and fortuitous, I found it necessary to distinguish those irregularities that are inherent in our tongue, and perhaps coeval with it, from others which the ignorance or negligence of later writers has produced. Every language has its anomalies, which, though inconvenient, and in themselves once unnecessary, must be tolerated among the imperfections of human things, and which require only to be registered, that they may not be increased, and ascertained, that they may not be confounded: but every language has likewise its improprieties and absurdities, which it is the duty of the lexicographer to correct or proscribe.

As language was at its beginning merely oral, all words of necessary or common use were spoken before they were written; and while they were unfixed by any visible signs, must have been spoken with great diversity, as we now observe those who cannot read catch sounds imperfectly, and utter them negligently. When this wild and barbarous jargon was first reduced to an alphabet, every penman endeavoured to express, as he could, the sounds which he was accustomed to pronounce or to receive, and vitiated in writing such words as were already vitiated in speech. The powers of the letters, when they were applied to a new language, must have been vague and unsettled, and therefore different hands would exhibit the same sound by different combinations.

From this uncertain pronunciation arise in a great part the various dialects of the same country, which will always be observed to grow fewer, and less different, as books are multiplied; and from this arbitrary representation of sounds by letters, proceeds that diversity of spelling observable in the *Saxon* remains, and I suppose in the first books of every nation, which perplexes or destroys analogy, and produces anomalous formations, that, being once incorporated, can never be afterward dismissed or reformed.

Of this kind are the derivatives *length* from *long, strength* from *strong, darling* from *dear, breadth* from *broad,* from *dry, drought,* and from *high, height,* which *Milton,* in zeal for analogy, writes *highth; Quid te exempta juvat spinis de pluribus una* [What does it avail to pluck out from many errors merely one?];[1] to change all would be too much, and to change one is nothing.

This uncertainty is most frequent in the vowels, which are so capriciously pronounced, and so differently modified, by accident or affectation, not only in every province, but in every mouth, that to them, as is well known to etymologists, little regard is to be shewn in the deduction of one language from another.

Such defects are not errours in orthography, but spots of barbarity impressed so deep in the *English* language, that criticism can never wash them away: these, therefore, must be permitted to remain untouched; but many words have likewise been altered by accident, or depraved by ignorance, as the pronunciation of the vulgar has been weakly followed; and some still continue to be variously written, as authours differ in their care or skill: of these it was proper to enquire the true orthography, which I have always considered as depending on their derivation, and have therefore referred them to their original languages: thus I write *enchant, enchantment, enchanter,* after the *French,* and *incantation* after the *Latin;* thus *entire* is chosen rather than *intire,* because it passed to us not from the *Latin integer,* but from the *French entier.*

Of many words it is difficult to say whether they were immediately received from the *Latin* or the *French,* since at the time when we had dominions in *France,* we had *Latin* service in our churches, It is, however, my opinion, that the *French* generally supplied us; for we have few *Latin* words, among the terms of domestick use, which are not *French;* but many *French,* which are very remote from *Latin.*

Even in words of which the derivation is apparent, I have been often obliged to sacrifice uniformity to custom; thus I write, in compliance with a numberless majority, *convey* and *inveigh, deceit* and *receipt, fancy* and *phantom;* sometimes the derivative varies from the primitive, as *explain* and *explanation, repeat* and *repetition.*

Some combinations of letters having the same power are used indifferently without any discoverable reason of choice, as in *choak, choke; soap, sope; fewel, fuel,* and many others; which I have sometimes inserted twice, that those who search for them under either form, may not search in vain.

In examining the orthography of any doubtful word, the mode of spelling by which it is inserted in the series of the dictionary, is to be considered as that to which I give, perhaps not often rashly, the preference. I have left, in the examples, to every authour his own practice unmolested, that the reader may balance suffrages, and judge between us: but this question is not always to be determined by reputed or by real learning; some men, intent upon greater things, have thought little on sounds and derivations; some, knowing in the ancient tongues, have neglected those in which our words are commonly to be sought. Thus *Hammond* writes *fecibleness* for *feasibleness,* because I suppose he imagined it derived immediately from the *Latin*; and some words, such as *dependant, dependent; dependance, dependence,* vary their final syllable, as one or another language is present to the writer.

In this part of the work, where caprice has long wantoned without controul, and vanity sought praise by petty reformation, I have endeavoured to proceed with a scholar's reverence for antiquity, and a grammarian's regard to the genius of our tongue. I have attempted few alterations, and among those few, perhaps the greater part is from the modern to the ancient practice; and I hope I may be allowed to recommend to those, whose thoughts have been perhaps employed too anxiously on verbal singularities, not to disturb, upon narrow views, or for minute propriety, the orthography of their fathers. It has been asserted, that for the law to be *known,* is of more importance than to be *right.* Change, says *Hooker,* is not made without inconvenience, even from worse to better.[2] There is in constancy and stability a general and lasting advantage, which will always overbalance the slow improvements of gradual correction. Much less ought our written language to comply with the corruptions of oral utterance, or copy that which every variation of time or place makes different from itself, and imitate those changes, which will again be changed, while imitation is employed in observing them.

This recommendation of steadiness and uniformity does not proceed from an opinion, that particular combinations of letters have much influence on human happiness; or that truth may not be successfully taught by modes of spelling fanciful and erroneous: I am not yet so lost in lexicography, as to forget that *words are the daughters of earth, and that things are the sons of heaven.*[3] Language is only the instrument of science, and words are but the signs of ideas: I wish, however, that the instrument might be less apt to decay, and that signs might be permanent, like the things which they denote.

In settling the orthography, I have not wholly neglected the pronunciation, which I have directed, by printing an accent upon the acute or elevated syllable. It will sometimes be found, that the accent is placed by the authour quoted, on a different syllable from that marked in the alphabetical series; it is then to be understood, that custom has varied, or that the authour has, in my opinion, pronounced wrong. Short directions are sometimes given where the sound of letters is irregular; and if they are sometimes omitted, defect in such minute observations will be more easily excused, than superfluity.

In the investigation both of the orthography and signification of words, their ETYMOLOGY was necessarily to be considered, and they were therefore to be divided into primitives and derivatives. A primitive word, is that which can be traced no further to any *English* root; thus *circumspect, circumvent, circumstance, delude, concave,* and *complicate,* though compounds in the *Latin,* are to us primitives. Derivatives are all those that can be referred to any word in *English* of greater simplicity.

The derivatives I have referred to their primitives, with an accuracy sometimes needless; for who does not see that *remoteness* comes from *remote, lovely* from *love, concavity* from *concave,* and *demonstrative* from *demonstrate?* but this grammatical exuberance the scheme of my work did not allow me to repress. It is of great importance in examining the general fabrick of a language, to trace one word from another, by noting the usual modes of derivation and inflection; and uniformity must be preserved in systematical works, though sometimes at the expence of particular propriety.

Among other derivatives I have been careful to insert and elucidate the anomalous plurals of nouns and preterites of verbs, which in the *Teutonick* dialects are very frequent, and though familiar to those who have always used them, interrupt and embarrass the learners of our language.

The two languages from which our primitives have been derived are the *Roman* and *Teutonick*: under the *Roman* I comprehend the *French* and provincial tongues; and under the *Teutonick* range the *Saxon, German,* and all their kindred dialects. Most of our polysyllables are *Roman,* and our words of one syllable are very often *Teutonick.*

In assigning the *Roman* original, it has perhaps sometimes happened that I have mentioned only the *Latin,* when the word was borrowed from the *French*; and considering myself as employed only in the illustration of my own language, I have not been very careful to observe whether the *Latin* word be pure or barbarous, or the *French* elegant or obsolete.

For the Teutonick etymologies, I am commonly indebted to *Junius* and *Skinner,* [4] the only names which I have forborn to quote when I copied their books; not that I might appropriate their labours or usurp their honours, but that I might spare a perpetual repetition by one general acknowledgment. Of these, whom I ought not to mention but with the reverence due to instructors and benefactors, *Junius* appears to have excelled in extent of learning, and *Skinner* in rectitude of understanding. *Junius* was accurately skilled in all the northen languages, *Skinner* probably examined the ancient and remoter dialects only by occasional inspection into dictionaries; but the learning of *Junius* is often of no other use than to show him a track by which he may deviate from his purpose, to which *Skinner* always presses forward by the shortest way. *Skinner* is often ignorant, but never ridiculous: *Junius* is always full of knowledge; but his variety distracts his judgment, and his learning is very frequently disgraced by his absurdities.

The votaries of the northern muses will not perhaps easily restrain their indignation, when they find the name of *Junius* thus degraded by a disadvantageous comparison; but whatever reverence is due to his diligence, or his attainments, it can be no criminal degree of censoriousness to charge that etymologist with want of judgment, who can seriously derive *dream* from *drama,* because *life is a drama, and a drama is a dream;* and who declares with a tone of defiance, that no man can fail to derive *moan* from μόνος, *monos, single* or *solitary,* who considers that grief naturally loves to be *alone.*[5]

Our knowledge of the northern literature is so scanty, that of words undoubtedly *Teutonick* the original is not always to be found in any ancient language; and I have therefore inserted *Dutch* or *German* substitutes, which I consider not as radical but parallel, not as the parents, but sisters of the *English.*

The words which are represented as thus related by descent or cognation, do not always agree in sense; for it is incident to words, as to their authours, to degenerate from their ancestors, and to change their manners when they change their country. It is sufficient, in etymological enquiries, if the senses of kindred words be found such as may easily pass into each other, or such as may both be referred to one general idea.

The etymology, so far as it is yet known, was easily found in the volumes where it is particularly and professedly delivered; and, by proper attention to the rules of derivation, the orthography was soon adjusted. But to COLLECT the WORDS of our language was a task of greater difficulty: the deficiency of dictionaries was immediately apparent; and when they were exhausted, what was yet wanting must be sought by fortuitous and unguided excursions into books, and gleaned as industry should find, or chance should offer it, in the boundless chaos of a living speech. My search, however, has been either skilful or lucky; for I have much augmented the vocabulary.

As my design was a dictionary, common or appellative, I have omitted all words which have relation to proper names; such as *Arian, Socinian, Calvinist, Benedictine, Mahometan;* but have retained those of a more general nature, as *Heathen, Pagan.*

Of the terms of art I have received such as could be found either in books of science or technical dictionaries; and have often inserted, from philosophical writers, words which are supported perhaps only by a single authority, and which being not admitted into general use, stand yet as candidates or probationers, and must depend for their adoption on the suffrage of futurity.

The words which our authours have introduced by their knowledge of foreign languages, or ignorance of their own, by vanity or wantonness, by compliance with fashion or lust of innovation, I have registred as they occurred, though commonly only to censure them, and warn others against the folly of naturalizing useless foreigners to the injury of the natives.

I have not rejected any by design, merely because they were unnecessary or exuberant; but have received those which by different writers have been differently formed, as *viscid,* and *viscidity, viscous,* and *viscosity.*

Compounded or double words I have seldom noted, except when they obtain a signification different from that which the components have in their simple state. Thus *highwayman, woodman,* and *horsecourser,* require an explanation; but of *thieflike* or *coachdriver* no notice was needed, because the primitives contain the meaning of the compounds.

Words arbitrarily formed by a constant and settled analogy, like diminutive adjectives in *ish,* as *greenish, bluish,* adverbs in *ly,* as *dully, openly,* substantives in *ness,* as *vileness, faultiness,* were less diligently sought, and sometimes have been omitted, when I had no authority that invited me to insert them; not that they are not genuine and regular offsprings of *English* roots, but because their relation to the primitive being always the same, their signification cannot be mistaken.

The verbal nouns in *ing,* such as the *keeping* of the *castle,* the *leading* of the *army,* are always neglected, or placed only to illustrate the sense of the verb, except when they signify things as well as actions, and have therefore a plural number, as *dwelling, living*; or have an absolute and abstract signification, as *colouring, painting, learning.*

The participles are likewise omitted, unless, by signifying rather habit or quality than action, they take the nature of adjectives; as a *thinking* man, a man of prudence; a *pacing* horse, a horse that can pace: these I have ventured to call *participial adjectives.* But neither are these always inserted, because they are commonly to be understood, without any danger of mistake, by consulting the verb.

Obsolete words are admitted, when they are found in authours not obsolete, or when they have any force or beauty that may deserve revival.

As composition is one of the chief characteristicks of a language, I have endeavoured to make some reparation for the universal negligence of my predecessors, by inserting great numbers of compounded words, as may be found under *after, fore, new, night, fair,* and many more. These, numerous as they are, might be multiplied, but that use and curiosity are here satisfied, and the frame of our language and modes of our combination amply discovered.

Of some forms of composition, such as that by which *re* is prefixed to note *repetition,* and *un* to signify *contrariety* or *privation,* all the examples cannot be accumulated, because the use of these particles, if not wholly arbitrary, is so little limited, that they are hourly affixed to new words as occasion requires, or is imagined to require them.

There is another kind of composition more frequent in our language than perhaps in any other, from which arises to foreigners the greatest difficulty. We modify the signification of many verbs by a particle subjoined; as to *come off,* to escape by a fetch; to *fall on,* to attack; to *fall off,* to apostatize; to *break off,* to stop abruptly; to *bear out,* to justify; to *fall in,* to comply; to *give over,* to cease; to *set off,* to embellish; to *set in,* to begin a continual tenour; to *set out,* to begin a course or journey; to *take off,* to copy; with innumerable expressions of the same kind of which some appear wildly irregular, being so far distant from the sense of the simple words, that no sagacity will be able to trace the steps by which they arrived at the present use. These I have noted with great care; and though I cannot flatter myself that the collection is complete, I believe I have so far assisted the students of our language, that this kind of phraseology will be no longer insuperable; and the combinations of verbs and particles, by chance omitted, will be easily explained by comparison with those that may be found.

Many words yet stand supported only by the name of *Bailey, Ainsworth, Philips,*[6] or the contracted *Dict.* for *Dictionaries* subjoined; of these I am not always certain that they are read in any book but the works of lexicographers. Of such I have omitted many, because I had never read them; and many I have inserted, because they may perhaps exist, though they have escaped my notice: they are, however, to be yet considered as resting only upon the credit of former dictionaries. Others, which I considered as useful, or know to be proper, though I could not at present support them by authorities, I have suffered to stand upon my own attestation, claiming the same privilege with my predecessors of being sometimes credited without proof.

The words, thus selected and disposed, are grammatically considered; they are referred to the different parts of speech; traced, when they are irregularly inflected, through their various terminations; and illustrated by observations, not indeed of great or striking importance, separately considered, but necessary to the elucidation of our language, and hitherto neglected or forgotten by *English* grammarians.

That part of my work on which I expect malignity most frequently to fasten, is the *Explanation*; in which I cannot hope to satisfy those, who are perhaps not inclined to be pleased, since I have not always been able to satisfy myself. To interpret a language by itself is very difficult; many words cannot be explained by synonimes, because the idea signified by them has not more than one appellation; nor by paraphrase, because simple ideas cannot be described. When the nature of things is unknown, or the notion unsettled and indefinite, and various in various minds, the words by which such notions are conveyed, or such things denoted, will be ambiguous and perplexed. And such is the fate of hapless lexicography, that not only darkness, but light, impedes and distresses it; things may be not only too little, but too much known, to be happily illustrated. To explain, requires the use of terms less abstruse than that which is to be explained, and such terms cannot always be found; for as nothing can be proved but by supposing something intuitively known, and evident without proof, so nothing can be defined but by the use of words too plain to admit a definition.

Other words there are, of which the sense is too subtle and evanescent to be fixed in a paraphrase; such are all those which are by the grammarians termed *expletives*, and, in dead languages, are suffered to pass for empty sounds, of no other use than to fill a verse, or to modulate a period, but which are easily perceived in living tongues to have power and emphasis, though it be sometimes such as no other form of expression can convey.

My labour has likewise been much increased by a class of verbs too frequent in the *English* language, of which the signification is so loose and general, the use so vague and indeterminate, and the senses detorted so widely from the first idea, that it is hard to trace them through the maze of variation, to catch them on the brink of utter inanity, to circumscribe them by any limitations, or interpret them by any words of distinct and settled meaning; such are *bear, break, come, cast, full, get, give, do, put, set, go, run, make, take, turn, throw.* If of these the whole power is not accurately delivered, it must be remembered, that while our language is yet living, and variable by the caprice of every one that speaks it, these words are hourly shifting their relations, and can no more be ascertained in a dictionary, than a grove, in the agitation of a storm, can be accurately delineated from its picture in the water.

The particles are among all nations applied with so great latitude, that they are not easily reducible under any regular scheme of explication: this difficulty is not less, nor perhaps greater, in *English,* than in other languages. I have laboured them with diligence, I hope with success; such at least as can be expected in a task, which no man, however, learned or sagacious, has yet been able to perform.

Some words there are which I cannot explain, because I do not understand them; these might have been omitted very often with little inconvenience, but I would not so far indulge my vanity as to decline this confession: for when *Tully* owns himself ignorant whether *lessus,* in the twelve tables, means a *funeral song,* or *mourning garment;* and *Aristotle* doubts whether οὐρεύς in the Iliad, signifies a *mule,* or *muleteer,*[7] I may surely, without shame, leave some obscurities to happier industry, or future information.

The rigour of interpretative lexicography requires that *the explanation, and the word explained, should be always reciprocal*; this I have always endeavoured, but could not always attain. Words are seldom exactly synonimous; a new term was not introduced, but because the former was thought inadequate: names, therefore, have often many ideas, but few ideas have many names. It was then necessary to use the proximate word, for the deficiency of single terms can very seldom be supplied by circumlocution; nor is the inconvenience great of such mutilated interpretations, because the sense may easily be collected entire from the examples.

In every word of extensive use, it was requisite to mark the progress of its meaning, and show by what gradations of intermediate sense it has passed from its primitive to its remote and accidental signification; so that every foregoing explanation should tend to that which follows, and the series be regularly concatenated from the first notion to the last.

This is specious, but not always practicable; kindred senses may be so interwoven, that the perplexity cannot be disentangled, nor any reason be assigned why one should be ranged before the other. When the radical idea branches out into parallel ramifications, how can a consecutive series be formed of senses in their nature collateral? The shades of meaning sometimes pass imperceptibly into each other; so that though on one side they apparently differ, yet it is impossible to mark the point of contact. Ideas of the same race, though not exactly alike, are sometimes so little different, that no words can express the dissimilitude, though the mind easily perceives it, when they are exhibited together; and sometimes there is such a confusion of acceptations, that discernment is wearied, and distinction puzzled, and perseverance herself hurries to an end, by crouding together what she cannot separate.

These complaints of difficulty will, by those that have never considered words beyond their popular use, be thought only the jargon of a man willing to magnify his labours, and procure veneration to his studies by involution and obscurity. But every art is obscure to those that have not learned it: this uncertainty of terms, and commixture of ideas, is well known to those who have joined philosophy with grammar; and if I have not expressed them very clearly, it must be remembered that I am speaking of that which words are insufficient to explain.

The original sense of words is often driven out of use by their metaphorical acceptations, yet must be inserted for the sake of a regular origination. Thus I know not whether *ardour* is used for *material heat,* or whether *flagrant,* in *English,* ever signifies the same with *burning*; yet such are the primitive ideas of these words, which are therefore set first, though without examples, that the figurative senses may be commodiously deduced.

Such is the exuberance of signification which many words have obtained, that it was scarcely possible to collect all their senses; sometimes the meaning of derivatives must be sought in the mother term, and sometimes deficient explanations of the primitive may be supplied in the train of derivation. In any case of doubt or difficulty, it will be always proper to examine all the words of the same race; for some words are slightly passed over to avoid repetition, some admitted easier and clearer explanation than others, and all will be better understood, as they are considered in greater variety of structures and relations.

All the interpretations of words are not written with the same skill, or the same happiness: things equally easy in themselves, are not all equally easy to any single mind. Every writer of a long work commits errours, where there appears neither ambiguity to mislead, nor obscurity to confound him; and in a search like this, many felicities of expression will be casually overlooked, many convenient parallels will be forgotten, and many particulars will admit improvement from a mind utterly unequal to the whole performance.

But many seeming faults are to be imputed rather to the nature of the undertaking, than the negligence of the performer. Thus some explanations are unavoidably reciprocal or circular, as *hind, the female of the stag; stag, the male of the hind*: sometimes easier words are changed into harder, as *burial* into *sepulture* or *interment, drier* into *desiccative, dryness* into *siccity* or *aridity, fit* into *paroxysm;* for the easiest word, whatever it be, can never be translated into one more easy. But easiness and difficulty are merely relative, and if the present prevalence of our language should invite foreigners to this dictionary, many will be assisted by those words which now seem only to increase or produce obscurity. For this reason I have endeavoured frequently to join a *Teutonick* and *Roman* interpretation, as to CHEER, to *gladden*, or *exhilarate*, that every learner of *English* may be assisted by his own tongue.

The solution of all difficulties, and the supply of all defects, must be sought in the examples, subjoined to the various senses of each word, and ranged according to the time of their authours.

When first I collected these authorities, I was desirous that every quotation should be useful to some other end than the illustration of a word; I therefore extracted from philosophers principles of science; from historians remarkable facts; from chymists complete processes; from divines striking exhortations; and from poets beautiful descriptions. Such is design, while it is yet at a distance from execution. When the time called upon me to range this accumulation of elegance and wisdom into an alphabetical series, I soon discovered that the bulk of my volumes would fright away the student, and was forced to depart from my scheme of including all that was pleasing or useful in *English* literature, and reduce my transcripts very often to clusters of words, in which scarcely any meaning is retained; thus to the weariness of copying, I was condemned to add the vexation of expunging. Some passages I have yet spared, which may relieve the labour of verbal searches, and intersperse with verdure and flowers the dusty desarts of barren philology.

The examples, thus mutilated, are no longer to be considered as conveying the sentiments or doctrine of their authours; the word for the sake of which they are inserted, with all its appendant clauses, has been carefully preserved; but it may sometimes happen, by hasty detruncation, that the general tendency of the sentence may be changed: the divine may desert his tenets, or the philosopher his system.

Some of the examples have been taken from writers who were never mentioned as masters of elegance or models of stile; but words must be sought where they are used; and in what pages, eminent for purity, can terms of manufacture or agriculture be found? Many quotations serve no other purpose, than that of proving the bare existence of words, and are therefore selected with less scrupulousness than those which are to teach their structures and relations.

My purpose was to admit no testimony of living authors, that I might not be misled by partiality, and that none of my cotemporaries might have reason to complain; nor have I departed from this resolution, but when some performance of uncommon excellence excited my veneration, when my memory supplied me, from late books, with an example that was wanting, or when my heart, in the tenderness of friendship, solicited admission for a favourite name.

So far have I been from any care to grace my pages with modern decorations, that I have studiously endeavoured to collect examples and authorities from the writers before the restoration, whose works I regard as *the wells of English undefiled,* as the pure sources of genuine diction. Our language for almost a century, has, by the concurrence of many causes, been gradually departing from its original *Teutonick* character, and deviating towards a *Gallick* structure and phraseology, from which it ought to be our endeavour to recal it, by making our ancient volumes the ground-work of stile, admitting among the additions of later times, only such as may supply real deficiencies, such as are readily adopted by the genius of our tongue, and incorporate easily with our native idioms.

But as every language has a time of rudeness antecedent to perfection, as well as of false refinement and declension, I have been cautious lest my zeal for antiquity might drive me into times too remote, and croud my book with words now no longer understood. I have fixed *Sidney's* work for the boundary, beyond which I make few excursions. From the authours, which rose in the time of *Elizabeth,* a speech might be formed adequate to all the purposes of use and elegance. If the language of theology were extracted from *Hooker* and the translation of the Bible; the terms of natural knowledge from *Bacon*; the phrases of policy, war, and navigation from *Raleigh*; the dialect of poetry and fiction from *Spenser* and *Sidney*; and the diction of common life from *Shakespeare,* few ideas would be lost to mankind, for want of *English* words, in which they might be expressed.

It is not sufficient that a word is found, unless it be so combined as that its meaning is apparently determined by the tract and tenour of the sentence; such passages I have therefore chosen, and when it happened that any authour gave a definition of a term, or such an explanation as is equivalent to a definition, I have placed his authority as a supplement to my own, without regard to the chronological order, that is otherwise observed.

Some words, indeed, stand unsupported by any authority, but they are commonly derivative nouns or adverbs, formed from their primitives by regular and constant analogy, or names of things seldom occurring in books, or words of which I have reason to doubt the existence.

There is more danger of censure from the multiplicity than paucity of examples; authorities will sometimes seem to have been accumulated without necessity or use, and perhaps some will be found, which might, without loss, have been omitted. But a work of this kind is not hastily to be charged with superfluities: those quotations, which to careless or unskilful perusers appear only to repeat the same sense, will often exhibit, to a more accurate examiner, diversities of signification, or, at least, afford different shades of the same meaning: one will shew the word applied to persons, another to things; one will express an ill, another a good, and a third a neutral sense; one will prove the expression genuine from an ancient authour; another will shew it elegant from a modern: a doubtful authority is corroborated by another of more credit; an ambiguous sentence is ascertained by a passage clear and determinate; the word, how often soever repeated, appears with new associates and in different combinations, and every quotation contributes something to the stability or enlargement of the language.

When words are used equivocally, I receive them in either sense; when they are metaphorical, I adopt them in their primitive acceptation.

I have sometimes, though rarely, yielded to the temptation of exhibiting a genealogy of sentiments, by shewing how one authour copied the thoughts and diction of another: such quotations are indeed little more than repetitions, which might justly be censured, did they not gratify the mind, by affording a kind of intellectual history.

The various syntactical structures occurring in the examples have been carefully noted; the licence or negligence with which many words have been hitherto used, has made our stile capricious and indeterminate; when the different combinations of the same word are exhibited together, the preference is readily given to propriety, and I have often endeavoured to direct the choice.

Thus have I laboured by settling the orthography, displaying the analogy, regulating the structures, and ascertaining the signification of *English* words, to perform all the parts of a faithful lexicographer: but I have not always executed my own scheme, or satisfied my own expectations. The work, whatever proofs of diligence and attention it may exhibit, is yet capable of many improvements: the orthography which I recommend is still controvertible, the etymology which I adopt is uncertain, and perhaps frequently erroneous; the explanations are sometimes too much contracted, and sometimes too much diffused, the significations are distinguished rather with subtilty than skill, and the attention is harrassed with unnecessary minuteness.

The examples are too often injudiciously truncated, and perhaps sometimes, I hope very rarely, alleged in a mistaken sense; for in making this collection I trusted more to memory, than, in a state of disquiet and embarrassment, memory can contain, and purposed to supply at the review what was left incomplete in the first transcription.

Many terms appropriated to particular occupations, though necessary and significant, are undoubtedly omitted; and of the words most studiously considered and exemplified, many senses have escaped observation.

Yet these failures, however frequent, may admit extenuation and apology. To have attempted much is always laudable, even when the enterprize is above the strength that undertakes it: To rest below his own aim is incident to every one whose fancy is active, and whose views are comprehensive; nor is any man satisfied with himself because he has done much, but because he can conceive little. When first I engaged in this work, I resolved to leave neither words nor things unexamined, and pleased myself with a prospect of the hours which I should revel away in feasts of literature, with the obscure recesses of northern learning, which I should enter and ransack, the treasures with which I expected every search into those neglected mines to reward my labour, and the triumph with which I should display my acquisitions to mankind. When I had thus enquired into the original of words, I resolved to show likewise my attention to things; to pierce deep into every science, to enquire the nature of every substance of which I inserted the name, to limit every idea by definition strictly logical, and exhibit every production of art or nature in an accurate description, that my book might be in place of all other dictionaries whether appellative or technical. But these were the dreams of a poet doomed at last to wake a lexicographer. I soon found that it is too late to look for instruments, when the work calls for execution, and that whatever abilities I brought to my task, with those I must finally perform it. To deliberate whenever I doubted, to enquire whenever I was ignorant, would have protracted the undertaking without end, and, perhaps, without much improvement; for I did not find by my first experiments, that what I had not of my own was easily to be obtained: I saw that one enquiry only gave occasion to another, that book referred to book, that to search was not always to find, and to find was not always to be informed; and that thus to persue perfection, was, like the first inhabitants of Arcadia, to chace the sun, which, when they had reached the hill where he seemed to rest, was still beheld at the same distance from them.

I then contracted my design, determining to confide in myself, and no longer to solicit auxiliaries, which produced more incumbrance than assistance: by this I obtained at least one advantage, that I set limits to my work, which would in time be ended, though not completed.

Despondency has never so far prevailed as to depress me to negligence; some faults will at last appear to be the effects of anxious diligence and persevering activity. The nice and subtle ramifications of meaning were not easily avoided by a mind intent upon accuracy, and convinced of the necessity of disentangling combinations, and separating similitudes. Many of the distinctions which to common readers appear useless and idle, will be found real and important by men versed in the school philosophy, without which no dictionary shall ever be accurately compiled, or skilfully examined.

Some senses however there are, which, though not the same,

are yet so nearly allied, that they are often confounded. Most men think indistinctly, and therefore cannot speak with exactness; and consequently some examples might be indifferently put to either signification: this uncertainty is not to be imputed to me, who do not form, but register the language; who do not teach men how they should think, but relate how they have hitherto expressed their thoughts.

The imperfect sense of some examples I lamented, but could not remedy, and hope they will be compensated by innumerable passages selected with propriety, and preserved with exactness; some shining with sparks of imagination, and some replete with treasures of wisdom.

The orthography and etymology, though imperfect, are not imperfect for want of care, but because care will not always be successful, and recollection or information come too late for use.

That many terms of art and manufacture are omitted, must be frankly acknowledged; but for this defect I may boldy allege that it was unavoidable: I could not visit caverns to learn the miner's language, nor take a voyage to perfect my skill in the dialect of navigation, nor visit the warehouses of merchants, and shops of artificers, to gain the names of wares, tools and operations, of which no mention is found in books; what favourable accident, or easy enquiry brought within my reach, has not been neglected; but it had been a hopeless labour to glean up words, by courting living information, and contesting with the sullenness of one, and the roughness of another.

To furnish the academicians *della Crusca*[8] with words of this kind, a series of comedies called *la Fiera*, or *the Fair*, was professedly written by *Buonaroti*; but I had no such assistant, and therefore was content to want what they must have wanted likewise, had they not luckily been so supplied.

Nor are all words which are not found in the vocabulary, to be lamented as omissions. Of the laborious and mercantile part of the people, the diction is in a great measure casual and mutable; many of their terms are formed for some temporary or local convenience, and though current at certain times and places, are in others utterly unknown. This fugitive cant, which is always in a state of increase or decay, cannot be regarded as any part of the durable materials of a language, and therefore must be suffered to perish with other things unworthy of preservation.

Care will sometimes betray to the appearance of negligence. He that is catching opportunities which seldom occur, will suffer those to pass by unregarded, which he expects hourly to return; he that is searching for rare and remote things, will neglect those that are obvious and familiar: thus many of the most common and cursory words have been inserted with little illustration, because in gathering the authorities, I forbore to copy those which I thought likely to occur whenever they were wanted. It is remarkable that, in reviewing my collection, I found the word SEA unexemplified.

Thus it happens, that in things difficult there is danger from ignorance, and in things easy from confidence; the mind, afraid of greatness, and disdainful of littleness, hastily withdraws herself from painful searches, and passes with scornful rapidity over tasks not adequate to her powers, sometimes too secure for caution, and again too anxious for vigorous effort; sometimes idle in a plain path, and sometimes distracted in labyrinths, and dissipated by different intentions.

A large work is difficult because it is large, even though all its parts might singly be performed with facility; where there are many things to be done, each must be allowed its share of time and labour, in the proportion only which it bears to the whole; nor can it be expected, that the stones which form the dome of a temple, should be squared and polished like the diamond of a ring.

Of the event of this work, for which, having laboured it with so much application, I cannot but have some degree of parental fondness, it is natural to form conjectures. Those who have been persuaded to think well of my design, will require that it should fix our language, and put a stop to those alterations which time and chance have hitherto been suffered to make in it without opposition. With this consequence I will confess that I flattered myself for a while; but now begin to fear that I have indulged expectation which neither reason nor experience can justify.

When we see men grow old and die at a certain time one after another, from century to century, we laugh at the elixir that promises to prolong life to a thousand years; and with equal justice may the lexicographer be derided, who being able to produce no example of a nation that has preserved their words and phrases from mutability, shall imagine that his dictionary can embalm his language, and secure it from corruption and decay, that it is in his power to change sublunary nature, and clear the world at once from folly, vanity, and affectation.

With this hope, however, academies have been instituted, to guard the avenues of their languages, to retain fugitives, and repulse intruders; but their vigilance and activity have hitherto been vain; sounds are too volatile and subtile for legal restraints; to enchain syllables, and to lash the wind, are equally the undertakings of pride, unwilling to measure its desires by its strength. The *French* language has visibly changed under the inspection of the academy; the stile of *Amelot*'s translation of Father *Paul* is observed by *Le Courayer* to be *un peu passé*;[9] and no *Italian* will maintain that the diction of any modern writer is not perceptibly different from that of *Boccace*, *Machiavel*, or *Caro*.

Total and sudden transformations of a language seldom happen; conquests and migrations are now very rare: but there are other causes of change, which, though slow in their operation, and invisible in their progress, are perhaps as much superiour to human resistance, as the revolutions of the sky, or intumescence of the tide. Commerce, however necessary, however lucrative, as it depraves the manners, corrupts the language; they that have frequent intercourse with strangers, to whom they endeavour to accommodate themselves, must in time learn a mingled dialect, like the jargon which serves the traffickers on the *Mediterranean* and *Indian* coasts. This will not always be confined to the exchange, the warehouse, or the port, but will be communicated by degrees to other ranks of the people, and be at last incorporated with the current speech.

There are likewise internal causes equally forcible. The language most likely to continue long without alteration, would be that of a nation raised a little, and but a little above barbarity, secluded from strangers, and totally employed in procuring the conveniencies of life; either without books, or, like some of the *Mahometan* countries, with very few: men thus busied and unlearned, having only such words as common use requires, would perhaps long continue to express the same notions by the same signs. But no such constancy can be expected in a people polished by arts, and classed by subordination, where one part of the community is sustained and accommodated by the labour of the other. Those who have much leisure to think, will always be enlarging the stock of ideas, and every increase of knowledge, whether real or fancied, will produce new words, or combinations of words. When the mind is unchained from necessity, it will range after convenience; when it is left at large in the fields of speculation, it will shift opinions; as any custom is disused, the words that expressed it must perish with it; as any opinion grows popular, it will innovate speech in the same proportion as it alters practice.

As by the cultivation of various sciences, a language is amplified, it will be more furnished with words deflected from original sense: the geometrician will talk of a courtier's zenith, or the eccentrick virtue of a wild hero, and the physician of sanguine expectations and phlegmatick delays. Copiousness of speech will give opportunities to capricious choice, by which some words will be preferred, and others degraded; vicissitudes of fashion will enforce the use of new, or extend the signification of known terms. The tropes of poetry will make hourly encroachments, and the metaphorical will become the current sense: pronunciation will be varied by levity or ignorance, and the pen must at length comply with the tongue; illiterate writers will at one time or other, by publick infatuation, rise into renown, who, not knowing the original import of words, will use them with colloquial licentiousness, confound distinction, and forget propriety. As politeness increases, some expressions will be considered as too gross and vulgar for the delicate, others as too formal and ceremonious for the gay and airy; new phrases are therefore adopted, which must, for the same reasons, be in time dismissed. *Swift*, in his petty treatise on the *English* language,[10] allows that new words must sometimes be introduced, but proposes that none should be suffered to become obsolete. But what makes a word obsolete, more than general agreement to forbear it? and how shall it be continued, when it conveys an offensive idea, or recalled again into the mouths of mankind, when it has once become unfamiliar by disuse, and unpleasing by unfamiliarity?

There is another cause of alteration more prevalent than any other, which yet in the present state of the world cannot be obviated. A mixture of two languages will produce a third distinct from both, and they will always be mixed, where the chief part of education, and the most conspicuous accomplishment, is skill in ancient or in foreign tongues. He that has long cultivated another language, will find its words and combinations croud upon his memory; and haste and negligence, refinement and affectation, will obtrude borrowed terms and exotick expressions.

The great pest of speech is frequency of translation. No book was ever turned from one language into another, without imparting something of its native idiom; this is the most mischievous and comprehensive innovation; single words may enter by thousands, and the fabrick of the tongue continue the same, but new phraseology changes much at once; it alters not the single stones of the building, but the order of the columns. If an academy should be established for the cultivation of our stile, which I, who can never wish to see dependance multiplied, hope the spirit of *English* liberty will hinder or destroy, let them, instead of compiling grammars and dictionaries, endeavour, with all their influence, to stop the licence of translatours, whose idleness and ignorance, if it be suffered to proceed, will reduce us to babble a dialect of *France.*

If the changes that we fear be thus irresistible, what remains but to acquiesce with silence, as in the other insurmountable distresses of humanity? it remains that we retard what we cannot repel, that we palliate what we cannot cure. Life may be lengthened by care, though death cannot be ultimately defeated: tongues, like governments, have a natural tendency to degeneration; we have long preserved our constitution, let us make some struggles for our language.

In hope of giving longevity to that which its own nature forbids
to be immortal, I have devoted this book, the labour of years, to
the honour of my country, that we may no longer yield the palm
of philology, without a contest, to the nations of the continent.
The chief glory of every people arises from its authours: whether
I shall add any thing by my own writings to the reputation of
English literature, must be left to time: much of my life has been
lost under the pressures of disease; much has been trifled away;
and much has always been spent in provision for the day that was
passing over me; but I shall not think my employment useless or
ignoble, if by my assistance foreign nations, and distant ages, gain
access to the propagators of knowledge, and understand the
teachers of truth; if my labours afford light to the repositories of
science, and add celebrity to *Bacon*, to *Hooker*, to *Milton*, and to
Boyle.

When I am animated by this wish, I look with pleasure on my
book, however defective, and deliver it to the world with the spirit
of a man that has endeavoured well. That it will immediately
become popular I have not promised to myself: a few wild blunders, and risible absurdities, from which no work of such multiplicity was ever free, may for a time furnish folly with laughter,
and harden ignorance in contempt; but useful diligence will at last
prevail, and there never can be wanting some who distinguish
desert; who will consider that no dictionary of a living tongue ever
can be perfect, since while it is hastening to publication, some
words are budding, and some falling away; that a whole life
cannot be spent upon syntax and etymology, and that even a
whole life would not be sufficient; that he, whose design includes
whatever language can express, must often speak of what he does
not understand; that a writer will sometimes be hurried by eagerness to the end, and sometimes faint with weariness under a task,
which *Scaliger* compares to the labours of the anvil and the mine;
that what is obvious is not always known, and what is known is not
always present; that sudden fits of inadvertency will surprize
vigilance, slight avocations will seduce attention, and casual
eclipses of the mind will darken learning; and that the writer shall
often in vain trace his memory at the moment of need, for that

which yesterday he knew with intuitive readiness, and which will come uncalled into his thoughts tomorrow.

In this work, when it shall be found that much is omitted, let it not be forgotten that much likewise is performed; and though no book was ever spared out of tenderness to the authour, and the world is little solicitous to know whence proceeded the faults of that which it condemns; yet it may gratify curiosity to inform it, that the *English Dictionary* was written with little assistance of the learned, and without any patronage of the great; not in the soft obscurities of retirement, or under the shelter of academick bowers, but amidst inconvenience and distraction, in sickness and in sorrow. It may repress the triumph of malignant criticism to observe, that if our language is not here fully displayed, I have only failed in an attempt which no human powers have hitherto completed. If the lexicons of ancient tongues, now immutably fixed, and comprised in a few volumes, be yet, after the toil of successive ages, inadequate and delusive; if the aggregated knowledge, and co-operating diligence of the *Italian* academicians, did not secure them from the censure of *Beni*; if the embodied cricks of *France*, when fifty years had been spent upon their work, were obliged to change its oeconomy, and give their second edition another form, I may surely be contented without the praise of perfection, which, if I could obtain, in this gloom of solitude, what would it avail me? I have protracted by work till most of those whom I wished to please have sunk into the grave,[11] and success and miscarriage are empty sounds: I therefore dismiss it with frigid tranquillity, having little to fear or hope from censure or from praise.

NOTES

1. Horace *Epistles* 2. 2. 212.

2. Richard Hooker, *Of the Laws of Ecclesiastical Polity*, 4. 14.

3. A paraphrase of a line in Samuel Madden, *Boulter's Monument* (1745); Johnson had been hired to revise this poem.

4. The seventeenth-century scholars Francis Junius and Stephen Skinner were still the received authorities on etymology.

5. A rather long footnote by Johnson has here been prescinded; in it he supplies additional instances of the "etymological extravagance" of Junius.

6. For Bailey see headnote. Robert Ainsworth published a Latin *Thesaurus* in 1736, and Edward Phillips *A New World of English Words* in 1658.

7. Cf. Cicero *De legibus* 2. 23. 59, and Aristotle *Poetics* 25. 16.

8. The Italian Academy was established in 1582 and published a dictionary in 1612.

9. The French Academy published its dictionary in 1694. A. N. Amelot's translation of Fr. Paulo Sarpi's *History of the Council of Trent* had appeared eleven years before, in 1683, while P. F. Le Courayer provided in 1736 a fresh translation of the same work.

10. *A Proposition for Correcting, Improving, and Ascertaining the English Tongue* (1712).

11. Johnson's wife had died three years before.

The History of Rasselas, Prince of Abissinia, Chapter X (1759)

In the tenth chapter of this oriental tale, Imlac, the sagacious counselor of Prince Rasselas, delineates the character of an ideal poet. It has been customary to see in Imlac's conception Johnson's own, and though Imlac shows an un-Johnsonian aptitude for exaggerated and dogmatic assertion, his opinions are not obviously inconsistent with those of his creator—at least not till the penultimate paragraph. He glances immediately at one of Johnson's favorite distinctions, the difference between the natural and the artificial writer. Equally representative are the paragraphs that follow, where, in the education of an aspiring poet, more labor than ecstasy is perceived: he must possess a wide-ranging experience, acuteness of observation, an avid and scrutinizing intellect. In this context must be read the famous, or notorious, sixth paragraph, denounced by romantic critics as aesthetic heresy: an author is to reproduce the general, not the particular; but he is to *select* the most "prominent and striking features." Imlac is not urging a facile reliance on vapid or hackneyed abstractions; quite the contrary, he desires a selective pattern preserving the most significant and salient elements. And a poet can do this effectively only if he has observed nature in detail and at first hand. Hence, six years later in his *Preface*, Johnson can applaud Shakespeare's keen powers of observation, and at the same time commend his dramatic characters for being, not individuals, but species (i.e., they are men animated by truly universal passions—ambition, jealousy, fear, etc.—rather than peculiar or eccentric ones). In

130

the final two paragraphs Imlac swells to something of a rhapsody, and though a classicist like Joshua Reynolds could share his desire that the artist rise above local customs and prejudices (see his *Discourses on Art* [1769–90], II), Imlac's tone more nearly anticipates Shelley, who in the *Defence of Poetry* (1821) also panegyrizes the poet as a universal legislator of mankind. Here, then, it is possible that he parts company with Johnson, whose opinion of Shelley's acclamatory and hyperbolic essay, to judge from the opening of the next chapter, would not have been favorable. It begins: "Imlac now felt the enthusiastic fit, and was beginning to aggrandize his own profession, when the prince cried out, 'Enough! Thou hast convinced me, that no human being can ever be a poet . . . .' " The text is that of the second edition (1759).

Imlac's History Continued. A Dissertation upon Poetry

"Wherever I went, I found that Poetry was considered as the highest learning, and regarded with a veneration somewhat approaching to that which man would pay to the Angelick Nature. And it yet fills me with wonder, that, in almost all countries, the most ancient poets are considered as the best: whether it be that every other kind of knowledge is an acquisition gradually attained, and poetry is a gift conferred at once; or that the first poetry of every nation surprised them as a novelty, and retained the credit by consent which it received by accident at first: or whether, as the province of poetry is to describe Nature and Passion, which are always the same, the first writers took possession of the most striking objects for description, and the most probable occurrences for fiction, and left nothing to those that followed them, but transcription of the same events, and new combinations of the same images. Whatever be the reason, it is commonly observed that the early writers are in possession of nature, and their followers of art: that the first excel in strength and invention, and the latter in elegance and refinement.

"I was desirous to add my name to this illustrious fraternity. I read all the poets of Persia and Arabia, and was able to repeat by memory the volumes that are suspended in the mosque of Mecca. But I soon found that no man was ever great by imitation. My desire of excellence impelled me to transfer my attention to nature and to life. Nature was to be my subject, and men to be my auditors: I could never describe what I had not seen: I could not hope to move those with delight or terrour, whose interests and opinions I did not understand.

"Being now resolved to be a poet, I saw every thing with a new purpose; my sphere of attention was suddenly magnified: no kind of knowledge was to be overlooked. I ranged mountains and deserts for images and resemblances, and pictured upon my mind every tree of the forest and flower of the valley. I observed with equal care the crags of the rock and the pinnacles of the palace. Sometimes I wandered along the mazes of the rivulet, and sometimes watched the changes of the summer clouds. To a poet nothing can be useless. Whatever is beautiful, and whatever is dreadful, must be familiar to his imagination: he must be conversant with all that is awfully vast or elegantly little. The plants of the garden, the animals of the wood, the minerals of the earth, and meteors of the sky, must all concur to store his mind with inexhaustible variety: for every idea is useful for the inforcement or decoration of moral or religious truth; and he, who knows most, will have most power of diversifying his scenes, and of gratifying his reader with remote allusions and unexpected instruction.

"All the appearances of nature I was therefore careful to study, and every country which I have surveyed has contributed something to my poetical powers."

"In so wide a survey," said the prince, "you must surely have left much unobserved. I have lived, till now, within the circuit of these mountains, and yet cannot walk abroad without the sight of something which I had never beheld before, or never heeded."

"The business of a poet," said Imlac, "is to examine, not the individual, but the species; to remark general properties and large appearances: he does not number the streaks of the tulip, or describe the different shades in the verdure of the forest. He is to exhibit in his portraits of nature such prominent and striking

features, as recal the original to every mind; and must neglect the
minuter discriminations, which one may have remarked, and
another have neglected, for those characteristicks which are alike
obvious to vigilance and carelessness.

"But the knowledge of nature is only half the task of a poet; he
must be acquainted likewise with all the modes of life. His character requires that he estimate the happiness and misery of every
condition; observe the power of all the passions in all their combinations, and trace the changes of the human mind as they are
modified by various institutions and accidental influences of cli-
mate or custom, from the spriteliness of infancy to the despon-
dence of decrepitude. He must divest himself of the prejudices of
his age or country; he must consider right and wrong in their
abstracted and invariable state; he must disregard present laws
and opinions, and rise to general and transcendental truths,
which will always be the same: he must therefore content himself
with the slow progress of his name; contemn the applause of his
own time, and commit his claims to the justice of posterity. He
must write as the interpreter of nature, and the legislator of
mankind, and consider himself as presiding over the thoughts
and manners of future generations; as a being superiour to time
and place.

"His labour is not yet at an end: he must know many languages
and many sciences; and, that his stile may be worthy of his
thoughts, must, by incessant practice, familiarize to himself every
delicacy of speech and grace of harmony."

Shakespeare Criticism

From the Restoration to the present, Shakespeare's popularity in the theater has never failed, though his plays have always been altered to satisfy the current vogue; but among critics he was controversial from the start. John Dryden, with some reservations, gives him high praise, while Dryden's contemporary Thomas Rymer ("of wrangling memory") heaps on him a passionate contempt. Perhaps a little abated, this dispute persists through Johnson's time. Shakespeare never wanted advocates, however, and from the beginning of the eighteenth century one edition of his works tread closely on another. Johnson's appeared in eight volumes in 1765, and had been preceded by the editions of Nicholas Rowe (1709), Pope (1725), Lewis Theobald (1734), Sir Thomas Hanmer (1744), and William Warburton (1747). Though Johnson, when evaluating his predecessors, assails Theobald with more severity than the rest, he was probably the least capricious; but Johnson is Shakespeare's first truly modern editor. A conservative emender, he resolutely avoided the vagaries of that "conjectural criticism" perpetrated spasmodically by the earlier editors, whose emendations too often evince what Shakespeare *ought* to have written, rather than what indeed he wrote. Thus Johnson restores the line from *Hamlet*, "In huggermugger to inter him," and evicts the more genteel version recognized in other editions: "In private to inter him." Johnson's is in fact the first Shakespeare variorum; it ran through several editions, and provided the basis for the great edition of Edmund Malone in 1790, from which derived, in turn, much of the best nineteenth-century textual work.

But the *Preface* excited more immediate interest and

controversy than the edition as a whole. The journals
reprinted it at once; and though it was not without its
detractors, it completed what the *Dictionary*, a decade
before, had so effectively begun: the irrevocable establishment of Johnson's reputation. Some recent scholars,
tracing its ideas to a profusion of incidental and forgotten
sources, have declared it derivative; yet it has remained,
in its scope and incisiveness, Johnson's paramount critical
essay. In judging the *Preface* one should consider two
points: that Shakespeare had not been definitively established as a classic by 1765, although for many years he
had had zealous partisans, and that literary criticism was
still engaged, sometimes greatly agitated, by such problems as the dramatic unities, the legitimacy of
tragicomedy, the nature of dramatic illusion, the desira-
bility of observing poetic justice. With respect to Shakespeare, Johnson's admiration is energetic but not undis-
criminating. Along with the virtues, Shakespeare has the
faults of a "natural poet," and so Johnson, as a judicial
critic, freely censures his language, plot structure, and
even the ethical suppositions of some of his plays. If this
less than eulogistic criticism gave scandal to the bardolators of Johnson's time and after, it should be recalled, first, that the bardolators have ever exhibited a
notable bigotry, bestowing their imprecations generously
on all blasphemers, and second, that Johnson was equally
capable of dismissing with contempt the petrific classicism of Rymer and Voltaire.

As criticism, the *Preface* stands securely in the empirical
English tradition. Johnson is reasonably representative
on such matters as the test of time and consensus, the
concern for morality in art, Shakespeare's faults of plot
and language, his genius and originality, the Elizabethan
age. On Shakespeare's dramatic characters, the unities,
dramatic illusion, his opinion is more individual; and
especially it is so in his remarkable defense of tragicomedy, a troublesome genre aspersed by conservative

and progressive critics alike. Earlier commentators had attacked the unities, but seldom with such cogency. Johnson's denial of dramatic illusion may appear too relentless, but it must be seen as an intelligent reaction against a belief, then fashionable, that the drama induced something akin to genuine delusion. Johnson disliked delusions, which intercept our grasp of reality; and he disliked critical theories that fly equally against common sense and common experience. The *Preface* is not, then, a "summing up" of neoclassical Shakespearean criticism, as it has so often been described and then dismissed, but rather Johnson's own conclusions on matters of controversy, conclusions that sometimes wholly concurred with the critical tradition, and sometimes did not. And since Johnson was the last great neoclassical critic, perhaps we should term his preface, more precisely, a final development. The best Shakespearean criticism after Johnson—that, say, of Coleridge and Hazlitt—pursues a different, though not certainly a more expansive, track.

Johnson's *Preface* should be read, not merely or even mainly as "the definitive neoclassical statement," but as a singularly penetrating examination of Shakespeare. From the opening paragraph throughout, it is empirical, pragmatic, and discriminating, far less entangled than most Shakespearean criticism with any modish or obsolescent ideology. Indeed, Johnson addresses his subject with distinct objectivity and, unlike so many critics of the last hundred years, refuses to impose on Shakespeare the philosophy of an Aquinas, a Hegel, or a Freud. He fastens on the dramatist's salient virtues: the universality of his characters and themes; his intuitive apprehension of human nature; the animation, the variety, and the unity of his performances; his extraordinary but not unfaltering aptitude for the pathetic mode. In throwing these qualities into such strong light, Johnson's criticism was, in the issue, to assist Shakespeare's reputation, although for

a while injured bardolatry resented its occasionally censorious tone. Boswell, whose reputation as a literary critic
was never high and soon entirely eclipsed, was here un-
usually perceptive: "A blind, indiscriminate admiration
of Shakspeare had exposed the British nation to the
ridicule of foreigners," he says, adding that Johnson's
judiciousness has served the dramatist far better than
puerile adulation.

The value of this essay, particularly for our time, has
not been lessened by its pejorative passages; for Shakespeare is now received as a classic, and we are no longer
required to vindicate every line as superlative or each
play as perfectly designed. The hierophantic criticism of
a Carlyle or a Herder has long been antiquated.
Moreover, in view of the many ingenious and diverse
interpretations of Shakespeare that are disgorged annu-
ally by our university presses or printed in our journals,
we cannot even deny with assurance Johnson's most serious charge against Shakespeare, the ambiguity of his
moral plan. Of course we may reply that the ambiguity is desirable, or that Johnson was incompetent to
fathom the profundities of Renaissance tragedy. (Recent
humanist critics have complained of his lack of a "tragic
sense of life," to use Unamuno's phrase.) Still, the prejudice in favor of ambiguity is only a prejudice. And it is
equally to be wondered whether any such dismissal of
Johnson would argue a superior understanding of
Shakespeare, or parochial, twentieth-century arrogance.
To say that Johnson would have interpreted Shakespearean tragedy better had he been illuminated by the
opinions of modern humanism is to forget that modern
humanism has so far produced no tragedy comparable to
those of classical Greece or Renaissance England. A
"tragic sense of life" may be conducive of pathos, but that
Shakespeare had already, and Johnson understood it
well enough. The sense of exceptional greatness degraded and wasted, of willful alienation from the divine

order—to comprehend these tragic senses as well, humanism, democratic and secular in its drift, is not better equipped than Johnson's Christianity. And so desperate have the exertions now become to make Shakespeare relevant—i.e., to fit him to conciliate the slender sensibility of our age—that it may be said of his commentators what A. E. Housman said of Lucan's: "The art of understanding Lucan makes no steady and continuous progress, and relapse accompanies advance. Later editors often miss what their predecessors clearly apprehended, and his earliest interpreters are still in many respects his best."

To complement the more theoretical and formal *Preface*, I have included afterwards a sampling of Johnson's notes and of the General Observations that he appended to each play. This criticism, although it is indeed more specific and occasionally more intimate than that of the *Preface*, is not, as some scholars have believed, more "romantic." Johnson's censure here of Shakespeare's faulty plots, facile contrivances, and puns; his rigorous moral judgment of the characters (e.g., Bertram, Hamlet, even Falstaff, whose wit is no exculpation of his cowardice and corruption); his concern everywhere with didacticism and poetic justice—what are all these but specific applications of the criteria established in the *Preface*?

The text of the *Preface* and notes follows the first edition; but in the interests of convenience and uniformity I have observed, for the notes, the example of the Yale edition and altered Johnson's act, scene, and line references, now obsolete, to those of W. Aldis Wright's Cambridge edition, revised 1891–93. At the end of this section I have placed a portion of the *Drury-Lane Prologue* (1747); the identification of Shakespeare with nature and Ben Jonson with art anticipates the account of Shakespeare in the *Preface*, although in fact this had long been a conventional distinction. The poem also foreshadows the *Preface* in its ethical emphasis, the flexible understanding of the rules, and the strictures on contemporary tragedy. The text of the prologue is that of the first edition.

PREFACE TO THE PLAYS OF WILLIAM SHAKESPEARE (1765)

That praises are without reason lavished on the dead, and that the honours due only to excellence are paid to antiquity, is a complaint likely to be always continued by those, who, being able to add nothing to truth, hope for eminence from the heresies of paradox; or those, who, being forced by disappointment upon consolatory expedients, are willing to hope from posterity what the present age refuses, and flatter themselves that the regard which is yet denied by envy, will be at last bestowed by time.

Antiquity, like every other quality that attracts the notice of mankind, has undoubtedly votaries that reverence it, not from reason, but from prejudice. Some seem to admire indiscriminately whatever has been long preserved, without considering that time has sometimes co-operated with chance; all perhaps are more willing to honour past than present excellence; and the mind contemplates genius through the shades of age, as the eye surveys the sun through artificial opacity. The great contention of criticism is to find the faults of the moderns, and the beauties of the ancients. While an authour is yet living we estimate his powers by his worst performance, and when he is dead we rate them by his best.

To works, however, of which the excellence is not absolute and definite, but gradual and comparative; to works not raised upon principles demonstrative and scientifick, but appealing wholly to observation and experience, no other test can be applied than length of duration and continuance of esteem. What mankind have long possessed they have often examined and compared, and if they persist to value the possession, it is because frequent comparisons have confirmed opinion in its favour. As among the works of nature no man can properly call a river deep or a mountain high, without the knowledge of many mountains and many rivers; so in the productions of genius, nothing can be stiled excellent till it has been compared with other works of the same kind. Demonstration immediately displays its power, and has nothing to hope or fear from the flux of years; but works tentative and experimental must be estimated by their proportion to the general and collective ability of man, as it is discovered in a long succession of endeavours. Of the first building that was raised, it might be with certainty determined that it was round or square, but whether it was spacious or lofty must have been referred to time. The Pythagorean scale of numbers was at once discovered to be perfect;[1] but the poems of *Homer* we yet know not to transcend the common limits of human intelligence, but by remarking, that nation after nation, and century after century, has been able to do little more than transpose his incidents, new name his characters, and paraphrase his sentiments.

The reverence due to writings that have long subsisted arises therefore not from any credulous confidence in the superior wisdom of past ages, or gloomy persuasion of the degeneracy of mankind, but is the consequence of acknowledged and indubitable positions, that what has been longest known has been most considered, and what is most considered is best understood.

The Poet, of whose works I have undertaken the revision, may now begin to assume the dignity of an ancient, and claim the privilege of established fame and prescriptive veneration. He has long outlived his century, the term commonly fixed as the test of literary merit.[2] Whatever advantages he might once derive from personal allusions, local customs, or temporary opinions, have for many years been lost; and every topick of merriment or motive of sorrow, which the modes of artificial life afforded him, now only obscure the scenes which they once illuminated. The effects of favour and competition are at an end; the tradition of his friendships and his enmities has perished; his works support no opinion with arguments, nor supply any faction with invectives; they can neither indulge vanity nor gratify malignity, but are read without any other reason than the desire of pleasure, and are therefore praised only as pleasure is obtained; yet, thus unassisted by interest or passion, they have past through variations of taste and changes of manners, and, as they devolved from one generation to another, have received new honours at every transmission.

But because human judgment, though it be gradually gaining upon certainty, never becomes infallible; and approbation, though long continued, may yet be only the approbation of prejudice or fashion; it is proper to inquire, by what peculiarities of excellence *Shakespeare* has gained and kept the favour of his countrymen.

Nothing can please many, and please long, but just representations of general nature. Particular manners can be known to few, and therefore few only can judge how nearly they are copied. The irregular combinations of fanciful invention may delight a-while, by that novelty of which the common satiety of life sends us all in quest; but the pleasures of sudden wonder are soon exhausted, and the mind can only repose on the stability of truth.

Shakespeare is above all writers, at least above all modern writers, the poet of nature; the poet that holds up to his readers a faithful mirrour of manners and of life. His characters are not modified by the customs of particular places, unpractised by the rest of the world; by the peculiarities of studies or professions, which can operate but upon small numbers; or by the accidents of transient fashions or temporary opinions: they are the genuine progeny of common humanity, such as the world will always supply, and observation will always find. His persons act and speak by the influence of those general passions and principles by which all minds are agitated, and the whole system of life is continued in motion. In the writings of other poets a character is too often an individual; in those of *Shakespeare* it is commonly a species.[3]

It is from this wide extension of design that so much instruction is derived. It is this which fills the plays of *Shakespeare* with practical axioms and domestick wisdom. It was said of *Euripides,* that every verse was a precept;[4] and it may be said of *Shakespeare,* that from his works may be collected a system of civil and oeconomical prudence. Yet his real power is not shown in the splendour of particular passages, but by the progress of his fable, and the tenour of his dialogue; and he that tries to recommend him by select quotations, will succeed like the pedant in *Hierocles*,[5] who, when he offered his house to sale, carried a brick in his pocket as a specimen.

It will not easily be imagined how much *Shakespeare* excells in accommodating his sentiments to real life, but by comparing him with other authours. It was observed of the ancient schools of declamation, that the more diligently they were frequented, the more was the student disqualified for the world, because he found nothing there which he should ever meet in any other place. The same remark may be applied to every stage but that of *Shakespeare*. The theatre, when it is under any other direction, is peopled by such characters as were never seen, conversing in a language which was never heard, upon topicks which will never arise in the commerce of mankind. But the dialogue of this authour is often so evidently determined by the incident which produces it, and is pursued with so much ease and simplicity, that it seems scarcely to claim the merit of fiction, but to have been gleaned by diligent selection out of common conversation, and common occurrences.[6]

Upon every other stage the universal agent is love, by whose power all good and evil is distributed, and every action quickened or retarded. To bring a lover, a lady and a rival into the fable; to entangle them in contradictory obligations, perplex them with oppositions of interest, and harrass them with violence of desires inconsistent with each other; to make them meet in rapture and part in agony; to fill their mouths with hyperbolical joy and outrageous sorrow; to distress them as nothing human ever was distressed; to deliver them as nothing human ever was delivered, is the business of a modern dramatist. For this probability is violated, life is misrepresented, and language is depraved. But love is only one of many passions, and as it has no great influence upon the sum of life, it has little operation in the dramas of a poet, who caught his ideas from the living world, and exhibited only what he saw before him. He knew, that any other passion, as it was regular or exorbitant, was a cause of happiness or calamity.

Characters thus ample and general were not easily discrimi-

nated and preserved, yet perhaps no poet ever kept his personages more distinct from each other. I will not say, with *Pope*, that
every speech may be assigned to the proper speaker,[7] because
many speeches there are which have nothing characteristical; but,
perhaps, though some may be equally adapted to every person, it
will be difficult to find, any that can be properly transferred from
the present possessor to another claimant. The choice is right,
when there is reason for choice.

Other dramatists can only gain attention by hyperbolical or
aggravated characters, by fabulous and unexampled excellence
or depravity, as the writers of barbarous romances invigorated
the reader by a giant and a dwarf; and he that should form his
expectations of human affairs from the play, or from the tale,
would be equally deceived. *Shakespeare* has no heroes; his scenes
are occupied only by men, who act and speak as the reader thinks
that he should himself have spoken or acted on the same occasion:
Even where the agency is supernatural the dialogue is level with
life. Other writers disguise the most natural passions and most
frequent incidents; so that he who contemplates them in the book
will not know them in the world: *Shakespeare* approximates the
remote, and familiarizes the wonderful; the event which he represents will not happen, but if it were possible, its effects would
probably be such as he has assigned; and it may be said, that he
has not only shewn human nature as it acts in real exigences, but
as it would be found in trials, to which it cannot be exposed.

This therefore is the praise of *Shakespeare,* that his drama is the
mirrour of life; that he who has mazed his imagination, in following the phantoms which other writers raise up before him, may
here be cured of his delirious extasies, by reading human sentiments in human language; by scenes from which a hermit may
estimate the transactions of the world, and a confessor predict the
progress of the passions.

His adherence to general nature has exposed him to the censure of criticks, who form their judgments upon narrower principles. *Dennis* and *Rhymer* think his *Romans* not sufficiently
Roman; and *Voltaire* censures his kings as not completely royal.
Dennis is offended, that *Menenius,* a senator of *Rome,* should play

the buffoon; and *Voltaire* perhaps thinks decency violated when the *Danish* Usurper is represented as a drunkard.[8] But *Shakespeare* always makes nature predominate over accident; and if he preserves the essential character, is not very careful of distinctions superinduced and adventitious. His story requires Romans or kings, but he thinks only on men. He knew that *Rome,* like every other city, had men of all dispositions; and wanting a buffoon, he went into the senate-house for that which the senate-house would certainly have afforded him. He was inclined to shew an usurper and a murderer not only odious but despicable, he therefore added drunkenness to his other qualities, knowing that kings love wine like other men, and that wine exerts its natural power upon kings. These are the petty cavils of petty minds; a poet overlooks the casual distinction of country and condition, as a painter, satisfied with the figure, neglects the drapery.

The censure which he has incurred by mixing comick and tragick scenes, as it extends to all his works, deserves more consideration. Let the fact be first stated, and then examined.[9]

Shakespeare's plays are not in the rigorous and critical sense either tragedies or comedies, but compositions of a distinct kind; exhibiting the real state of sublunary nature, which partakes of good and evil, joy and sorrow, mingled with endless variety of proportion and innumerable modes of combination; and expressing the course of the world, in which the loss of one is the gain of another; in which, at the same time, the reveller is hasting to his wine, and the mourner burying his friend; in which the malignity of one is sometimes defeated by the frolick of another; and many mischiefs and many benefits are done and hindered without design.

Out of this chaos of mingled purposes and casualties the ancient poets, according to the laws which custom had prescribed, selected some the crimes of men, and some their absurdities; some the momentous vicissitudes of life, and some the lighter occurrences; some the terrours of distress, and some the gayeties of prosperity. Thus rose the two modes of imitation, known by the names of *tragedy* and *comedy,* compositions intended to promote different ends by contrary means, and considered as so little allied, that I do not recollect among the *Greeks* or *Romans* a single writer who attempted both.

Shakespeare has united the powers of exciting laughter and sorrow not only in one mind, but in one composition. Almost all his plays are divided between serious and ludicrous characters, and, in the successive evolutions of the design, sometimes produce seriousness and sorrow, and sometimes levity and laughter.

That this is a practice contrary to the rules of criticism will be readily allowed; but there is always an appeal open from criticism to nature. The end of writing is to instruct; the end of poetry is to instruct by pleasing.[10] That the mingled drama may convey all the instruction of tragedy or comedy cannot be denied, because it includes both in its alter[n]ations of exhibition, and approaches nearer than either to the appearance of life, by shewing how great machinations and slender designs may promote or obviate one another, and the high and the low co-operate in the general system by unavoidable concatenation.

It is objected, that by this change of scenes the passions are interrupted in their progression, and that the principal event, being not advanced by a due gradation of preparatory incidents, wants at last the power to move, which constitutes the perfection of dramatick poetry. This reasoning is so specious, that it is received as true even by those who in daily experience feel it to be false. The interchanges of mingled scenes seldom fail to produce the intended vicissitudes of passion. Fiction cannot move so much, but that the attention may be easily transferred; and though it must be allowed that pleasing melancholy be sometimes interrupted by unwelcome levity, yet let it be considered likewise, that melancholy is often not pleasing, and that the distrubance of one man may be the relief of another; that different auditors have different habitudes; and that, upon the whole, all pleasure consists in variety.

The players, who in their edition[11] divided our authour's works into comedies, histories, and tragedies, seem not to have distinguished the three kinds, by any very exact or definite ideas.

An action which ended happily to the principal persons, however serious or distressful through its intermediate incidents, in their opinion constituted a comedy. This idea of a comedy continued long amongst us, and plays were written, which, by changing the catastrophe, were tragedies to-day and comedies to-morrow.

Tragedy was not in those times a poem of more general dignity or elevation than comedy; it required only a calamitous conclusion, with which the common criticism of that age was satisfied; whatever lighter pleasure it afforded in its progress.

History was a series of actions, with no other than chronological succession, independent on each other, and without any tendency to introduce or regulate the conclusion. It is not always very nicely distinguished from tragedy. There is not much nearer approach to unity of action in the tragedy of *Antony and Cleopatra*, than in the history of *Richard the Second*. But a history might be continued through many plays; as it had no plan, it had no limits.

Through all these denominations of the drama, *Shakespeare*'s mode of composition is the same; an interchange of seriousness and merriment, by which the mind is softened at one time, and exhilarated at another. But whatever be his purpose, whether to gladden or depress, or to conduct the story, without vehemence or emotion, through tracts of easy and familiar dialogue, he never fails to attain his purpose; as he commands us, we laugh or mourn, or sit silent with quiet expectation, in tranquillity without indifference.

When *Shakespeare*'s plan is understood, most of the criticisms of *Rhymer* and *Voltaire* vanish away. The play of *Hamlet* is opened, without impropriety, by two sentinels; *Iago* bellows at *Brabantio*'s window, without injury to the scheme of the play, though in terms which a modern audience would not easily endure; the character of *Polonius* is seasonable and useful; and the Grave-diggers themselves may be heard with applause.

Shakespeare engaged in dramatick poetry with the world open before him; the rules of the ancients were yet known to few; the publick judgment was unformed; he had no example of such fame as might force him upon imitation, nor criticks of such authority as might restrain his extravagance: He therefore indulged his natural disposition, and his disposition, as *Rhymer* has remarked, led him to comedy. In tragedy he often writes with great appearance of toil and study, what is written at last with little felicity; but in his comick scenes, he seems to produce without labour, what no labour can improve. In tragedy he is always struggling after some occasion to be comick, but in comedy he seems to repose, or to luxuriate, as in a mode of thinking congenial to his nature. In his tragick scenes there is always something wanting, but his comedy often surpasses expectation or desire. His comedy pleases by the thoughts and the language, and his tragedy for the greater part by incident and action. His tragedy seems to be skill, his comedy to be instinct.

The force of his comick scenes has suffered little diminution from the changes made by a century and a half, in manners or in words. As his personages act upon principles arising from genuine passion, very little modified by particular forms, their pleasures and vexations are communicable to all times and to all places; they are natural, and therefore durable; the adventitious peculiarities of personal habits, are only superficial dies, bright and pleasing for a little while, yet soon fading to a dim tinct, without any remains of former lustre; but the discriminations of true passion are the colours of nature; they pervade the whole mass, and can only perish with the body that exhibits them. The accidental compositions of heterogeneous modes are dissolved by the chance which combined them; but the uniform simplicity of primitive qualities neither admits increase, nor suffers decay. The sand heaped by one flood is scattered by another, but the rock always continues in its place. The stream of time, which is continually washing the dissoluble fabricks of other poets, passes without injury by the adamant of *Shakespeare*.

If there be, what I believe there is, in every nation, a stile which never becomes obsolete, a certain mode of phraseology so consonant and congenial to the analogy and principles of its respective language as to remain settled and unaltered; this stile is probably to be sought in the common intercourse of life, among those who speak only to be understood, without ambition of elegance. The polite are always catching modish innovations, and the learned depart from established forms of speech, in hope of finding or making better; those who wish for distinction forsake the vulgar, when the vulgar is right; but there is a conversation above grossness and below refinement, where propriety resides, and where this poet seems to have gathered his comick dialogue. He is therefore more agreeable to the ears of the present age than any other authour equally remote, and among his other excellencies deserves to be studied as one of the original masters of our language.

These observations are to be considered not as unexceptionably constant, but as containing general and predominant truth. *Shakespeare*'s familiar dialogue is affirmed to be smooth and clear, yet not wholly without ruggedness or difficulty; as a country may be eminently fruitful, though it has spots unfit for cultivation: His characters are praised as natural, though their sentiments are sometimes forced, and their actions improbable; as the earth upon the whole is spherical, though its surface is varied with protuberances and cavities.

Shakespeare with his excellencies has likewise faults, and faults sufficient to obscure and overwhelm any other merit.[12] I shall shew them in the proportion in which they appear to me, without envious malignity or superstitious veneration. No question can be more innocently discussed than a dead poet's pretensions to renown; and little regard is due to that bigotry which sets candour higher than truth.

His first defect is that to which may be imputed most of the evil in books or in men. He sacrifices virtue to convenience, and is so much more careful to please than to instruct, that he seems to write without any moral purpose. From his writings indeed a system of social duty may be selected, for he that thinks reasonably must think morally; but his precepts and axioms drop casually from him; he makes no just distribution of good or evil, nor is always careful to shew in the virtuous a disapprobation of the wicked; he carries his persons indifferently through right and wrong, and at the close dismisses them without further care, and leaves their examples to operate by chance. This fault the barbarity of his age cannot extenuate; for it is always a writer's duty to make the world better, and justice is a virtue independant on time or place.

The plots are often so loosely formed, that a very slight consideration may improve them, and so carelessly pursued, that he seems not always fully to comprehend his own design. He omits opportunities of instructing or delighting which the train of his story seems to force upon him, and apparently rejects those exhibitions which would be more affecting, for the sake of those which are more easy.

It may be observed, that in many of his plays the latter part is evidently neglected. When he found himself near the end of his work, and, in view of his reward, he shortened the labour, to snatch the profit. He therefore remits his efforts where he should most vigorously exert them, and his catastrophe is improbably produced or imperfectly represented.

He had no regard to distinction of time or place, but gives to one age or nation, without scruple, the customs, institutions, and opinions of another, at the expence not only of likelihood, but of possibility. These faults *Pope* has endeavoured, with more zeal than judgment, to transfer to his imagined interpolators.[13] We need not wonder to find *Hector* quoting *Aristotle*, when we see the loves of *Theseus* and *Hippolyta* combined with the *Gothick* mythology of fairies. *Shakespeare*, indeed, was not the only violator of chronology, for in the same age *Sidney*, who wanted not the advantages of learning, has, in his *Arcadia*, confounded the pastoral with the feudal times, the days of innocence, quiet and security, with those of turbulence, violence and adventure.

In his comick scenes he is seldom very successful, when he engages his characters in reciprocations of smartness and contests of sarcasm; their jests are commonly gross, and their pleasantry licentious; neither his gentlemen nor his ladies have much delicacy, nor are sufficiently distinguished from his clowns by any appearance of refined manners. Whether he represented the real conversation of his time is not easy to determine; the reign of *Elizabeth* is commonly supposed to have been a time of stateliness, formality and reserve, yet perhaps the relaxations of that severity were not very elegant. There must, however, have been always some modes of gayety preferable to others, and a writer ought to chuse the best.

In tragedy his performance seems constantly to be worse, as his labour is more. The effusions of passion which exigence forces out are for the most part striking and energetick; but whenever he solicits his invention, or strains his faculties, the offspring of his throes is tumour, meanness, tediousness, and obscurity.

In narration he affects a disproportionate pomp of diction and a wearisome train of circumlocution, and tells the incident imperfectly in many words, which might have been more plainly delivered in few. Narration in dramatick poetry is naturally tedious, as it is unanimated and inactive, and obstructs the progress of the action; it should therefore always be rapid, and enlivened by frequent interruption. *Shakespeare* found it an encumbrance, and instead of lightening it by brevity, endeavoured to recommend it by dignity and splendour.

His declamations or set speeches are commonly cold and weak, for his power was the power of nature; when he endeavoured, like other tragick writers, to catch opportunities of amplification, and instead of inquiring what the occasion demanded, to show how much his stores of knowledge could supply, he seldom escapes without the pity or resentment of his reader.

It is incident to him to be now and then entangled with an unwieldy sentiment, which he cannot well express, and will not reject; he struggles with it a while, and if it continues stubborn, comprises it in words such as occur, and leaves it to be disentangled and evolved by those who have more leisure to bestow upon it.

Not that always where the language is intricate the thought is subtle, or the image always great where the line is bulky; the equality of words to things is very often neglected, and trivial sentiments and vulgar ideas disappoint the attention, to which they are recommended by sonorous epithets and swelling figures.

But the admirers of this great poet[14] have never less reason to indulge their hopes of supreme excellence, than when he seems fully resolved to sink them in dejection, and mollify them with tender emotions by the fall of greatness, the danger of innocence, or the crosses of love. He is not long soft and pathetick without some idle conceit, or contemptible equivocation. He no sooner begins to move, than he counteracts himself; and terrour and pity, as they are rising in the mind, are checked and blasted by sudden frigidity.

A quibble is to *Shakespeare*, what luminous vapours are to the traveller; he follows it at all adventures, it is sure to lead him out of his way, and sure to engulf him in the mire. It has some malignant power over his mind, and its fascinations are irresistible. Whatever be the dignity or profundity of his disquisition, whether he be enlarging knowledge or exalting affection, whether he be amusing attention with incidents, or enchaining it in suspense, let but a quibble spring up before him, and he leaves his work unfinished. A quibble is the golden apple for which he will always turn aside from his career, or stoop from his elevation. A quibble, poor and barren as it is, gave him such delight, that he was content to purchase it, by the sacrifice of reason, propriety and truth. A quibble was to him the fatal *Cleopatra* for which he lost the world, and was content to lose it.

It will be thought strange, that, in enumerating the defects of this writer, I have not yet mentioned his neglect of the unities; his violation of those laws which have been instituted and established by the joint authority of poets and of criticks.

For his other deviations from the art of writing, I resign him to critical justice, without making any other demand in his favour, than that which must be indulged to all human excellence; that his virtues be rated with his failings: But, from the censure which this irregularity may bring upon him, I shall, with due reverence to that learning which I must oppose, adventure to try how I can defend him.

His histories, being neither tragedies nor comedies, are not subject to any of their laws; nothing more is necessary to all the praise which they expect, than that the changes of action be so prepared as to be understood, that the incidents be various and affecting, and the characters consistent, natural and distinct. No other unity is intended, and therefore none is to be sought.

In his other works he has well enough preserved the unity of action. He has not, indeed, an intrigue regularly perplexed and regularly unravelled; he does not endeavour to hide his design only to discover it, for this is seldom the order of real events, and *Shakespeare* is the poet of nature: But his plan has commonly what *Aristotle* requires, a beginning, a middle, and an end,[15] one event is concatenated with another, and the conclusion follows by easy consequence. There are perhaps some incidents that might be spared, as in other poets there is much talk that only fills up time upon the stage; but the general system makes gradual advances, and the end of the play is the end of expectation.

To the unities of time and place he has shewn no regard, and perhaps a nearer view of the principles on which they stand will diminish their value, and withdraw from them the veneration which, from the time of *Corneille*,[16] they have very generally received, by discovering that they have given more trouble to the poet, than pleasure to the auditor.

The necessity of observing the unities of time and place arises from the supposed necessity of making the drama credible. The criticks hold it impossible, that an action of months or years can be possibly believed to pass in three hours; or that the spectator can suppose himself to sit in the theatre, while ambassadors go and return between distant kings, while armies are levied and towns besieged, while an exile wanders and returns, or till he whom they saw courting his mistress, shall lament the untimely fall of his son. The mind revolts from evident falsehood, loses its force when it departs from the resemblance of reality.

From the narrow limitation of time necessarily arises the contraction of place. The spectator, who knows that he saw the first act at *Alexandria*, cannot suppose that he sees the next at *Rome*, at a distance to which not the dragons of *Medea* could, in so short a time, have transported him; he knows with certainty that he has not changed his place; and he knows that place cannot change itself; that what was a house cannot become a plain; that what was *Thebes* can never be *Persepolis*.

Such is the triumphant language with which a critick exults over the misery of an irregular poet, and exults commonly without resistance or reply. It is time therefore to tell him, by the authority of *Shakespeare*, that he assumes, as an unquestionable principle, a position, which, while his breath is forming it into words, his understanding pronounces to be false. It is false, that any representation is mistaken for reality; that any dramatick fable in its materiality was ever credible, or, for a single moment, was ever credited.

The objection arising from the impossibility of passing the first hour at *Alexandria*, and the next at *Rome*, supposes, that when the play opens the spectator really imagines himself at *Alexandria*, and believes that his walk to the theatre has been a voyage to *Egypt*, and that he lives in the days of *Antony* and *Cleopatra*. Surely he that imagines this may imagine more. He that can take the stage at one time for the palace of the *Ptolemies*, may take it in half an hour for the promontory of *Actium*. Delusion, if delusion be admitted, has no certain limitation; if the spectator can be once persuaded, that his old acquaintances are *Alexander* and *Caesar*, that a room illuminated with candles is the plain of *Pharsalia*, or the bank of *Granicus*, he is in a state of elevation above the reach of reason, or of truth, and from the heights of empyrean poetry, may despise the circumscriptions of terrestrial nature. There is no reason why a mind thus wandering in extasy should count the clock, or why an hour should not be a century in that calenture of the brains that can make the stage a field.

The truth is, that the spectators are always in their senses, and know, from the first act to the last, that the stage is only a stage, and that the players are only players. They come to hear a certain number of lines recited with just gesture and elegant modulation. The lines relate to some action, and an action must be in some place; but the different actions that compleat a story may be in places very remote from each other; and where is the absurdity of allowing that space to represent first *Athens*, and then *Sicily*, which was always known to be neither *Sicily* nor *Athens*, but a modern theatre?

By supposition, as place is introduced, time may be extended; the time required by the fable elapses for the most part between the acts; for of so much of the action as is represented, the real and poetical duration is the same. If, in the first act, preparations for war against *Mithridates* are represented to be made in *Rome*, the event of the war may, without absurdity, be represented, in the catastrophe, as happening in *Pontus*; we know that there is neither war, nor preparation for war; we know that we are neither in *Rome* nor *Pontus*; that neither *Mithridates* nor *Lucullus* are before us. The drama exhibits successive imitations of successive actions, and why may not the second imitation represent an action that happened years after the first; if it be so connected with it, that nothing but time can be supposed to intervene? Time is, of all modes of existence, most obsequious to the imagination; a lapse of years is as easily conceived as a passage of hours. In contemplation we easily contract the time of real actions, and therefore willingly permit it to be contracted when we only see their imitation.

It will be asked, how the drama moves, if it is not credited. It is credited with all the credit due to a drama. It is credited, whenever it moves, as a just picture of a real original; as representing to the auditor what he would himself feel, if he were to do or suffer what is there feigned to be suffered or to be done. The reflection that strikes the heart is not, that the evils before us are real evils, but that they are evils to which we ourselves may be exposed. If there be any fallacy, it is not that we fancy the players, but that we fancy ourselves unhappy for a moment; but we rather lament the possibility than suppose the presence of misery, as a mother weeps over her babe, when she remembers that death may take it from her. The delight of tragedy proceeds from our consciousness of fiction; if we thought murders and treasons real, they would please no more.

Imitations produce pain or pleasure, not because they are mistaken for realities, but because they bring realities to mind. When the imagination is recreated by a painted landscape, the trees are not supposed capable to give us shade, or the fountains coolness; but we consider, how we should be pleased with such fountains playing beside us, and such woods waving over us. We are agitated in reading the history of *Henry* the Fifth, yet no man takes his book for the field of *Agencourt.* A dramatick exhibition is a book recited with concomitants that encrease or diminish its effect. Familiar comedy is often more powerful on the theatre, than in the page; imperial tragedy is always less. The humour of *Petruchio* may be heightened by grimace; but what voice or what gesture can hope to add dignity or force to the soliloquy of *Cato.* [17]

A play read, affects the mind like a play acted. It is therefore evident, that the action is not supposed to be real, and it follows that between the acts a longer or shorter time may be allowed to pass, and that no more account of space or duration is to be taken by the auditor of a drama, than by the reader of a narrative, before whom may pass in an hour the life of a hero, or the revolutions of an empire.

Whether *Shakespeare* knew the unities, and rejected them by design, or deviated from them by happy ignorance, it is, I think, impossible to decide, and useless to enquire. We may reasonably suppose, that, when he rose to notice, he did not want the counsels and admonitions of scholars and cricks, and that he at last deliberately persisted in a practice, which he might have begun by chance. As nothing is essential to the fable, but unity of action, and as the unities of time and place arise evidently from false assumptions, and, by circumscribing the extent of the drama, lessen its variety, I cannot think it much to be lamented, that they were not known by him, or not observed: Nor, if such another poet could arise, should I very vehemently reproach him, that his first act passed at *Venice*, and his next in *Cyprus*. Such violations of rules merely positive, become the comprehensive genius of *Shakespeare*, and such censures are suitable to the minute and slender criticism of *Voltaire*:

> *Non usque adeo permiscuit imis*
> *Longus summa dies, ut non, si voce Metelli*
> *Serventur leges, malint a Caesare tolli.*

[Nor time, nor chance breed such confusions yet,
Nor are the mean so rais'd, nor sunk the great;
But laws themselves would rather chuse to be
Suppress'd by Caesar, than preserved by thee.][18]

Yet when I speak thus slightly of dramatick rules, I cannot but recollect how much wit and learning may be produced against me; before such authorities I am afraid to stand, not that I think the present question one of those that are to be decided by mere authority, but because it is to be suspected, that these precepts have not been so easily received but for better reasons than I have yet been able to find. The result of my enquiries, in which it would be ludicrous to boast of impartiality, is, that the unities of time and place are not essential to a just drama, that though they may sometimes conduce to pleasure, they are always to be sacrificed to the nobler beauties of variety and instruction; and that a play, written with nice observation of critical rules, is to be contemplated as an elaborate curiosity, as the product of superfluous and ostentatious art, by which is shewn, rather what is possible, than what is necessary.

He that, without diminution of any other excellence, shall preserve all the unities unbroken, deserves the like applause with the architect, who shall display all the orders of architecture in a citadel, without any deduction from its strength; but the principal beauty of a citadel is to exclude the enemy; and the greatest graces of a play, are to copy nature and instruct life.

Perhaps, what I have here not dogmatically but deliberatively[19] written, may recal the principles of the drama to a new examination. I am almost frighted at my own temerity; and when I estimate the fame and the strength of those that maintain the contrary opinion, am ready to sink down in reverential silence; as *Aeneas* withdrew from the defence of *Troy*, when he saw *Neptune* shaking the wall, and *Juno* heading the besiegers.[20]

Those whom my arguments cannot persuade to give their approbation to the judgment of *Shakespeare*, will easily, if they consider the condition of his life, make some allowance for his ignorance.

Every man's performances, to be rightly estimated, must be compared with the state of the age in which he lived, and with his own particular opportunities; and though to the reader a book be not worse or better for the circumstances of the authour, yet as there is always a silent reference of human works to human abilities, and as the enquiry, how far man may extend his designs, or how high he may rate his native force, is of far greater dignity than in what rank we shall place any particular performance, curiosity is always busy to discover the instruments, as well as to survey the workmanship, to know how much is to be ascribed to original powers, and how much to casual and adventitious help. The palaces of *Peru* or *Mexico* were certainly mean and incommodious habitations, if compared to the houses of *European* monarchs; yet who could forbear to view them with astonishment, who remembered that they were built without the use of iron?

The *English* nation, in the time of *Shakespeare*, was yet struggling to emerge from barbarity. The philology of *Italy* had been transplanted hither in the reign of *Henry* the Eighth; and the learned languages had been successfully cultivated by *Lilly*, *Linacer*, and *More*; by *Pole*, *Cheke*, and *Gardiner*; and afterwards by *Smith*, *Clerk*, *Haddon*, and *Ascham*.[21] Greek was now taught to boys in the principal schools; and those who united elegance with learning, read, with great diligence, the *Italian* and *Spanish* poets. But literature was yet confined to professed scholars, or to men and women of high rank. The publick was gross and dark; and to be able to read and write, was an accomplishment still valued for its rarity.

Nations, like individuals, have their infancy. A people newly awakened to literary curiosity, being yet unacquainted with the true state of things, knows not how to judge of that which is proposed as its resemblance. Whatever is remote from common appearances is always welcome to vulgar, as to childish credulity; and of a country unenlightened by learning, the whole people is the vulgar. The study of those who then aspired to plebeian learning was laid out upon adventures, giants, dragons, and enchantments. *The Death of Arthur* was the favourite volume.[22]

The mind, which has feasted on the luxurious wonders of fiction, has no taste of the insipidity of truth. A play which imitated only the common occurrences of the world, would, upon the admirers of *Palmerin* and *Guy* of *Warwick*, have made little impression; he that wrote for such an audience was under the necessity of looking round for strange events and fabulous transactions, and that incredibility, by which maturer knowledge is offended, was the chief recommendation of writings, to unskilful curiosity.

Our authour's plots are generally borrowed from novels, and it is reasonable to suppose, that he chose the most popular, such as were read by many, and related by more; for his audience could not have followed him through the intricacies of the drama, had they not held the thread of the story in their hands.

The stories, which we now find only in remoter authours, were in his time accessible and familliar. The fable of *As you like it,* which is supposed to be copied from *Chaucer*'s Gamelyn, was a little pamphlet of those times; and old Mr. *Cibber* remembered the tale of *Hamlet* in plain *English* prose, which the criticks have now to seek in *Saxo Grammaticus.*

His *English* histories he took from *English* chronicles and *English* ballads; and as the ancient writers were made known to his countrymen by versions, they supplied him with new subjects; he dilated some of *Plutarch*'s lives into plays, when they had been translated by *North.*

His plots, whether historical or fabulous, are always crouded with incidents, by which the attention of a rude people was more easily caught than by sentiment or argumentation; and such is the power of the marvellous even over those who despise it, that every man finds his mind more strongly seized by the tragedies of *Shakespeare* than of any other writer; others please us by particular speeches, but he always makes us anxious for the event, and has perhaps excelled all but *Homer* in securing the first purpose of a writer, by exciting restless and unquenchable curiosity, and compelling him that reads his work to read it through.

The shows and bustle with which his plays abound have the same original. As knowledge advances, pleasure passes from the eye to the ear, but returns, as it declines, from the ear to the eye. Those to whom our authour's labours were exhibited had more skill in pomps or processions than in poetical language, and perhaps wanted some visible and discriminated events, as comments on the dialogue. He knew how he should most please; and whether his practice is more agreeable to nature, or whether his example has prejudiced the nation, we still find that on our stage something must be done as well as said, and inactive declamation is very coldly heard, however musical or elegant, passionate or sublime.

Voltaire expresses his wonder,[23] that our authour's extravagancies are endured by a nation, which has seen the tragedy of *Cato.*

Let him be answered, that *Addison* speaks the language of poets, and *Shakespeare*, of men. We find in *Cato* innumerable beauties which enamour us of its authour, but we see nothing that acquaints us with human sentiments or human actions; we place it with the fairest and the noblest progeny which judgment propagates by conjunction with learning, but *Othello* is the vigorous and vivacious offspring of observation impregnated by genius. *Cato* affords a splendid exhibition of artificial and fictitious manners, and delivers just and noble sentiments, in diction easy, elevated and harmonious, but its hopes and fears communicate no vibration to the heart; the composition refers us only to the writer; we pronounce the name of *Cato*, but we think on *Addison*.

The work of a correct and regular writer is a garden accurately formed and diligently planted, varied with shades, and scented with flowers; the composition of *Shakespeare* is a forest, in which oaks extend their branches, and pines tower in the air, interspersed sometimes with weeds and brambles, and sometimes giving shelter to myrtles and to roses; filling the eye with awful pomp, and gratifying the mind with endless diversity. Other poets display cabinets of precious rarities, minutely finished, wrought into shape, and polished unto brightness. *Shakespeare* opens a mine which contains gold and diamonds in unexhaustible plenty, though clouded by incrustations, debased by impurities, and mingled with a mass of meaner minerals.

It has been much disputed, whether *Shakespeare* owed his excellence to his own native force, or whether he had the common helps of scholastick education, the precepts of critical science, and the examples of ancient authours.

There has always prevailed a tradition, that *Shakespeare* wanted learning, that he had no regular education, nor much skill in the dead languages. *Johnson*, his friend, affirms, that *he had small Latin, and no Greek*;[24] who, besides that he had no imaginable temptation to falsehood, wrote at a time when the character and acquisitions of *Shakespeare* were known to multitudes. His evidence ought therefore to decide the controversy, unless some testimony of equal force could be opposed.

Some have imagined, that they have discovered deep learning

in many imitations of old writers; but the examples which I have known urged, were drawn from books translated in his time; or were such easy coincidences of thought, as will happen to all who consider the same subjects; or such remarks on life or axioms of morality as float in conversation, and are transmitted through the world in proverbial sentences.

I have found it remarked, that, in this important sentence, *Go before, I'll follow*, we read a translation of, *I prae, sequar.*[25] I have been told, that when *Caliban*, after a pleasing dream, says, *I cry'd to sleep again*, the authour imitates *Anacreon*, who had, like every other man, the same wish on the same occasion.

There are a few passages which may pass for imitations, but so few, that the exception only confirms the rule; he obtained them from accidental quotations, or by oral communication, and as he used what he had, would have used more if he had obtained it.

The *Comedy of Errors* is confessedly taken from the *Menaechmi* of *Plautus*; from the only play of *Plautus* which was then in *English*. What can be more probable, than that he who copied that, would have copied more; but that those which were not translated were inaccessible?

Whether he knew the modern languages is uncertain. That his plays have some *French* scenes proves but little; he might easily procure them to be written, and probably, even though he had known the language in the common degree, he could not have written it without assistance. In the story of *Romeo* and *Juliet* he is observed to have followed the *English* translation, where it deviates from the *Italian*; but this on the other part proves nothing against his knowledge of the original. He was to copy, not what he knew himself, but what was known to his audience.

It is most likely that he had learned *Latin* sufficiently to make him acquainted with construction, but that he never advanced to an easy perusal of the *Roman* authours. Concerning his skill in modern languages, I can find no sufficient ground of determination; but as no imitations of *French* or *Italian* authours have been discovered, though the *Italian* poetry was then high in esteem, I am inclined to believe, that he read little more than *English*, and chose for his fables only such tales as he found translated.

That much knowledge is scattered over his works is very justly observed by *Pope*, [26] but it is often such knowledge as books did not supply. He that will understand *Shakespeare*, must not be content to study him in the closet, he must look for his meaning sometimes among the sports of the field, and sometimes among the manufactures of the shop.

There is however proof enough that he was a very diligent reader, nor was our language then so indigent of books, but that he might very liberally indulge his curiosity without excursion into foreign literature. Many of the *Roman* authours were translated, and some of the *Greek*; the reformation had filled the kingdom with theological learning; most of the topicks of human disquisition had found *English* writers; and poetry had been cultivated, not only with diligence, but success. This was a stock of knowledge sufficient for a mind so capable of appropriating and improving it.

But the greater part of his excellence was the product of his own genius. He found the *English* stage in a state of the utmost rudeness; no essays either in tragedy or comedy had appeared, from which it could be discovered to what degree of delight either one or other might be carried. Neither character nor dialogue were yet understood. *Shakespeare* may be truly said to have introduced them both amongst us, and in some of his happier scenes to have carried them both to the utmost height.

By what gradations of improvement he proceeded, is not easily known; for the chronology of his works is yet unsettled. *Rowe* is of opinion, that *perhaps we are not to look for his beginning, like those of other writers, in his least perfect works; art had so little, and nature so large a share in what he did, that for ought I know,* says he, *the performances of his youth, as they were the most vigorous, were the best.* [27] But the power of nature is only the power of using to any certain purpose the materials which diligence procures, or opportunity supplies. Nature gives no man knowledge, and when images are collected by study and experience, can only assist in combining or applying them. *Shakespeare,* however favoured by nature, could impart only what he had learned; and as he must increase his ideas, like other mortals, by gradual acquisition, he, like them, grew wiser as he grew older, could display life better, as he knew it more, and instruct with more efficacy, as he was himself more amply instructed.

There is a vigilance of observation and accuracy of distinction which books and precepts cannot confer; from this almost all original and native excellence proceeds. *Shakespeare* must have looked upon mankind with perspicacity, in the highest degree curious and attentive. Other writers borrow their characters from preceding writers, and diversify them only by the accidental appendages of present manners; the dress is a little varied, but the body is the same. Our authour had both matter and form to provide; for except the characters of *Chaucer,* to whom I think he is not much indebted, there were no writers in *English,* and perhaps not many in other modern languages, which shewed life in its native colours.

The contest about the original benevolence or malignity of man had not yet commenced. Speculation had not yet attempted to analyse the mind, to trace the passions to their sources, to unfold the seminal principles of vice and virtue, or sound the depths of the heart for the motives of action. All those enquiries, which from that time that human nature became the fashionable study, have been made sometimes with nice discernment, but often with idle subtilty, were yet unattempted. The tales, with which the infancy of learning was satisfied, exhibited only the superficial appearances of action, related the events but omitted the causes, and were formed for such as delighted in wonders rather than in truth. Mankind was not then to be studied in the closet; he that would know the world, was under the necessity of gleaning his own remarks, by mingling as he could in its business and amusements.

Boyle congratulated himself upon his high birth, because it favoured his curiosity, by facilitating his access. *Shakespeare* had no such advantage; he came to *London* a needy adventurer, and lived for a time by very mean employments. Many works of genius and learning have been performed in states of life, that appear very little favourable to thought or to enquiry; so many, that he who considers them is inclined to think that he sees enterprise and perseverance predominating over all external agency, and bidding help and hindrance vanish before them. The genius of *Shakespeare* was not to be depressed by the weight of poverty, nor limited by the narrow conversation to which men in want are inevitably condemned; the incumbrances of his fortune were shaken from his mind, *as dewdrops from a lion's mane.*[28]

Though he had so many difficulties to encounter, and so little assistance to surmount them, he has been able to obtain an exact knowledge of many modes of life, and many casts of native dispositions; to vary them with great multiplicity; to mark them by nice distinctions; and to shew them in full view by proper combinations. In this part of his performances he had none to imitate, but has himself been imitated by all succeeding writers; and it may be doubted, whether from all his successors more maxims of theoretical knowledge, or more rules of practical prudence, can be collected, than he alone has given to his country.

Nor was his attention confined to the actions of men; he was an exact surveyor of the inanimate world; his descriptions have always some peculiarities, gathered by contemplating things as they really exist. It may be observed, that the oldest poets of many nations preserve their reputation, and that the following generations of wit, after a short celebrity, sink into oblivion. The first, whoever they be, must take their sentiments and descriptions immediately from knowledge; the resemblance is therefore just, their descriptions are verified by every eye, and their sentiments acknowledged by every breast. Those whom their fame invites to the same studies, copy partly them, and partly nature, till the books of one age gain such authority, as to stand in the place of nature to another, and imitation, always deviating a little, becomes at last capricious and casual. *Shakespeare,* whether life or nature be his subject, shews plainly, that he has seen with his own eyes; he gives the image which he receives, not weakened or distorted by the intervention of any other mind; the ignorant feel his representations to be just, and the learned see that they are compleat.

Perhaps it would not be easy to find any authour, except *Homer,* who invented so much as *Shakespeare,* who so much advanced the studies which he cultivated, or effused so much novelty upon his age or country. The form, the characters, the language, and the shows of the *English* drama are his. *He seems, says Dennis, to have been the very original of our* English *tragical harmony, that is, the harmony of blank verse, diversified often by dissyllable and trissyllable terminations. For the diversity distinguishes it from heroick harmony, and by bringing it nearer to common use makes it more proper to gain attention, and more fit for action and dialogue. Such verse we make when we are writing prose; we make such verse in common conversation.* [29]

I know not whether this praise is rigorously just. The dissyllable termination, which the critick rightly appropriates to the drama, is to be found, though, I think, not in *Gorboduc* which is confessedly before our authour; yet in *Hieronnymo*, [30] of which the date is not certain, but which there is reason to believe at least as old as his earliest plays. This however is certain, that he is the first who taught either tragedy or comedy to please, there being no theatrical piece of any older writer, of which the name is known, except to antiquaries and collectors of books, which are sought because they are scarce, and would not have been scarce, had they been much esteemed.

To him we must ascribe the praise, unless *Spenser* may divide it with him, of having first discovered to how much smoothness and harmony the *English* language could be softened. He has speeches, perhaps sometimes scenes, which have all the delicacy of *Rowe*, without his effeminacy. He endeavours indeed commonly to strike by the force and vigour of his dialogue, but he never executes his purpose better, than when he tries to sooth by softness.

Yet it must be at last confessed, that as we owe every thing to him, he owes something to us; that, if much of his praise is paid by perception and judgement, much is likewise given by custom and veneration. We fix our eyes upon his graces, and turn them from his deformities, and endure in him what we should in another loath or despise. If we endured without praising, respect for the father of our drama might excuse us; but I have seen, in the book of some modern critick; [31] a collection of anomalies, which shew that he has corrupted language by every mode of depravation, but which his admirer has accumulated as a monument of honour.

He has scenes of undoubted and perpetual excellence, but perhaps not one play, which, if it were now exhibited as the work of a contemporary writer, would be heard to the conclusion. I am indeed far from thinking, that his works were wrought to his own ideas of perfection; when they were such as would satisfy the audience, they satisfied the writer. It is seldom that authours, though more studious of fame than *Shakespeare*, rise much above the standard of their own age; to add a little of what is best will always be sufficient for present praise, and those who find themselves exalted into fame, are willing to credit their encomiasts, and to spare the labour of contending with themselves.

It does not appear, that *Shakespeare* thought his works worthy of posterity, that he levied any ideal tribute upon future times, or had any further prospect, than of present popularity and present profit. When his plays had been acted, his hope was at an end; he solicited no addition of honour from the reader. He therefore made no scruple to repeat the same jests in many dialogues, or to entangle different plots by the same knot of perplexity, which may be at least forgiven him, by those who recollect, that of *Congreve*'s four comedies, two are concluded by a marriage in a mask, by a deception, which perhaps never happened, and which, whether likely or not, he did not invent.

So careless was this great poet of future fame, that, though he retired to ease and plenty, while he was yet little *declined into the vale of years*, [32] before he could be disgusted with fatigue, or disabled by infirmity, he made no collection of his works, nor desired to rescue those that had been already published from the depravations that obscured them, or secure to the rest a better destiny, by giving them to the world in their genuine state.

Of the plays which bear the name of *Shakespeare* in the late editions, the greater part were not published till about seven years after his death, and the few which appeared in his life are apparently thrust into the world without the care of the authour, and therefore probably without his knowledge.

Of all the publishers, clandestine or professed, their negligence and unskilfulness has by the late revisers been sufficiently shown. The faults of all are indeed numerous and gross, and have not only corrupted many passages perhaps beyond recovery, but have brought others into suspicion, which are only obscured by obsolete phraseology, or by the writer's unskilfulness and affectation. To alter is more easy than to explain, and temerity is a more common quality than diligence. Those who saw that they must employ conjecture to a certain degree, were willing to indulge it a little further. Had the authour published his own works, we should have sat quietly down to disentangle his intricacies, and clear his obscurities; but now we tear what we cannot loose, and eject what we happen not to understand.

The faults are more than could have happened without the concurrence of many causes. The stile of *Shakespeare* was in itself ungrammatical, perplexed and obscure; his works were transcribed for the players by those who may be supposed to have seldom understood them; they were transmitted by copiers equally unskilful, who still multiplied errours; they were perhaps sometimes mutilated by the actors, for the sake of shortening the speeches; and were at last printed without correction of the press.

In this state they remained, not as Dr. *Warburton* supposes, because they were unregarded,[33] but because the editor's art was not yet applied to modern languages, and our ancestors were accustomed to so much negligence of *English* printers, that they could very patiently endure it. At last an edition was undertaken by *Rowe*; not because a poet was to be published by a poet, for *Rowe* seems to have thought very little on correction or explanation, but that our authour's works might appear like those of his fraternity, with the appendages of a life and recommendatory preface. *Rowe* has been clamorously blamed for not performing what he did not undertake, and it is time that justice be done him, by confessing, that though he seems to have had no thought of corruption beyond the printer's errours, yet he has made many emendations, if they were not made before, which his successors have received without acknowledgement, and which, if they had produced them, would have filled pages and pages with censures of the stupidity by which the faults were committed, with displays of the absurdities which they involved, with ostentatious expositions of the new reading, and self congratulations on the happiness of discovering it.

Of *Rowe*, as of all the editors, I have preserved the preface, and have likewise retained the authour's life,[34] though not written with much elegance or spirit; it relates however what is now to be known, and therefore deserves to pass through all succeeding publications.

The nation had been for many years content enough with Mr. *Rowe*'s performance, when Mr. *Pope* made them acquainted with the true state of *Shakespeare*'s text, shewed that it was extremely corrupt, and gave reason to hope that there were means of reforming it. He collated the old copies, which none had thought to examine before, and restored many lines to their integrity; but, by a very compendious criticism, he rejected whatever he disliked, and thought more of amputation than of cure.

I know not why he is commended by Dr. *Warburton* for distinguishing the genuine from the spurious plays.[35] In this choice he exerted no judgement of his own; the plays which he received, were given by *Hemings* and *Condel*, the first editors; and those which he rejected, though, according to the licentiousness of the press in those times, they were printed during *Shakespeare*'s life, with his name, had been omitted by his friends, and were never added to his works before the edition of 1664, from which they were copied by the later printers.

This was a work which *Pope* seems to have thought unworthy of his abilities, being not able to suppress his contempt of *the dull duty of an editor*.[36] He understood but half his undertaking. The duty of a collator is indeed dull, yet, like other tedious tasks, is very necessary; but an emendatory critick would ill discharge his duty, without qualities very different from dulness. In perusing a corrupted piece, he must have before him all possibilities of meaning, with all possibilities of expression. Such must be his comprehension of thought, and such his copiousness of language. Out of many readings possible, he must be able to select that which best suits with the state, opinions, and modes of language prevailing in every age, and with his authour's particular cast of thought, and turn of expression. Such must be his knowledge, and such his taste. Conjectural criticism demands more than humanity possesses, and he that exercises it with most praise has very frequent need of indulgence. Let us now be told no more of the dull duty of an editor.

Confidence is the common consequence of success. They whose excellence of any kind has been loudly celebrated, are ready to conclude, that their powers are universal. *Pope*'s edition fell below his own expectations, and he was so much offended, when he was found to have left any thing for others to do, that he past the latter part of his life in a state of hostility with verbal criticism.

I have retained all his notes, that no fragment of so great a writer may be lost; his preface, valuable alike for elegance of composition and justness of remark, and containing a general criticism on his author, so extensive that little can be added, and so exact, that little can be disputed, every editor has an interest to suppress, but that every reader would demand its insertion.

Pope was succeeded by *Theobald*, a man of narrow comprehension and small acquisitions, with no native and intrinsick splendour of genius, with little of the artificial light of learning, but zealous for minute accuracy, and not negligent in pursuing it. He collated the ancient copies, and rectified many errors. A man so anxiously scrupulous might have been expected to do more, but what little he did was commonly right.

In his report of copies and editions he is not to be trusted, without examination. He speaks sometimes indefinitely of copies, when he has only one. In his enumeration of editions, he mentions the two first folios as of high, and the third folio as of middle authority; but the truth is, that the first is equivalent to all others, and that the rest only deviate from it by the printer's negligence. Whoever has any of the folios has all, excepting those diversities which mere reiteration of editions will produce. I collated them all at the beginning, but afterwards used only the first.

Of his notes I have generally retained those which he retained himself in his second edition, except when they were confuted by subsequent annotators, or were too minute to merit preservation. I have sometimes adopted his restoration of a comma, without inserting the panegyrick in which he celebrated himself for his achievement. The exuberant excrescence of his diction I have often lopped, his triumphant exultations over *Pope* and *Rowe* I have sometimes suppressed, and his contemptible ostentation I have frequently concealed; but I have in some places shewn him, as he would have shewn himself, for the reader's diversion, that the inflated emptiness of some notes may justify or excuse the contraction of the rest.

Theobald, thus weak and ignorant, thus mean and faithless, thus petulant and ostentatious, by the good luck of having *Pope* for his enemy, has escaped, and escaped alone, with reputation, from this undertaking. So willingly does the world support those who solicite favour, against those who command reverence; and so easily is he praised, whom no man can envy.

Our authour fell then into the hands of Sir *Thomas Hanmer*, the *Oxford* editor, a man, in my opinion, eminently qualified by nature for such studies. He had, what is the first requisite to emendatory criticism, that intuition by which the poet's intention is immediately discovered, and that dexterity of intellect which dispatches its work by the easiest means. He had undoubtedly read much; his acquaintance with customs, opinions, and traditions, seem to have been large; and he is often learned without shew. He seldom passes what he does not understand, without an attempt to find or to make a meaning, and sometimes hastily makes what a little more attention would have found. He is solicitous to reduce to grammar, what he could not be sure that his authour intended to be grammatical. *Shakespeare* regarded more the series of ideas, than of words; and his language, not being designed for the reader's desk, was all that he desired it to be, if it conveyed his meaning to the audience.

Hanmer's care of the metre has been too violently censured. He found the measures reformed in so many passages, by the silent labours of some editors, with the silent acquiescence of the rest, that he thought himself allowed to extend a little further the license, which had already been carried so far without reprehension; and of his corrections in general, it must be confessed, that they are often just, and made commonly with the least possible violation of the text.

But, by inserting his emendations, whether invented or borrowed, into the page, without any notice of varying copies, he has appropriated the labour of his predecessors, and made his own edition of little authority. His confidence indeed, both in himself and others, was too great; he supposes all to be right that was done by *Pope* and *Theobald*; he seems not to suspect a critick of fallibility, and it was but reasonable that he should claim what he so liberally granted.

As he never writes without careful enquiry and diligent consideration, I have received all his notes, and believe that every reader will wish for more.

Of the last editor it is more difficult to speak. Respect is due to high place,[37] tenderness to living reputation, and veneration to genius and learning; but he cannot be justly offended at that liberty of which he has himself so frequently given an example, nor very solicitous what is thought of notes, which he ought never to have considered as part of his serious employments, and which, I suppose, since the ardour of composition is remitted, he no longer numbers among his happy effusions.

The original and predominant errour of his commentary, is acquiescence in his first thoughts; that precipitation which is produced by consciousness of quick discernment; and that confidence with presumes to do by surveying the surface, what labour only can perform, by penetrating the bottom. His notes exhibit sometimes perverse interpretations, and sometimes improbable conjectures; he at one time gives the authour more profundity of meaning, than the sentence admits, and at another discovers absurdities, where the sense is plain to every other reader. But his emendations are likewise often happy and just; and his interpretation of obscure passages learned and sagacious.

Of his notes, I have commonly rejected those, against which the general voice of the publick has exclaimed, or which their own incongruity immediately condemns, and which, I suppose, the authour himself would desire to be forgotten. Of the rest, to part I have given the highest approbation, by inserting the offered reading in the text; part I have left to the judgment of the reader, as doubtful, though specious; and part I have censured without reserve, but I am sure without bitterness of malice, and, I hope, without wantonness of insult.

It is no pleasure to me, in revising my volumes, to observe how much paper is wasted in confutation. Whoever considers the revolutions of learning, and the various questions of greater or less importance, upon which wit and reason have exercised their powers, must lament the unsuccessfulness of enquiry, and the slow advances of truth, when he reflects, that great part of the labour of every writer is only the destruction of those that went before him. The first care of the builder of a new system, is to demolish the fabricks which are standing. The chief desire of him that comments an authour, is to shew how much other commentators have corrupted and obscured him. The opinions prevalent in one age, as truths above the reach of controversy, are confuted and rejected in another, and rise again to reception in remoter times. Thus the human mind is kept in motion without progress. Thus sometimes truth and errour, and sometimes contrarieties of errour, take each other's place by reciprocal invasion. The tide of seeming knowledge which is poured over one generation, retires and leaves another naked and barren; the sudden meteors of intelligence which for a while appear to shoot their beams into the regions of obscurity, on a sudden withdraw their lustre, and leave mortals again to grope their way.

These elevations and depressions of renown, and the contradictions to which all improvers of knowledge must for ever be exposed, since they are not escaped by the highest and brightest of mankind, may surely be endured with patience by criticks and annotators, who can rank themselves but as the satellites of their authours. How canst thou beg for life, says *Achilles* to his captive, when thou knowest that thou art now to suffer only what must another day be suffered by *Achilles*?[38]

Dr. *Warburton* had a name sufficient to confer celebrity on those who could exalt themselves into antagonists, and his notes have raised a clamour too loud to be distinct. His chief assailants are the authours of *the Canons of criticism* and of the *Review of Shakespeare's text*;[39] of whom one ridicules his errours with airy petulance, suitable enough to the levity of the controversy; the other attacks them with gloomy malignity, as if he were dragging to justice an assassin or incendiary. The one stings like a fly, sucks a little blood, takes a gay flutter, and returns for more; the other bites like a viper, and would be glad to leave inflammations and gangrene behind him. When I think on one, with his confederates, I remember the danger of *Coriolanus*, who was afraid that *girls with spits, and boys with stones, should slay him in puny battle*; when the other crosses my imagination, I remember the prodigy in *Macbeth*,

> *An eagle tow'ring in his pride of place,*
> *Was by a mousing owl hawk'd at and kill'd.*[40]

Let me however do them justice. One is a wit, and one a scholar. They have both shewn acuteness sufficient in the discovery of faults, and have both advanced some probable interpretations of obscure passages; but when they aspire to conjecture and emendation, it appears how falsely we all estimate our own abilities, and the little which they have been able to perform might have taught them more candour to the endeavours of others.

Before Dr. *Warbuton*'s edition, *Critical observations on Shakespeare* had been published by Mr. *Upton*, a man skilled in languages, and acquainted with books, but who seems to have had no great vigour of genius or nicety of taste. Many of his explanations are curious and useful, but he likewise, though he professed to oppose the licentious confidence of editors, and adhere to the old copies, is unable to restrain the rage of emendation, though his ardour is ill seconded by his skill. Every cold empirick, when his heart is expanded by a successful experiment, swells into a theorist, and the laborious collator at some unlucky moment frolicks in conjecture.

Critical, historical and explanatory notes have been likewise published upon *Shakespeare* by Dr. *Grey*, whose diligent perusal of the old *English* writers has enabled him to make some useful observations. What he undertook he has[41] well enough performed, but as he neither attempts judicial nor emendatory criticism, he employs rather his memory than his sagacity. It were to be wished that all would endeavour to imitate his modesty who have not been able to surpass his knowledge.

I can say with great sincerity of all my predecessors, what I hope will hereafter be said of me, that not one has left *Shakespeare* without improvement, nor is there one to whom I have not been indebted for assistance and information. Whatever I have taken from them it was my intention to refer to its original authour, and it is certain, that what I have not given to another, I believed when I wrote it to be my own. In some perhaps I have been anticipated; but if I am ever found to encroach upon the remarks of any other commentator, I am willing that the honour, be it more or less, should be transferred to the first claimant, for his right, and his alone, stands above dispute; the second can prove his pretensions only to himself, nor can himself always distinguish invention, with sufficient certainty, from recollection.

They have all been treated by me with candour, which they have not been careful of observing to one another. It is not easy to discover from what cause the acrimony of a scholiast can naturally proceed. The subjects to be discussed by him are of very small importance; they involve neither property nor liberty; nor favour the interest of sect or party. The various readings of copies, and different interpretations of a passage, seem to be questions that might exercise the wit, without engaging the passions. But, whether it be, that *small things make mean men proud*,[42] and vanity catches small occasions; or that all contrariety of opinion, even in those that can defend it no longer, makes proud men angry; there is often found in commentaries a spontaneous strain of invective and contempt, more eager and venomous than is vented by the most furious controvertist in politicks against those whom he is hired to defame.

Perhaps the lightness of the matter may conduce to the vehemence of the agency; when the truth to be investigated is so near to inexistence, as to escape attention, its bulk is to be enlarged by rage and exclamation: That to which all would be indifferent in its original state, may attract notice when the fate of a name is appended to it. A commentator has indeed great temptations to supply by turbulence what he wants of dignity, to beat his little gold to a spacious surface, to work that to foam which no art or diligence can exalt to spirit.

The notes which I have borrowed or written are either illustrative, by which difficulties are explained; or judicial, by which faults and beauties are remarked; or emendatory, by which depravations are corrected.

The explanations transcribed from others, if I do not subjoin any other interpretation, I suppose commonly to be right, at least I intend by acquiscence to confess, that I have nothing better to propose.

After the labours of all the editors, I found many passages which appeared to me likely to obstruct the greater number of readers, and thought it my duty to facilitate their passage. It is impossible for an expositor not to write too little for some, and too much for others. He can only judge what is necessary by his own experience; and how long soever he may deliberate, will at last explain many lines which the learned will think impossible to be mistaken, and omit many for which the ignorant will want his help. These are censures merely relative, and must be quietly endured. I have endeavoured to be neither superfluously copious, nor scrupulously reserved, and hope that I have made my authour's meaning accessible to many who before were frighted from perusing him, and contributed something to the publick, by diffusing innocent and rational pleasure.

The compleat explanation of an authour not systematick and consequential, but desultory and vagrant, abounding in casual allusions and light hints, is not to be expected from any single scholiast. All personal reflections, when names are suppressed, must be in a few years irrecoverably obliterated; and customs, too minute to attract the notice of law, such as modes of dress, formalities of conversation, rules of visits, disposition of furniture, and practices of ceremony, which naturally find places in familiar dialogue, are so fugitive and unsubstantial, that they are not easily retained or recovered. What can be known, will be collected by chance, from the recesses of obscure and obsolete papers, perused commonly with some other view. Of this knowledge every man has some, and none has much; but when an authour has engaged the publick attention, those who can add any thing to his illustration, communicate their discoveries, and time produces what had eluded diligence.

To time I have been obliged to resign many passages, which,

though I did not understand them, will perhaps hereafter be explained, having, I hope, illustrated some, which others have neglected or mistaken, sometimes by short remarks, or marginal directions, such as every editor has added at his will, and often by comments more laborious than the matter will seem to deserve; but that which is most difficult is not always most important, and to an editor nothing is a trifle by which his authour is obscured.

The poetical beauties or defects I have not been very diligent to observe. Some plays have more, and some fewer judicial observations, not in proportion to their difference of merit, but because I gave this part of my design to chance and to caprice. The reader, I believe, is seldom pleased to find his opinion anticipated; it is natural to delight more in what we find or make, than in what we receive. Judgement, like other faculties, is improved by practice, and its advancement is hindered by submission to dictatorial decisions, as the memory grows torpid by the use of a table book. Some initiation is however necessary; of all skill, part is infused by precept, and part is obtained by habit; I have therefore shewn so much as may enable the candidate of criticism to discover the rest.

To the end of most plays, I have added short strictures, containing a general censure of faults, or praise of excellence; in which I know not how much I have concurred with the current opinion; but I have not, by any affectation of singularity, deviated from it. Nothing is minutely and particularly examined, and therefore it is to be supposed, that in the plays which are condemned there is much to be praised, and in these which are praised much to be condemned.

The part of criticism in which the whole succession of editors has laboured with the greatest diligence, which has occasioned the most arrogant ostentation, and excited the keenest acrimony, is the emendation of corrupted passages, to which the publick attention having been first drawn by the violence of contention between *Pope* and *Theobald*, has been continued by the persecution which, with a kind of conspiracy, has been since raised against all the publishers of *Shakespeare*.

That many passages have been passed in a state of depravation through all the editions is indubitably certain; of these the restoration is only to be attempted by collation of copies or sagacity of conjecture. The collator's province is safe and easy, the conjecturer's perilous and difficult. Yet as the greater part of the plays are extant only in one copy, the peril must not be avoided, nor the difficulty refused.

Of the readings which this emulation of amendment has hitherto produced, some from the labours of every publisher I have advanced into the text; those are to be considered as in my opinion sufficiently supported; some I have rejected without mention, as evidently erroneous; some I have left in the notes without censure or approbation, as resting in equipoise between objection and defence; and some, which seemed specious but not right, I have inserted with a subsequent animadversion.

Having classed the observations of others, I was at last to try what I could substitute for their mistakes, and how I could supply their omissions. I collated such copies as I could procure, and wished for more, but have not found the collectors of these rarities very communicative. Of the editions which chance or kindness put into my hands I have given an enumeration, that I may not be blamed for neglecting what I had not the power to do.

By examining the old copies, I soon found that the later publishers, with all their boasts of diligence, suffered many passages to stand unauthorised, and contented themselves with *Rowe's* regulation of the text, even where they knew it to be arbitrary, and with a little consideration might have found it to be wrong. Some of these alterations are only the ejection of a word for one that appeared to him more elegant or more intelligible. These corruptions I have often silently rectified; for the history of our language, and the true force of our words, can only be preserved, by keeping the text of authours free from adulteration. Others, and those very frequent, smoothed the cadence, or regulated the measure; on these I have not exercised the same rigour; if only a word was transposed, or a particle inserted or omitted, I have sometimes suffered the line to stand; for the inconstancy of the copies is such, as that some liberties may be easily permitted. But this practice I have not suffered to proceed far, having restored the primitive diction wherever it could for any reason be preferred.

The emendations, which comparison of copies supplied, I have inserted in the text; sometimes where the improvement was slight, without notice, and sometimes with an account of the reasons of the change.

Conjecture, though it be sometimes unavoidable, I have not wantonly nor licentiously indulged. It has been my settled principle, that the reading of the ancient books is probably true, and therefore is not to be disturbed for the sake of elegance, perspicuity, or mere improvement of the sense. For though much credit is not due to the fidelity, nor any to the judgement of the first publishers, yet they who had the copy before their eyes were more likely to read it right, than we who read it only by imagination. But it is evident that they have often made strange mistakes by ignorance or negligence, and that therefore something may be properly attempted by criticism, keeping the middle way between presumption and timidity.

Such criticism I have attempted to practise, and where any passage appeared inextricably perplexed, have endeavoured to discover how it may be recalled to sense, with least violence. But my first labour is, always to turn the old text on every side, and try if there be any interstice, through which light can find its way; nor would *Huetius*[43] himself condemn me, as refusing the trouble of research, for the ambition of alteration. In this modest industry I have not been unsuccessful. I have rescued many lines from the violations of temerity, and secured many scenes from the inroads of correction. I have adopted the *Roman* sentiment, that it is more honourable to save a citizen, than to kill an enemy, and have been more careful to protect than to attack.

I have preserved the common distribution of the plays into acts, though I believe it to be in almost all the plays void of authority. Some of those which are divided in the later editions have no division in the first folio, and some that are divided in the folio have no division in the preceding copies. The settled mode of the theatre requires four intervals in the play, but few, if any, of our authour's compositions can be properly distributed in that manner. An act is so much of the drama as passes without intervention of time or change of place. A pause makes a new act. In every real, and therefore in every imitative action, the intervals may be more or fewer, the restriction of five acts being accidental and arbitrary. This *Shakespeare* knew, and this he practised; his plays were written, and at first printed in one unbroken continuity, and ought now to be exhibited with short pauses, interposed as often as the scene is changed, or any considerable time is required to pass. This method would at once quell a thousand absurdities.

In restoring the authour's works to their integrity, I have considered the punctuation as wholly in my power; for what could be their care of colons and commas, who corrupted words and sentences. Whatever could be done by adjusting points is therefore silently performed, in some plays with much diligence, in others with less; it is hard to keep a busy eye steadily fixed upon evanescent atoms, or a discursive mind upon evanescent truth.

The same liberty has been taken with a few particles, or other words of slight effect. I have sometimes inserted or omitted them without notice. I have done that sometimes, which the other editors have done always, and which indeed the state of the text may sufficiently justify.

The greater part of readers, instead of blaming us for passing trifles, will wonder that on mere trifles so much labour is expended, with such importance of debate, and such solemnity of diction. To these I answer with confidence, that they are judging of an art which they do not understand; yet cannot much reproach them with their ignorance, nor promise that they would become in general, by learning criticism, more useful, happier or wiser.

As I practised conjecture more, I learned to trust it less; and after I had printed a few plays, resolved to insert none of my own readings in the text. Upon this caution I now congratulate myself, for every day encreases my doubt of my emendations.

Since I have confined my imagination to the margin, it must not be considered as very reprehensible, if I have suffered it to play some freaks in its own dominion. There is no danger in conjecture, if it be proposed as conjecture; and while the text remains uninjured, those changes may be safely offered, which are not considered even by him that offers them as necessary or safe.

If my readings are of little value, they have not been ostentatiously displayed or importunately obtruded. I could have written longer notes, for the art of writing notes is not of difficult attainment. The work is performed, first by railing at the stupidity, negligence, ignorance, and asinine tastelessness of the former editors, and shewing, from all that goes before and all that follows, the inelegance and absurdity of the old reading; then by proposing something, which to superficial readers would seem specious, but which the editor rejects with indignation; then by producing the true reading, with a long paraphrase, and concluding with loud acclamations on the discovery, and a sober wish for the advancement and prosperity of genuine criticism.

All this may be done, and perhaps done sometimes without impropriety. But I have always suspected that the reading is right, which requires many words to prove it wrong; and the emendation wrong, that cannot without so much labour appear to be right. The justness of a happy restoration strikes at once, and the moral precept may be well applied to criticism, *quod dubitas ne feceris* [while you doubt, do not].[44]

To dread the shore which he sees spread with wrecks, is natural to the sailor. I had before my eye, so many critical adventures ended in miscarriage, that caution was forced upon me. I encountered in every page Wit struggling with its own sophistry, and Learning confused by the multiplicity of its views. I was forced to censure those whom I admired, and could not but reflect, while I was dispossessing their emendations, how soon the same fate might happen to my own, and how many of the readings which I have corrected may be by some other editor defended and established.

> *Criticks, I saw, that other's names efface,*
> *And fix their own, with labour, in the place;*
> *Their own, like others, soon their place resign'd,*
> *Or disappear'd, and left the first behind.*   POPE.[45]

That a conjectural critick should often be mistaken, cannot be wonderful, either to others or himself, if it be considered, that in his art there is no system, no principal and axiomatical truth that regulates subordinate positions. His chance of errour is renewed at every attempt; an oblique view of the passage, a slight misapprehension of a phrase, a casual inattention to the parts connected, is sufficient to make him not only fail, but fail ridiculously; and when he succeeds best, he produces perhaps but one reading of many probable, and he that suggests another will always be able to dispute his claims.

It is an unhappy state, in which danger is hid under pleasure. The allurements of emendation are scarcely resistible. Conjecture has all the joy and all the pride of invention, and he that has once started a happy change, is too much delighted to consider what objections may rise against it.

Yet conjectural criticism has been of great use in the learned world; nor is it my intention to depreciate a study, that has exercised so many mighty minds, from the revival of learning to our own age, from the Bishop of *Aleria* to English *Bentley*.[46] The criticks on ancient authours have, in the exercise of their sagacity, many assistances, which the editor of *Shakespeare* is condemned to want. They are employed upon grammatical and settled languages, whose construction contributes so much to perspicuity, that *Homer* has fewer passages unintelligible than *Chaucer*. The words have not only a known regimen, but invariable quantities, which direct and confine the choice. There are commonly more manuscripts than one; and they do not often conspire in the same mistakes. Yet *Scaliger* could confess to *Salmasius* how little satisfaction his emendations gave him. *Illudunt nobis conjecturae nostrae, quarum nos pudet, posteaquam in meliores codices incidimus* [Our conjectures play us for fools, and we are put to shame, when subsequently we light on better texts]. And *Lipsius* could complain, that criticks were making faults, by trying to remove them, *Ut olim vitiis, ita nunc remediis laboratur* [As once we labored over corruptions, so now we do the same with our corrections].[47] And indeed, where mere conjecture is to be used, the emendations of *Scaliger* and *Lipsius*, notwithstanding their wonderful sagacity and erudition, are often vague and disputable, like mine or *Theobald*'s.

Perhaps I may not be more censured for doing wrong, than for doing little; for raising in the publick expectations, which at last I have not answered. The expectation of ignorance is indefinite, and that of knowledge is often tyrannical. It is hard to satisfy those who know not what to demand, or those who demand by design what they think impossible to be done. I have indeed disappointed no opinion more than my own; yet I have endeavoured to perform my task with no slight solicitude. Not a single passage in the whole work has appeared to me corrupt, which I have not attempted to restore; or obscure, which I have not endeavoured to illustrate. In many I have failed like others; and from many, after all my efforts, I have retreated, and confessed the repulse. I have not passed over, with affected superiority, what is equally difficult to the reader and to myself, but where I could not instruct him, have owned my ignorance. I might easily have accumulated a mass of seeming learning upon easy scenes; but it ought not to be imputed to negligence, that, where nothing was necessary, nothing has been done, or that, where others have said enough, I have said no more.

Notes are often necessary, but they are necessary evils. Let him, that is yet unacquainted with the powers of *Shakespeare,* and who desires to feel the highest pleasure that the drama can give, read every play from the first scene to the last, with utter negligence of all his commentators. When his fancy is once on the wing, let it not stoop at correction or explanation. When his attention is strongly engaged, let it disdain alike to turn aside to the name of *Theobald* and of *Pope.* Let him read on through brightness and obscurity, through integrity and corruption; let him preserve his comprehension of the dialogue and his interest in the fable. And when the pleasures of novelty have ceased, let him attempt exactness, and read the commentators.

Particular passages are cleared by notes, but the general effect of the work is weakened. The mind is refrigerated by interruption; the thoughts are diverted from the principal subject; the reader is weary, he suspects not why; and at last throws away the book, which he has too diligently studied.

Parts are not to be examined till the whole has been surveyed; there is a kind of intellectual remoteness necessary for the comprehension of any great work in its full design and its true proportions; a close approach shews the smaller niceties, but the beauty of the whole is discerned no longer.

It is not very grateful to consider how little the succession of editors has added to this authour's power of pleasing. He was read, admired, studied, and imitated, while he was yet deformed with all the improprieties which ignorance and neglect could accumulate upon him; while the reading was yet not rectified, nor his allusions understood; yet then did *Dryden* pronounce "that *Shakespeare* was the man, who, of all modern and perhaps ancient poets, had the largest and most comprehensive soul. All the images of nature were still present to him, and he drew them not laboriously, but luckily: When he describes any thing, you more than see it, you feel it too. Those who accuse him to have wanted learning, give him the greater commendation: he was naturally learned: he needed not the spectacles of books to read nature; he looked inwards, and found her there. I cannot say he is every where alike; were he so, I should do him injury to compare him with the greatest of mankind. He is many times flat and insipid; his comick wit degenerating into clenches, his serious swelling into bombast. But he is always great, when some great occasion is presented to him: No man can say, he ever had a fit subject for his wit, and did not then raise himself as high above the rest of poets,

Quantum lenta solent inter viburna cupressi.

[As cypresses are wont to tower amidst the supple willows]."[48]

It is to be lamented, that such a writer should want a commentary; that his language should become obsolete, or his sentiments obscure. But it is vain to carry wishes beyond the condition of human things; that which must happen to all, has happened to *Shakespeare,* by accident and time; and more than has been suffered by any other writer since the use of types, has been suffered by him through his own negligence of fame, or perhaps by that superiority of mind, which despised its own performances, when it compared them with its powers, and judged those works unworthy to be preserved, which the criticks of following ages were to contend for the fame of restoring and explaining.

Among these candidates of inferiour fame, I am now to stand the judgment of the publick; and wish that I could confidently produce my commentary as equal to the encouragement which I have had the honour of receiving. Every work of this kind is by its nature deficient, and I should feel little solicitude about the sentence, were it to be pronounced only by the skilful and the learned.

From Johnson's *NOTES TO SHAKESPEARE* (1765)

Measure for Measure

[3. 1. 32]
> DUKE. Thou hast nor youth, nor age;
>   But as it were an after-dinner's sleep,
>   Dreaming on both

This is exquisitely imagined. When we are young we busy ourselves in forming schemes for succeeding time, and miss the gratifications that are before us; when we are old we amuse the languour of age with the recollection of youthful pleasures or performances; so that our life, of which no part is filled with the business of the present time, resembles our dreams after dinner, when the events of the morning are mingled with the designs of the evening.

As You Like It

[General Observation]:
Of this play the fable is wild and pleasing. I know not how the ladies will approve the facility with which both *Rosalind* and *Celia* give away their hearts. To *Celia* much may be forgiven for the heroism of her friendship. The character of *Jaques* is natural and well preserved. The comick dialogue is very sprightly, with less mixture of low buffoonery than in some other plays; and the graver part is elegant and harmonious. By hastening to the end of his work *Shakespeare* suppressed the dialogue between the usurper and the hermit, and lost an opportunity of exhibiting a moral lesson in which he might have found matter worthy of his highest powers.

Twelfth Night

[General Observation]:
This play is in the graver part elegant and easy, and in some of

the lighter scenes exquisitely humorous. *Ague-cheek* is drawn with great propriety, but his character is, in a great measure, that of natural fatuity, and is therefore not the proper prey of a satirist. The soliloquy of *Malvolio* is truly comick; he is betrayed to ridicule merely by his pride. The marriage of *Olivia,* and the succeeding perplexity, though well enough contrived to divert on the stage, wants credibility, and fails to produce the proper instruction required in the drama, as it exhibits no just picture of life.

All's Well That Ends Well

[5. 3. 21]
> KING. We're reconcil'd, and the first view shall kill
> All repetition

The first interview shall put an end to all recollection of the past. Shakespeare is now hastening to the end of the play, finds his matter sufficient to fill up his remaining scenes, and therefore, as on other such occasions, contracts his dialogue and precipitates his action. Decency required that *Bertram*'s double crime of cruelty and disobedience joined likewise with some hypocrisy, should raise more resentment; and that though his mother might easily forgive him, his king should more pertinaciously vindicate his own authority and *Helen*'s merit: of all this *Shakespeare* could not be ignorant, but *Shakespeare* wanted to conclude his play.

[General Observation]:

This play has many delightful scenes, though not sufficiently probable, and some happy characters, though not new, nor produced by any deep knowledge of human nature. *Parolles* is a boaster and a coward, such as has always been the sport of the stage, but perhaps never raised more laughter or contempt than in the hands of *Shakespeare.*

I cannot reconcile my heart to *Bertram*; a man noble without generosity, and young without truth; who marries *Helen* as a coward and leaves her as a profligate: when she is dead by his unkindness, sneaks home to a second marriage, is accused by a woman whom he has wronged, defends himself by falshood, and is dismissed to happiness.

The story of *Bertram* and *Diana* had been told before of *Mariana* and *Angelo,* and, to confess the truth, scarcely merited to be heard a second time.

2 Henry IV

[5. 5. 64]

> KING HENRY V. Till then I banish thee, on pain of death,
> As I have done the rest of my mis-leaders,
> Not to come near our person by ten miles.

Mr. *Rowe* observes, that many readers lament to see *Falstaff* so hardly used by his old friend. But if it be considered that the fat knight has never uttered one sentiment of generosity, and with all his power of exciting mirth, has nothing in him that can be esteemed, no great pain will be suffered from the reflection that he is compelled to live honestly, and maintained by the king, with a promise of advancement when he shall deserve it.

I think the poet more blameable for *Poins,* who is always represented as joining some virtues with his vices, and is therefore treated by the prince with apparent distinction, yet he does nothing in the time of action, and though after the bustle is over he is again a favourite, at last vanishes without notice. *Shakespeare* certainly lost him by heedlessness, in the multiplicity of his characters, the variety of his action, and his eagerness to end the play.

[5. 5. 92]

> CHIEF JUSTICE. Go, carry Sir *John Falstaff* to the *Fleet.*

I do not see why *Falstaff* is carried to the Fleet. We have never lost sight of him since his dismission from the king; he has committed no new fault, and therefore incurred no punishment; but the different agitations of fear, anger, and surprise in him and his company, made a good scene to the eye; and our authour, who wanted them no longer on the stage, was glad to find this method of sweeping them away.

[General Observation]:

I fancy every reader, when he ends this play, cries out with *Desdemona, O most lame and impotent conclusion!* As this play was not, to our knowledge, divided into acts by the authour, I could be content to conclude it with the death of *Henry* the fourth.

In that Jerusalem shall Harry *dye*. These scenes which now make the fifth act of *Henry* the fourth, might then be the first of *Henry* the fifth; but the truth is, that they do unite very commodiously to either play. When these plays were represented, I believe they ended as they are now ended in the books; but *Shakespeare* seems to have designed that the whole series of action from the beginning of *Richard* the second, to the end of *Henry* the fifth, should be considered by the reader as one work, upon one plan, only broken into parts by the necessity of exhibition.

None of *Shakespeare's* plays are more read than the first and second parts of *Henry* the fourth. Perhaps no authour has ever in two plays afforded so much delight. The great events are interesting, for the fate of kingdoms depends upon them; the slighter occurrences are diverting, and, except one or two, sufficiently probable; the incidents are multiplied with wonderful fertility of invention, and the characters diversified with the utmost nicety of discernment, and the profoundest skill in the nature of man.

The prince, who is the hero both of the comick and tragick part, is a young man of great abilities and violent passions, whose sentiments are right, though his actions are wrong; whose virtues are obscured by negligence, and whose understanding is dissipated by levity. In his idle hours he is rather loose than wicked, and when the occasion forces out his latent qualities, he is great without effort, and brave without tumult. The trifler is roused into a hero, and the hero again reposes in the trifler. This character is great, original, and just.

Piercy is a rugged soldier, cholerick, and quarrelsome, and has only the soldier's virtues, generosity and courage.

But *Falstaff* unimitated, unimitable *Falstaff*, how shall I describe thee? Thou compound of sense and vice; of sense which may be admired but not esteemed, of vice which may be despised, but hardly detested. *Falstaff* is a character loaded with faults, and with those faults which naturally produce contempt. He is a thief, and a glutton, a coward, and a boaster, always ready to cheat the weak, and prey upon the poor; to terrify the timorous and insult the defenceless. At once obsequious and malignant, he satirises in their absence those whom he lives by flattering. He is familiar with the prince only as an agent of vice, but of this familiarity he is so proud as not only to be supercilious and haughty with common men, but to think his interest of importance to the duke of *Lancaster*. Yet the man thus corrupt, thus despicable, makes himself necessary to the prince that despises him, by the most pleasing of all qualities, perpetual gaiety, by an unfailing power of exciting laughter, which is the more freely indulged, as his wit is not of the splendid or ambitious kind, but consists in easy escapes and sallies of levity, which make sport but raise no envy. It must be observed that he is stained with no enormous or sanguinary crimes, so that his licentiousness is not so offensive but that it may be borne for his mirth.

The moral to be drawn from this representation is, that no man is more dangerous than he that with a will to corrupt, hath the power to please; and that neither wit nor honesty ought to think themselves safe with such a companion when they see *Henry* seduced by *Falstaff*.

King Lear

[4. 6. 11]
> EDGAR. How fearful
> And dizzy 'tis, to cast one's eyes so low!

This description has been much admired since the time of *Addison*, who has remarked, with a poor attempt at pleasantry, that *he who can read it without being giddy has a very good head, or a very bad one*. The description is certainly not mean, but I am far from thinking it wrought to the utmost excellence of poetry. He that looks from a precipice finds himself assailed by one great and dreadful image of irresistible destruction. But this overwhelming idea is dissipated and enfeebled from the instant that the mind can restore itself to the observation of particulars, and diffuse its attention to distinct objects. The enumeration of the choughs and crows, the samphire-man and the fishers, counteracts the great effect of the prospect, as it peoples the desert of intermediate vacuity, and stops the mind in the rapidity of its descent through emptiness and horrour.

[General Observation]:
The Tragedy of *Lear* is deservedly celebrated among the dramas of *Shakespeare*. There is perhaps no play which keeps the

attention so strongly fixed; which so much agitates our passions and interests our curiosity. The artful involutions of distinct interests, the striking opposition of contrary characters, the sudden changes of fortune, and the quick succession of events, fill the mind with a perpetual tumult of indignation, pity, and hope. There is no scene which does not contribute to the aggravation of the distress or conduct of the action, and scarce a line which does not conduce to the progress of the scene. So powerful is the current of the poet's imagination, that the mind, which once ventures within it, is hurried irresistibly along.

On the seeming improbability of *Lear*'s conduct it may be observed, that he is represented according to histories at that time vulgarly received as true. And perhaps if we turn our thoughts upon the barbarity and ignorance of the age to which this story is referred, it will appear not so unlikely as while we estimate *Lear*'s manners by our own. Such preference of one daughter to another, or resignation of dominion on such conditions, would be yet credible, if told of a pretty prince of *Guinea* or *Madagascar*. *Shakespeare*, indeed, by the mention of his Earls and Dukes, has given us the idea of times more civilised, and of life regulated by softer manners; and the truth is, that though he so nicely discriminates, and so minutely describes the characters of men, he commonly neglects and confounds the characters of ages, by mingling customs ancient and modern, *English* and foreign.

My learned friend Mr. *Warton*, who has in the *Adventurer*[49] very minutely criticised this play, remarks, that the instances of cruelty are too savage and shocking, and that the intervention of *Edmund* destroys the simplicity of the story. These objections may, I think, be answered, by repeating, that the cruelty of the daughters is an historical fact, to which the poet has added little, having only drawn it into a series by dialogue and action. But I am not able to apologise with equal plausibility for the extrusion of *Gloucester*'s eyes, which seems an act too horrid to be endured in dramatick exhibition, and such as must always compel the mind to relieve its distress by incredulity. Yet let it be remembered that our authour well knew what would please the audience for which he wrote.

The injury done by *Edmund* to the simplicity of the action is abundantly recompensed by the addition of variety, by the art with which he is made to co-operate with the chief design, and the opportunity which he gives the poet of combining perfidy with perfidy, and connecting the wicked son with the wicked daughters, to impress this important moral, that villany is never at a stop, that crimes lead to crimes, and at last terminate in ruin.

But though this moral be incidentally enforced, *Shakespeare* has suffered the virtue of *Cordelia* to perish in a just cause, contrary to the natural ideas of justice, to the hope of the reader, and, what is yet more strange, to the faith of chronicles. Yet this conduct is justified by the Spectator, who blames *Tate* for giving *Cordelia* success and happiness in his alteration, and declares that, in his opinion, *the tragedy has lost half its beauty.*[50] *Dennis* has remarked, whether justly or not, that, to secure the favourable reception of *Cato, the town was poisoned with much false and abominable criticism,* and that endeavours had been used to discredit and decry poetical justice.[51] A play in which the wicked prosper, and the virtuous miscarry, may doubtless be good, because it is a just representation of the common events of human life: but since all reasonable beings naturally love justice, I cannot easily be persuaded, that the observation of justice makes a play worse; or, that if other excellencies are equal, the audience will not always rise better pleased from the final triumph of persecuted virtue.

In the present case the publick has decided. *Cordelia*, from the time of *Tate*, has always retired with victory and felicity. And, if my sensations could add any thing to the general suffrage, I might relate, that I was many years ago so shocked by *Cordelia*'s death, that I know not whether I ever endured to read again the last scenes of the play till I undertook to revise them as an editor.

Macbeth

[1. 7. 28]
    [Stage direction.] Enter Lady Macbeth.

The arguments by which Lady *Macbeth* persuades her husband to commit the murder, afford a proof of *Shakespeare*'s knowledge of human nature. She urges the excellence and dignity of courage, a glittering idea which has dazzled mankind from age to age, and animated sometimes the housebreaker, and sometimes the conqueror; but this sophism *Macbeth* has for ever destroyed by distinguishing true from false fortitude, in a line and a half; of which it may also be said, that they ought to bestow immortality on the author, though all his other productions had been lost.

> *I dare do all that may become a man,*
> *Who dares do more, is none.*

This topic, which has been always employed with too much success, is used in this scene with peculiar propriety, to a soldier by a woman. Courage is the distinguishing virtue of a soldier, and the reproach of cowardice cannot be borne by any man from a woman, without great impatience.

She then urges the oaths by which he had bound himself to murder *Duncan*, another art of sophistry by which men have sometimes deluded their consciences, and persuaded themselves that what would be criminal in others is virtuous in them; this argument *Shakespeare*, whose plan obliged him to make *Macbeth* yield, has not confuted, though he might easily have shown that a former obligation could not be vacated by a latter: that obligations laid on us by a higher power, could not be overruled by obligations which we lay upon ourselves.

[2. 1. 49]
> MACBETH. Now o'er one half the world
> Nature seems dead, and wicked dreams abuse
> The curtain'd sleep; now witchcraft celebrates
> Pale *Hecat*'s offerings

That is, *over our hemisphere all action and motion seem to have ceased.* This image, which is perhaps the most striking that poetry can produce, has been adopted by *Dryden* in his *Conquest of* Mexico.

> *All things are hush'd as Nature's self lay dead,*
> *The mountains seem to nod their drowsy head;*
> *The little birds in dreams their songs repeat,*
> *And sleeping flow'rs beneath the night dews sweat.*
> *Even lust and envy sleep!*

These lines, though so well known, I have transcribed, that the contrast between them and this passage of *Shakespeare* may be more accurately observed.

Night is described by two great poets, but one describes a night of quiet, the other of perturbation. In the night of *Dryden*, all the disturbers of the world are laid asleep; in that of *Shakespeare*, nothing but sorcery, lust and murder, is awake. He that reads *Dryden*, finds himself lull'd with serenity, and disposed to solitude and contemplation. He that peruses *Shakespeare*, looks round alarmed, and starts to find himself alone. One is the night of a lover, the other, of a murderer.

Romeo and Juliet

[General Observation]:

This play is one of the most pleasing of our Author's performances. The scenes are busy and various, the incidents numerous and important, the catastrophe irresistibly affecting, and the process of the action carried on with such probability, at least with such congruity to popular opinions, as tragedy requires.

Here is one of the few attempts of *Shakespeare* to exhibit the conversation of gentlemen, to represent the airy sprightliness of juvenile elegance. Mr. *Dryden* mentions a tradition, which might easily reach his time, of a declaration made by *Shakespeare*, that *he was obliged to kill* Mercutio *in the third act, lest he should have been killed by him.* Yet he thinks him *no such formidable person, but that he might have lived through the play, and died in his bed,* without danger to a poet.[52] *Dryden* well knew, had he been in quest of truth, that, in a pointed sentence, more regard is commonly had to the words than the thought, and that it is very seldom to be rigorously understood. *Mercutio*'s wit, gaiety and courage, will always procure him friends that wish him a longer life; but his death is not precipitated, he has lived out the time allotted him in the construction of the play; nor do I doubt the ability of *Shakespeare* to have continued his existence, though some of his sallies are perhaps out of the reach of *Dryden*; whose genius was not very fertile of merriment, nor ductile of humour, but acute, argumentative, comprehensive, and sublime.

The Nurse is one of the characters in which the Authour

delighted: he has, with great subtilty of distinction, drawn her at once loquacious and secret, obsequious and insolent, trusty and dishonest.

His comick scenes are happily wrought, but his pathetick strains are always polluted with some unexpected depravations. His persons, however distressed *have a conceit left them in their misery, a miserable conceit.*[53]

Hamlet

[2. 2. 86]

> POLONIUS. My liege, and Madam, to expostulate
> What Majesty should be, what duty is,
> Why day is day, night night, and time is time,
> Were nothing but to waste night, day, and time.

Polonius is a man bred in courts, exercised in business, stored with observation, confident of his knowledge, proud of his eloquence, and declining into dotage. His mode of oratory is truly represented as designed to ridicule the practice of those times, of prefaces that made no introduction, and of method that embarrassed rather than explained. This part of his character is accidental, the rest is natural. Such a man is positive and confident, because he knows that his mind was once strong, and knows not that it is become weak. Such a man excels in general principles, but fails in the particular application. He is knowing in retrospect, and ignorant in foresight. While he depends upon his memory, and can draw from his repositories of knowledge, he utters weighty sentences, and gives useful counsel; but as the mind in its enfeebled state cannot be kept long busy and intent, the old man is subject to sudden dereliction of his faculties, he loses the order of his ideas, and entangles himself in his own thoughts, till he recovers the leading principle, and falls again into his former train. This idea of dotage encroaching upon wisdom, will solve all the phaenomena of the character of *Polonius*.

[3. 1. 56–88]

> HAMLET. To be, or not to be? that is the question.

Of this celebrated soliloquy, which bursting from a man distracted with contrariety of desires, and overwhelmed with the magnitude of his own purposes, is connected rather in the speaker's mind, than on his tongue, I shall endeavour to discover the train, and to shew how one sentiment produces another.

Hamlet, knowing himself injured in the most enormous and atrocious degree, and seeing no means of redress, but such as must expose him to the extremity of hazard, meditates on his situation in this manner: *Before I can form any rational scheme of action under this pressure of distress*, it is necessary to decide, whether, *after our present state, we are* to be or not to be. That is the question, which, as it shall be answered, will determine, *whether 'tis nobler*, and more suitable to the dignity of reason, *to suffer the outrages of fortune* patiently, or to take arms aginst *them*, and by opposing end them, *though perhaps* with the loss of life. If *to die*, were *to sleep, no more, and by a sleep to end* the miseries of our nature, such a sleep were *devoutly to be wished*; but if *to sleep* in death, be *to dream*, to retain our powers of sensibility, we must *pause* to consider, *in that sleep of death what dreams may come*. This consideration *makes calamity* so long endured; *for who would bear* the vexations of life, which might be ended *by a bare bodkin*, but that he is afraid of something in unknown futurity? This fear it is that gives efficacy to conscience, which, by turning the mind upon *this regard*, chills the ardour of *resolution*, checks the vigour of *enterprise*, and makes the *current* of desire stagnate in inactivity.

We may suppose that he would have applied these general observations to his own case, but that he discovered *Ophelia*.

[General Observation]:

If the dramas of *Shakespeare* were to be characterised, each by the particular excellence which distinguishes it from the rest, we must allow to the tragedy of *Hamlet* the praise of variety. The incidents are so numerous, that the argument of the play would make a long tale. The scenes are interchangeably diversified with merriment and solemnity; with merriment that includes judicious and instructive observations, and solemnity, not strained by poetical violence above the natural sentiments of man. New characters appear from time to time in continual succession, exhibiting various forms of life and particular modes of conversation. The pretended madness of *Hamlet* causes much mirth, the mournful distraction of *Ophelia* fills the heart with tenderness, and every personage produces the effect intended, from the apparition that in the first act chills the blood with horror, to the fop in the last, that exposes affectation to just contempt.

The conduct is perhaps not wholly secure against objections. The action is indeed for the most part in continual progression, but there are some scenes which neither forward nor retard it. Of the feigned madness of *Hamlet* there appears no adequate cause, for he does nothing which he might not have done with the reputation of sanity. He plays the madman most, when he treats *Ophelia* with so much rudeness, which seems to be useless and wanton cruelty.

Hamlet is, through the whole play, rather an instrument than an agent. After he has, by the stratagem of the play, convicted the King, he makes no attempt to punish him, and his death is at last effected by an incident which *Hamlet* has no part in producing.

The catastrophe is not very happily produced; the exchange of weapons is rather an expedient of necessity, than a stroke of art. A scheme might easily have been formed, to kill *Hamlet* with the dagger, and *Laertes* with the bowl.

The poet is accused of having shewn little regard to poetical justice, and may be charged with equal neglect of poetical probability. The apparition left the regions of the dead to little purpose; the revenge which he demands is not obtained but by the death of him that was required to take it; and the gratification which would arise from the destruction of an usurper and a murderer, is abated by the untimely death of *Ophelia*, the young, the beautiful, the harmless, and the pious.

Othello

[General Observation]:

The beauties of this play impress themselves so strongly upon the attention of the reader, that they can draw no aid from critical illustration. The fiery openness of *Othello*, magnanimous, artless, and credulous, boundless in his confidence, ardent in his affection, inflexible in his resolution, and obdurate in his revenge; the cool malignity of *Iago*, silent in his resentment, subtle in his designs, and studious at once of his interest and his vengeance; the soft simplicity of *Desdemona*, confident of merit, and conscious of innocence, her artless perseverance in her suit, and her slowness to suspect that she can be suspected, are such proofs of *Shakespeare*'s skill in human nature, as, I suppose, it is vain to seek in any modern writer. The gradual progress which *Iago* makes in the Moor's conviction, and the circumstances which he employs to inflame him, are so artfully natural, that, though it will perhaps not be said of him as he says of himself, that he is *a man not easily jealous*, yet we cannot but pity him when at last we find him *perplexed in the extreme*.

There is always danger lest wickedness conjoined with abilities should steal upon esteem, though it misses of approbation; but the character of *Iago* is so conducted, that he is from the first scene to the last hated and despised.

Even the inferiour characters of this play would be very conspicuous in any other piece, not only for their justness but their strength. *Cassio* is brave, benevolent, and honest, ruined only by his want of stubbornness to resist an insidious invitation. *Roderigo*'s suspicious credulity, and impatient submission to the cheats which he sees practised upon him, and which by persuasion he suffers to be repeated, exhibit a strong picture of a weak mind betrayed by unlawful desires, to a false friend: and the virtue of *Aemilia* is such as we often find, worn loosely, but not cast off, easy to commit small crimes, but quickened and alarmed at atrocious villanies.

The Scenes from the beginning to the end are busy, varied by happy interchanges, and regularly promoting the progression of the story; and the narrative in the end, though it tells but what is known already, yet is necessary to produce the death of *Othello*.

Had the scene opened in *Cyprus*, and the preceding incidents been occasionally related, there had been little wanting to a drama of the most exact and scrupulous regularity.

PROLOGUE SPOKEN AT THE OPENING OF THE THEATRE IN DRURY-LANE, 1747

[The first thirty-two lines only are here printed.]

When Learning's Triumph o'er her barb'rous Foes
First rear'd the Stage, immortal SHAKESPEAR rose;
Each Change of many-colour'd Life he drew,
Exhausted Worlds, and then imagin'd new:
Existence saw him spurn her bounded Reign,
And panting Time toil'd after him in vain:
His pow'rful Strokes presiding Truth impress'd,
And unresisted Passion storm'd the Breast.

Then JOHNSON[54] came, instructed from the School,
To please in Method, and invent by Rule;
His studious Patience, and laborious Art,
By regular Approach essay'd the Heart;
Cold Approbation gave the ling'ring Bays,
For those who durst not censure, scarce cou'd praise.
A Mortal born he met the general Doom,
But left, like *Egypt*'s Kings, a lasting Tomb.

The Wits of *Charles* found easier Ways to Fame,
Nor wish'd for JOHNSON's Art, or SHAKESPEAR's Flame;
Themselves they studied, as they felt, they writ,
Intrigue was Plot, Obscenity was Wit.
Vice always found a sympathetick Friend;
They pleas'd their Age, and did not aim to mend.
Yet Bards like these aspir'd to lasting Praise,
And proudly hop'd to pimp in future Days.
Their Cause was gen'ral, their Supports were strong,
Their Slaves were willing, and their Reign was long;
Till Shame regain'd the Post that Sense betray'd,
And Virtue call'd Oblivion to her Aid.

Then crush'd by Rules, and weaken'd as refin'd,
For Years the Pow'r of Tragedy declin'd;
From Bard, to Bard, the frigid Caution crept,
Till Declamation roar'd, while Passion slept.

NOTES

1. Cf. Aristotle *Metaphysics* 1. 5.

2. Cf. Horace *Epistles* 2. 1. 39.

3. Cf. *Rasselas*, chap. 10, and editor's commentary, pp. 130–33.

4. Cf. Cicero *Ad familiares* 16. 8. 4.

5. Hierocles Alexandrinus, Greek philosopher of the fifth century A.D.

6. Cf. Johnson's *Preface to the English Dictionary*, p. 118.

7. Cf. Pope's *Preface to Shakespeare* (1725), par. 4.

8. Cf. John Dennis, *An Essay on the Genius and Writings of Shakespear* (1712); Thomas Rymer, *A Short View of Tragedy* (1692); Voltaire, *Appel à toutes les nations de l'Europe* (1761) and *Dissertation sur la tragédie ancienne et moderne* (1749).

9. On tragicomedy see *Rambler* no. 156, p. 60.

10. Cf. Horace *Ars poetica* 11. 333–34, 343–44.

11. John Heminge and Henry Condell, actors in Shakespeare's dramatic company, published the First Folio (1623).

12. I.e., Shakespeare has faults which would obscure any merits less estimable than those Johnson has just imputed to him. Cf. Johnson's discussion of his first defect—his lack of a moral purpose—with his remarks on *The Beggar's Opera*, p. 248.

13. Cf. Pope's *Preface*, par. 18.

14. The 1778 edition reads: "have most reason to complain when he approachest nearest to his highest excellence, and seems fully resolved . . . crosses of love. What he does best, he soon ceases to do. He is . . . ."

15. Cf. Aristotle *Poetics* 7. 2–3.

16. See particularly Pierre Corneille's *Discours dramatiques* (1660). Cf. the following account of the dramatic unities and dramatic illusion with that in the *Life of Rowe*, pp. 242–43.

17. Addison's *Cato* (1713), 5. 1. 1–40.

18. Lucan *Pharsalia* 3. 138–40 (tr. Rowe).

19. Altered in later editions to "deliberately."

20. *Aeneid* 1. 610.

21. Lilly . . . Ascham: fifteenth- and sixteenth-century British educators and scholars.

22. Possibly, but not certainly, the reference is to Malory's *Morte d'Arthur* (1485).

23. In his *Appel à toutes les nations*. Cf. Johnson's discussion of *Cato* with that in the *Life of Addison*, p. 245.

24. Ben Jonson, in his verses in the First Folio on Shakespeare; the quotation is corrected in the 1773 edition to "less Greek."

25. Cf. Zachary Grey, *Critical, Historical, and Explanatory Notes on Shakespeare* (1754); the references are to *Richard III*, 1. 1. 144, and Terence, *Andria*, 1. 171.

26. Cf. Pope's *Preface*, par. 15.

27. Cf. Rowe, *Some Account of the Life &c. of . . . Shakespear* (1709), par. 4.

28. *Troilus and Cressida*, 3. 3. 224.

29. Cf. *Essay on the Genius and Writings of Shakespear*, par. 2. "Heroic harmony" refers to the tighter, rimed couplets characteristic of seventeenth-century heroic drama.

30. The reference is probably to Kyd's *Spanish Tragedy*.

31. John Upton, *Critical Observations on Shakespeare* (1746).

32. *Othello*, 3. 3. 269–70.

33. Cf. William Warburton's *Preface* (1747), par. 2.

34. The 1773 and later editions read: "As of the other editors, I have preserved the prefaces, I have likewise borrowed the author's life from Rowe . . . ."

35. Cf. Warburton's *Preface*, par. 4.

36. Cf. Pope's *Preface*, penultimate paragraph.

37. This is Warburton, who in 1759 had been made Bishop of Gloucester.

38. Cf. *Iliad* 21. 106–14. In the 1773 and later editions this sentence begins: "How canst thou beg for life, says Homer's hero to his captive . . . ."

39. Thomas Edwards wrote *Canons of Criticism* (1748) and Benjamin Heath *The Revisal of Shakespeare's Text* (1765). Johnson's inaccurate title for Heath is corrected in the 1778 edition.

40. *Macbeth*, 2. 4. 12–13. "An eagle" is corrected to "A falcon" in the 1773 edition.

41. The 1768 edition reads: "undertook was."

42. *2 Henry VI*, 4. 1. 106.

43. Pierre Huet, *De interpretatione libri duo* (1661).

44. Pliny *Epistles* 1. 18.

45. *Temple of Fame*, 11. 37–40 (for "efface" read "deface").

46. Joannes Andreas and Richard Bentley, both famous editors.

47. Scaliger, Salmasius, and Lipsius were all renowned classical scholars.

48. Dryden, *Essay of Dramatic Poesy* (1668); the Latin is from Virgil, *Eclogues*, 1. 25.

49. Cf. nos. 113, 116, 122.

50. *Spectator* no. 40.

51. *Remarks upon Cato* (1713).

52. *Defense of the Epilogue* (1672).

53. Quoted from Dryden, Preface to *Fables Ancient and Modern* (1700).

54. Ben Jonson is meant. The "wits of Charles" mentioned below are of course the Restoration playwrights. Among the declamatory bards described at the end is Addison, whose *Cato* Johnson criticizes in the *Preface*.

From *The Lives of the English Poets*
(1779–81)

The genesis of the *Lives* is a familiar story. Some forty reputable London booksellers, reacting to the publication in Edinburgh of a cheap edition of the major English poets to be peddled throughout Great Britain, united to issue a more elaborate edition, and requested Johnson, as much for the prestige of his name as his critical competence, to write the prefaces. There is evidence that Johnson had already contemplated such a project. Twelve years earlier, during his interview with George III, the king had suggested that he undertake "the literary biography of this country," and Johnson indicated his willingness to comply; but only under the added spur of the booksellers' proposal was he persuaded to begin work. He had little to do with establishing the scheme of the edition, which excluded living poets and poets antecedent to Cowley and Waller; nor was he required to select the texts or to perform any of the other editorial duties. His office was only to furnish a series of "Prefaces, Biographical and Critical, to the Works of the English Poets." These fifty-two separate prefaces were issued, together with the poets they introduced, in ten volumes from 1779 to 1781; in 1781 they were also published in four volumes separately from the texts, and again in 1783. Johnson, writing in circumstances less irksome than usual and with the confidence of a man at the zenith of his profession, seems to have delighted as much in this work as in any; surely he saw it, and properly, as the culmination of his critical career.

What the booksellers had desired were short sketches; what they received was much more. The prefaces vary greatly in length, from three or four hundred words to as many paragraphs; but the greatest of the lives, the *Cowley, Milton, Dryden,* and *Pope* particularly, are far more than mere prefaces, and hence the popular title, *Lives of the English Poets,* first used in the second edition, is probably more apt. The *Lives* were not without their predecessors: Gerard Langbaine's *Account of the English Dramatic Poets* (1691), *Lives of the Poets* (1753—a piece of hack journalism by Robert Shiels and Theophilus Cibber), the rudimentary biographical prefaces in Elizabeth Cooper's *Muses Library* (1737); from the first two sources Johnson extracted some of his material. But his work is in all respects superior, and while critical biographies had been executed before the *Lives*—Johnson himself wrote a few earlier in his career— he may be said here to have drawn the form most nearly to perfection. They follow generally a tripartite scheme: first a biographical account, then a character sketch somewhat after the Theophrastan model, and finally a criticism of the poet's works in chronological order. But not all the lives fit the pattern: in *Cowley,* for instance, the discussion of the metaphysical poets, here reproduced, replaces the central character sketch. Nor does Johnson observe with any pedantic scrupulosity the tripartite division itself: in *Pope,* for example, both moral and critical commentary can be found scattered throughout the biographical section. In unifying so deftly the portions of biography with those of criticism, and in casting on his subjects a coherence and depth of critical and moral perception, Johnson far surpasses any competitors. There are debilities, to be sure: the biographical parts are corrupted with factual errors which Johnson was too indolent to correct. This aspect of the work he takes least pleasure in; for him apparently, as indeed for the modern reader, the most engaging sections are the character sketches, which he uses, after the fashion of Tacitus and Plutarch, as moral exempla, and the literary criticism, which represents the final and, many would affirm, the finest efflorescence of neoclassicism.

With the *Lives* in their entirety, nevertheless, any serious student of Johnson or neoclassicism must be acquainted. These excerpts fail to capture effectively that relationship between the authors' lives and works which Johnson so consistently stressed. For the purposes of this volume I have extracted the more significant critical commentaries on the more significant writers, although I have preserved a few fragments from the lesser lives, rather more for what they reveal of Johnson than for what they inform us of the poets (e.g., the discussions of blank verse in *Thomson* and *Akenside* may be compared with the one in *Milton*). The first life, *Cowley*, was Johnson's favorite, and what he favored in it was the segment here reprinted on wit and the metaphysical poets. Since Cowley represents that poetic movement immediately antecedent to Johnson's own, his evaluation of this school fittingly preludes his examination of neoclassical poetry. At the same time, it constitutes Johnson's fullest account of one of the central terms of neoclassicism: wit. He dismisses Pope's famous definition ("What oft was thought, but ne'er so well express'd") as too inane, and supplies what he rightly calls a more philosophical one: wit is a *discordia concors*, a discovering of significant resemblances in things apparently unlike. The plodding poetaster, to be sure, will content himself with comparing the obvious; but at the opposite extremity, a poet may be too ingenious, fetching his resemblances from afar, or rather from too far. The similarities in true wit must surprise us, but they must also strike us as natural and just. Thus the similes of the metaphysicals are too labored and factitious: fascinated as we are by the ingenuity of these poets, our attention is distracted from their poems, and they consequently fail in their effect. Our minds, but not our feelings, are engaged. Because of their artifice, their minute analyses, their intricacy and paradox, the metaphysicals cannot attain the beautiful, the pathetic or sublime. W.J. Bate has noted that modern critics, seeking to rehabilitate the metaphysicals, have fastened upon precisely those qualities here discommended by Johnson; thus they have not discredited his critical acumen, but only have discovered depth where Johnson saw puerility. Whether the earlier or the later judgment is more just must wait the test of time, although it may be asked if, in even the greatest of the metaphysicals, Donne, more than a handful of poems have survived the shifts of fashion or have impressed themselves firmly on the sensibilities of modern readers.

The *Milton*, unlike the *Cowley*, was controversial in Johnson's time: not so much for his strictures on *Lycidas*, which excite today the most resentment, as for his reprehension of Milton's character (here omitted). Still, by 1780 rebellious critics were apt to favor Milton's earlier and allegedly minor poems—a vagary of taste at which Johnson, at the start of his account, is apparently squinting. Whether or not we agree with his criticisms of *Lycidas*, they in no way contradict his other principles, and may be compared with his evaluation of Gray's odes. Like the odes, and like metaphysical verse, the poem is judged too artificial and unnatural, too much the school-boy exercise, too clichéd in its language and theme, too irregular in its versification to give pleasure. Johnson's objection to its mingling of pagan with Christian elements is not exceptional for his time or inconsistent with his other views. In Johnson, as the extract from *Waller* shows, the Christian never sank into the aesthetician; and we may glance at his own elegy on Dr. Levet for a modest example of what he preferred: an unpretentious and sincere memorial, with a touch of the pathetic. Johnson is most valiantly a judicial critic on *Paradise Lost*. Let us consider that this poem presumes to treat of religious matters, mingles Christian and pagan materials (though admittedly in a less intimate manner than

Lycidas), is executed in blank verse (a form to which
Johnson responded with frigidity), by a man whose sec-
tarian and political persuasions Johnson detested and
who, as an artificial poet observing life through books
rather than nature, embodies the opposite of nearly everything Johnson venerated in Shakespeare. Moreover,
in treating of prelapsarian man, the poem is largely de-
void of that immediate human interest by which Johnson
is always most pleased. Yet he praises unstintingly the
vigor of Milton's genius and the sublimity of his masterpiece. And if he asserts that reading this masterpiece is
sometimes tiresome, and that none ever desired it longer
—can we confidently disagree with either?—nevertheless he celebrates at the close Milton's heroic character
and places him second only to Homer among the epic
poets.

Dryden and Pope, though somewhat inferior to Milton, are to Johnson clearly more congenial. Dryden's
criticism, like Addison's, closely approaches his own de-
sideratum: he describes it as intelligent but not pedantic
or tediously confined to a system. Dryden's style, again
like Addison's, is informal, easy, elegant but clear. He
rightly credits Dryden with establishing the new mode of
poetry replacing the metaphysical, but he censures him
as deficient in the pathetic, a vein in which, as the next
selection shows, a lesser genius like Rowe could excel.

Lawrence Lipking has described the comparison between Dryden and Pope in the latter's life as something of
a climax to the entire *Lives*; and indeed many important
distinctions in neoclassicism are here assembled and applied to its two supreme poets: Dryden knows more of
general nature, Pope of local manners; Dryden's genius
is more vigorous, Pope's more regular and accurate.
Within the neoclassical scheme, Dryden is shown to be
the more natural, Pope the more artificial, though both
are superlative examples of their respective types. This
life also touches on other fundamental matters:

Johnson's opinions on the function of a simile, and on onomatopoetic verse, are amply developed in his discussion of *The Essay on Criticism*. Of all of Pope's major works, *The Essay on Man* gratifies him least. For Johnson, Pope is here a Dick Minim of philosophy, enouncing truisms as though they were profound, and mere conjectures as though they were surely true. His contempt for the poetic clichés and puerilities of *Lycidas* he now expends on the intellectual clichés and wild surmises of *The Essay on Man*. It is probably as much to the facility of Pope's style as to his ideas that he takes exception. His *Vanity of Human Wishes* drives to a conclusion very similar to that of Pope's fourth epistle, but there the facility is replaced with a solemn and pensive dignity. Yet finally Pope is the poet of the beautiful, the quintessential craftsman. By mid-century Joseph Warton and others had begun, with not a little condescension, to deprecate this species of poet. But even now—particularly now, with the decay of romanticism—Johnson's concluding point has not been blunted: "If Pope be not a poet, where is poetry to be found?"

Gray was also one of the more controversial lives, and it is true that Johnson here lapses into a perversely literalistic criticism recalling some of his more doubtful strictures on *Lycidas*. His remarks, for instance, on the closing lines of the "Death of a Favorite Cat" seem unreasonably humorless, pedantic, almost obtuse, although it is perhaps understandable that that critic who could delight in the exquisite volatility of *The Rape of the Lock* would revolt from this more cumbrous, but in no way contemptible, flight of whimsy. Then too, Gray's odes have never recovered their original popularity, and posterity has confirmed the depreciations of Johnson. Finally, his ingenuous admiration of the *Elegy Written in a Country Church-yard* exhibits his candor and good taste. Like all the great neoclassical poems, of which Johnson's own *Vanity of Human Wishes* is not least, it is vigorous, straight forward, and in its way original, yet "abounds with images which find a mirror in every mind, and with sentiments to which every bosom returns an echo." It is also, like Johnson's great poem, a powerful exercise in one of his favorite modes, the pathetic.

The Lives of the Poets no more "sum up" the judgment of neoclassicism on its own poets than the Preface to Shakespeare sums up its Shakespearean criticism. As in that Preface, Johnson is here independant: he will defend Pope when Pope is being aspersed, and censure Gray's odes and Milton's lesser pieces as they are pressing into favor. Yet he occupies, in the main, conservative and judicious positions, and so has survived the supervening cycles of taste. Merely fashionable criticism has alternately embraced and despised Milton, Pope, and the metaphysicals, but these persist, while the criticism has been blown away or ploughed under. Finally, the ending of Gray, in which Johnson rejoices to concur with the common reader, reminds us of one of his first principles: that literary criticism must never be severed from the common experience of humanity. This principle and the others—his emphasis on justness and vivacity of wit, propriety of diction, precision of metaphor and image, universality of theme, moral profundity—he applies throughout his critical work, usually with discrimination and always with vigor, avoiding, as he says in praise of Addison's criticism, "the pomp of system and severity of science." T. S. Eliot has remarked that in no other series of English critical essays can one discern such coherence and breadth. Criticism before Johnson's time had been too undeveloped or miscellaneous to permit it, and any critical consensus since has been too diffuse. For modern aesthetics, lapsing sometimes into a random impressionism, and sometimes into a furor systematicus, and in either case retreating from common discourse, the Lives, indeed the entire body of Johnson's criticism, may yet have meaning and a use.

The text is taken from the 1783 edition, the last to be revised by Johnson. Portions omitted from within the selections are indicated by three asterisks (* * *).

COWLEY

Cowley, like other poets who have written with narrow views, and, instead of tracing intellectual pleasure to its natural sources in the mind of man, paid their court to temporary prejudices, has been at one time too much praised, and too much neglected at another.

Wit, like all other things, subject by their nature to the choice of man, has its changes and fashions, and at different times takes different forms. About the beginning of the seventeenth century appeared a race of writers that may be termed the metaphysical poets; of whom, in a criticism on the works of Cowley, it is not improper to give some account.

The metaphysical poets were men of learning, and to shew their learning was their whole endeavour; but, unluckily resolving to shew it in rhyme, instead of writing poetry, they only wrote verses, and very often such verses as stood the trial of the singer better than of the ear; for the modulation was so imperfect, that they were only found to be verses by counting the syllables.

If the father of criticism has rightly denominated poetry τέχνη μιμητικὴ, an imitative art,[1] these writers will, without great wrong, lose their right to the name of poets; for they cannot be said to have imitated any thing; they neither copied nature nor life; neither painted the forms of matter, nor represented the operations of intellect.

Those however who deny them to be poets, allow them to be wits. Dryden confesses of himself and his contemporaries, that they fall below Donne in wit, but maintains that they surpass him in poetry.

If Wit be well described by Pope, as being, "that which has been often thought, but was never before so well expressed,"[2] they certainly never attained, nor ever sought it; for they endeavoured to be singular in their thoughts, and were careless of their diction. But Pope's account of wit is undoubtedly erroneous: he depresses it below its natural dignity, and reduces it from strength of thought to happiness of language.

If by a more noble and more adequate conception that be considered as Wit, which is at once natural and new, that which, though not obvious, is, upon its first production, acknowledged to be just; if it be that, which he that never found it, wonders how he missed; to wit of this kind the metaphysical poets have seldom risen. Their thoughts are often new, but seldom natural; they are not obvious, but neither are they just; and the reader, far from wondering that he missed them, wonders more frequently by what perverseness of industry they were ever found.

But Wit, abstracted from its effects upon the hearer, may be more rigorously and philosophically considered as a kind of *discordia concors*;[3] a combination of dissimilar images, or discovery of occult resemblances in things apparently unlike. Of wit, thus defined, they have more than enough. The most heterogeneous ideas are yoked by violence together; nature and art are ransacked for illustrations, comparisons, and allusions; their learning instructs, and their subtilty surprises; but the reader commonly thinks his improvement dearly bought, and though he sometimes admires, is seldom pleased.

From this account of their compositions it will be readily inferred, that they were not successful in representing or moving the affections. As they were wholly employed on something unexpected and surprising, they had no regard to that uniformity of sentiment which enables us to conceive and to excite the pains and the pleasure of other minds: they never enquired what, on any occasion, they should have said or done; but wrote rather as beholders than partakers of human nature; as Beings looking upon good and evil, impassive and at leisure; as Epicurean deities making remarks on the actions of men, and the vicissitudes of life, without interest and without emotion. Their courtship was void of fondness, and their lamentation of sorrow. Their wish was only to say what they hoped had been never said before.

Nor was the sublime more within their reach than the

pathetick; for they never attempted that comprehension and expanse of thought which at once fills the whole mind, and of which the first effect is sudden astonishment, and the second rational admiration. Sublimity is produced by aggregation, and littleness by dispersion. Great thoughts are always general, and consist in positions not limited by exceptions, and in descriptions not descending to minuteness. It is with great propriety that Subtlety, which in its original import means exility of particles, is taken in its metaphorical meaning for nicety of distinction. Those writers who lay on the watch for novelty could have little hope of greatness; for great things cannot have escaped former observation. Their attempts were always analytick; they broke every image into fragments: and could no more represent, by their slender conceits and laboured particularities, the prospects of nature, or the scenes of life, than he, who dissects a sun-beam with a prism, can exhibit the wide effulgence of a summer noon.

What they wanted however of the sublime, they endeavoured to supply by hyperbole; their amplification had no limits; they left not only reason but fancy behind them; and produced combinations of confused magnificence, that not only could not be credited, but could not be imagined.

Yet great labour, directed by great abilities, is never wholly lost: if they frequently threw away their wit upon false conceits, they likewise sometimes struck out unexpected truth: if their conceits were farfetched, they were often worth the carriage. To write on their plan, it was at least necessary to read and think. No man could be born a metaphysical poet, nor assume the dignity of a writer, by descriptions copied from descriptions, by imitations borrowed from imitations, by traditional imagery, and hereditary similes, by readiness of rhyme, and volubility of syllables.

In perusing the works of this race of authors, the mind is exercised either by recollection or inquiry; either something already learned is to be retrieved, or something new is to be examined. If their greatness seldom elevates, their acuteness often surprises; if the imagination is not always gratified, at least the powers of reflection and comparison are employed; and in the mass of materials which ingenious absurdity has thrown together, genuine wit and useful knowledge may be sometimes found, buried perhaps in grossness of expression, but useful to those who know their value; and such as, when they are expanded to perspicuity, and polished to elegance, may give lustre to works which have more propriety though less copiousness of sentiment.

* * *

[Cowley's] diction was in his own time censured as negligent. He seems not to have known, or not to have considered, that words being arbitrary must owe their power to association, and have the influence, and that only, which custom has given them. Language is the dress of thought; and as the noblest mien, or most graceful action, would be degraded and obscured by a garb appropriated to the gross employments of rusticks or mechanicks, so the most heroick sentiments will lose their efficacy, and the most splendid ideas drop their magnificence, if they are conveyed by words used commonly upon low and trivial occasions, debased by vulgar mouths, and contaminated by inelegant applications.

Truth indeed is always truth, and reason is always reason; they have an intrinsick and unalterable value, and constitute that intellectual gold which defies destruction: but gold may be so concealed in baser matter, that only a chymist can recover it; sense may be so hidden in unrefined and plebeian words, that none but philosophers can distinguish it; and both may be so buried in impurities, as not to pay the cost of their extraction.

MILTON

Those who admire the beauties of this great poet, sometimes force their own judgement into false approbation of his little pieces, and prevail upon themselves to think that admirable which is only singular. All that short compositions can commonly attain is neatness and elegance. Milton never learned the art of doing little things with grace; he overlooked the milder excellence of suavity and softness; he was a *Lion* that had no skill *in dandling the Kid*.[4]

One of the poems on which much praise has been bestowed is

Lycidas; of which the diction is harsh, the rhymes uncertain, and the numbers unpleasing. What beauty there is, we must therefore seek in the sentiments and images. It is not to be considered as the effusion of real passion; for passion runs not after remote allusions and obscure opinions. Passion plucks no berries from the myrtle and ivy, nor calls upon Arethuse and Mincius, nor tells of rough *satyrs* and *fauns with cloven heel*. Where there is leisure for fiction there is little grief.

In this poem there is no nature, for there is no truth; there is no art, for there is nothing new. Its form is that of a pastoral, easy, vulgar, and therefore disgusting: whatever images it can supply, are long ago exhausted; and its inherent improbability always forces dissatisfaction on the mind. When Cowley tells of Hervey that they studied together, it is easy to suppose how much he must miss the companion of his labours, and the partner of his discoveries; but what image of tenderness can be excited by these lines!

> We drove a field, and both together heard
> What time the grey fly winds her sultry horn.
> Battening our flocks with the fresh dew of night.[5]

We know that they never drove a field, and that they had no flocks to batten; and though it be allowed that the representation may be allegorical, the true meaning is so uncertain and remote, that it is never sought because it cannot be known when it is found.

Among the flocks, and copses, and flowers, appear the heathen deities; Jove and Phoebus, Neptune and Aeolus, with a long train of mythological imagery, such as a College easily supplies. Nothing can less display knowledge, or less exercise invention, than to tell how a shepherd has lost his companion, and must now feed his flocks alone, without any judge of his skill in piping; and how one god asks another god what is become of Lycidas, and how neither god can tell. He who thus grieves will excite no sympathy; he who thus praises will confer no honour.

This poem has yet a grosser fault. With these trifling fictions are mingled the most awful and sacred truths, such as ought never to be polluted with such irreverend combinations. The shepherd likewise is now a feeder of sheep, and afterwards an ecclesiastical pastor, a superintendent of a Christian flock. Such equivocations are always unskilful; but here they are indecent, and at least approach to impiety, of which, however, I believe the writer not to have been conscious.

Such is the power of reputation justly acquired; that its blaze drives away the eye from nice examination. Surely no man could have fancied that he read *Lycidas* with pleasure, had he not known its author.

Of the two pieces, *L'Allegro* and *Il Penseroso,* I believe opinion is uniform; every man that reads them, reads them with pleasure. The author's design is not, what Theobald has remarked, merely to shew how objects derive their colours from the mind, by representing the operation of the same things upon the gay and the melancholy temper, or upon the same man as he is differently disposed; but rather how, among the successive variety of appearances, every disposition of mind takes hold on those by which it may be gratified.

The *chearful* man hears the lark in the morning; the *pensive* man hears the nightingale in the evening. The *chearful* man sees the cock strut, and hears the horn and hounds echo in the wood; then walks *not unseen* to observe the glory of the rising sun, or listen to the singing milk-maid, and view the labours of the plowman and the mower; then casts his eyes about him over scenes of smiling plenty, and looks up to the distant tower, the residence of some fair inhabitant; thus he pursues rural gaiety through a day of labour or of play, and delights himself at night with the fanciful narratives of superstitious ignorance.

The *pensive* man, at one time, walks *unseen* to muse at midnight; and at another hears the sullen curfew. If the weather drives him home, he sits in a room lighted only by *glowing embers*; or by a lonely lamp outwatches the North Star, to discover the habitation of separate souls, and varies the shades of meditation, by contemplating the magnificent or pathetick scenes of tragick and epic poetry. When the morning comes, a morning gloomy with rain and wind, he walks into the dark trackless woods, falls asleep by some murmuring water, and with melancholy enthusiasm expects some dream of prognostication, or some musick played by aerial performers.

Both Mirth and Melancholy are solitary, silent inhabitants of the breast that neither receive nor transmit communication; no mention is therefore made of a philosophical friend, or a pleasant companion. The seriousness does not arise from any participation of calamity, nor the gaiety from the pleasures of the bottle.

The man of *chearfulness*, having exhausted the country, tries what *towered cities* will afford, and mingles with scenes of splendor, gay assemblies, and nuptial festivities; but he mingles a mere spectator, as, when the learned comedies of Jonson, or the wild dramas of Shakespeare, are exhibited, he attends the theatre.

The *pensive* man never loses himself in crowds, but walks the cloister, or frequents the cathedral. Milton probably had not yet forsaken the Church.

Both his characters delight in musick; but he seems to think that chearful notes would have obtained from Pluto a compleat dismission of Eurydice, of whom solemn sounds only procured a conditional release.

For the old age of Chearfulness he makes no provision; but Melancholy he conducts with great dignity to the close of life. His Chearfulness is without levity, and his Pensiveness without asperity.

Through these two poems the images are properly selected, and nicely distinguished; but the colours of the diction seem not sufficiently discriminated. I know not whether the characters are kept sufficiently apart. No mirth can, indeed, be found in his melancholy; but I am afraid that I always meet some melancholy in his mirth. They are two noble efforts of imagination.

The greatest of his juvenile performances is the *Mask of Comus*; in which may very plainly be discovered the dawn or twilight of *Paradise Lost*. Milton appears to have formed very early that system of diction, and mode of verse, which his maturer judgement approved, and from which he never endeavoured nor desired to deviate.

Nor does *Comus* afford only a specimen of his language; it exhibits likewise his power of description and his vigour of sentiment, employed in the praise and defence of virtue. A work more truly poetical is rarely found; allusions, images, and descriptive epithets, embellish almost every period with lavish decoration. As a series of lines, therefore, it may be considered as worthy of all the admiration with which the votaries have received it.

As a drama it is deficient. The action is not probable. A Masque, in those parts where supernatural intervention is admitted, must indeed be given up to all the freaks of imagination; but, so far as the action is merely human, it ought to be reasonable, which can hardly be said of the conduct of the two brothers; who, when their sister sinks with fatigue in a pathless wilderness, wander both away together in search of berries too far to find their way back, and leave a helpless Lady to all the sadness and danger of solitude. This however is a defect overbalanced by its convenience.

What deserves more reprehension is, that the prologue spoken in the wild wood by the attendant Spirit is addressed to the audience; a mode of communication so contrary to the nature of dramatick representation, that no precedents can support it.

The discourse of the Spirit is too long; an objection that may be made to almost all the following speeches: they have not the spriteliness of a dialogue animated by reciprocal contention, but seem rather declamations deliberately composed, and formally repeated, on a moral question. The auditor therefore listens as to a lecture, without passion, without anxiety.

* * *

Throughout the whole, the figures are too bold, and the language too luxuriant for dialogue. It is a drama in the epic style, inelegantly splendid, and tediously instructive.

The *Sonnets* were written in different parts of Milton's life, upon different occasions. They deserve not any particular criticism; for of the best it can only be said, that they are not bad; and perhaps only the eighth and the twenty-first are truly entitled to this slender commendation. The fabrick of a sonnet, however adapted to the Italian language, has never succeeded in ours, which, having greater variety of termination, requires the rhymes to be often changed.

Those little pieces may be dispatched without much anxiety; a greater work calls for greater care. I am now to examine *Paradise Lost*; a poem, which, considered with respect to design, may claim the first place, and with respect to performance the second, among the productions of the human mind.

By the general consent of criticks, the first praise of genius is due to the writer of an epick poem, as it requires an assemblage of all the powers which are singly sufficient for other compositions. Poetry is the art of uniting pleasure with truth, by calling imagination to the help of reason. Epick poetry undertakes to teach the most important truths by the most pleasing precepts, and therefore relates some great event in the most affecting manner. History must supply the writer with the rudiments of narration, which he must improve and exalt by a nobler art, must animate by dramatick energy, and diversify by retrospection and anticipation; morality must teach him the exact bounds, and different shades, of vice and virtue; from policy, and the practice of life, he has to learn the discriminations of character, and the tendency of the passions, either single or combined; and physiology must supply him with illustrations and images. To put these materials to poetical use, is required an imagination capable of painting nature, and realizing fiction. Nor is he yet a poet till he has attained the whole extension of his language, distinguished all the delicacies of phrase, and all the colours of words, and learned to adjust their different sounds to all the varieties of metrical modulation.

Bossu is of opinion that the poet's first work is to find a *moral*, which his fable is afterwards to illustrate and establish.[6] This seems to have been the process only of Milton; the moral of other poems is incidental and consequent; in Milton's only it is essential and intrinsick. His purpose was the most useful and the most arduous; *to vindicate the ways of God to man*; to shew the reasonableness of religion, and the necessity of obedience to the Divine Law.

To convey this moral, there must be a *fable*, a narration artfully constructed, so as to excite curiosity, and surprise expectation. In this part of his work, Milton must be confessed to have equalled every other poet. He has involved in his account of the Fall of Man the events which preceded, and those that were to follow it: he has interwoven the whole system of theology with such propriety, that every part appears to be necessary; and scarcely any recital is wished shorter for the sake of quickening the progress of the main action.

The subject of an epic poem is naturally an event of great importance. That of Milton is not the destruction of a city, the conduct of a colony, or the foundation of an empire. His subject is the fate of worlds, the revolutions of heaven and of earth; rebellion against the Supreme King, raised by the highest order of created beings; the overthrow of their host, and the punishment of their crime; the creation of a new race of reasonable creatures; their original happiness and innocence, their forfeiture of immortality, and their restoration to hope and peace.

Great events can be hastened or retarded only by persons of elevated dignity. Before the greatness displayed in Milton's poem, all other greatness shrinks away. The weakest of his agents are the highest and noblest of human beings, the original parents of mankind; with whose actions the elements consented; on whose rectitude, or deviation of will, depended the state of terrestrial nature, and the condition of all the future inhabitants of the globe.

Of the other agents in the poem, the chief are such as it is irreverence to name on slight occasions. The rest were lower powers:

> —Of which the least could wield
> Those elements, and arm him with the force
> Of all their regions;[7]

powers, which only the controul of Omnipotence restrains from laying creation waste, and filling the vast expanse of space with ruin and confusion. To display the motives, and actions of beings thus superiour, so far as human reason can examine them, or human imagination represent them, is the talk which this mighty poet has undertaken and performed.

In the examination of epick poems much speculation is commonly employed upon the *characters*. The characters in the *Paradise Lost*, which admit of examination, are those of angels and of man; of angels good and evil; of man in his innocent and sinful state.

Among the angels, the virtue of Raphael is mild and placid, of easy condescension and free conmmunication; that of Michael is regal and lofty, and, as may seem, attentive to the dignity of his own nature. Abdiel and Gabriel appear occasionally, and act as every incident requires; the solitary fidelity of Abdiel is very amiably painted.

Of the evil angels the characters are more diversified. To Satan, as Addison observes, such sentiments are given as suit *the most exalted and most depraved being*. Milton has been censured, by Clarke, for the impiety which sometimes breaks from Satan's mouth.[8] For there are thoughts, as he justly remarks, which no observation of character can justify, because no good man would willingly permit them to pass, however transiently, through his own mind. To make Satan speak as a rebel, without any such expressions as might taint the reader's imagination, was indeed one of the great difficulties in Milton's undertaking, and I cannot but think that he has extricated himself with great happiness. There is in Satan's speeches little that can give pain to a pious ear. The language of rebellion cannot be the same with that of obedience. The malignity of Satan foams in haughtiness and obstinacy; but his expressions are commonly general, and no otherwise offensive than as they are wicked.

The other chiefs of the celestial rebellion are very judiciously discriminated in the first and second books; and the ferocious character of Moloch appears, both in the battle and the council, with exact consistency.

To Adam and to Eve are given, during their innocence, such sentiments as innocence can generate and utter. Their love is pure benevolence and mutual veneration; their repasts are without luxury, and their diligence without toil. Their addresses to their Maker have little more than the voice of admiration and gratitude. Fruition left them nothing to ask, and Innocence left them nothing to fear.

But with guilt enter distrust and discord, mutual accusation, and stubborn self-defence; they regard each other with alienated minds, and dread their Creator as the avenger of their transgression. At last they seek shelter in his mercy, soften to repentance, and melt in supplication. Both before and after the Fall, the superiority of Adam is diligently sustained.

Of the *probable* and the *marvellous*, two parts of a vulgar epic poem, which immerge the critick in deep consideration, the *Paradise Lost* requires little to be said. It contains the history of a miracle, of Creation and Redemption; it displays the power and the mercy of the Supreme Being; the probable therefore is marvellous, and the marvellous is probable. The substance of the narrative is truth; and as truth allows no choice, it is, like necessity, superior to rule. To the accidental or adventitious parts, as to every thing human, some slight exceptions may be made. But the main fabrick is immovably supported.

It is justly remarked by Addison, that this poem has, by the nature of its subject, the advantage above all others, that it is universally and perpetually interesting.[9] All mankind will, through all ages, bear the same relation to Adam and to Eve, and must partake of that good and evil which extend to themselves.

Of the *machinery*, so called from Θεὸς ἀπὸ μηχανῆς [*deus ex machina*],[10] by which is meant the occasional interposition of supernatural power, another fertile topic of critical remarks, here is no room to speak, because every thing is done under the immediate and visible direction of Heaven; but the rule is so far observed, that no part of the action could have been accomplished by any other means.

Of *episodes*, I think there are only two, contained in Raphael's relation of the war in heaven, and Michael's prophetick account of the changes to happen in this world. Both are closely connected with the great action; one was necessary to Adam as a warning, the other as a consolation.

To the compleatness or *integrity* of the design nothing can be objected; it has distinctly and clearly what Aristotle requires, a beginning, a middle, and an end. There is perhaps no poem, of the same length, from which so little can be taken without apparent mutilation. Here are no funeral games, nor is there any long description of a shield. The short digressions at the beginning of the third, seventh, and ninth books, might doubtless be spared; but superfluities so beautiful, who would take away? or who does not wish that the author of the *Iliad* had gratified succeeding ages with a little knowledge of himself? Perhaps no passages are more frequently or more attentively read than those extrinsick paragraphs; and, since the end of poetry is pleasure, that cannot be unpoetical with which all are pleased.

The questions, whether the action of the poem be strictly *one*, whether the poem can be properly termed *heroick*, and who is the hero, are raised by such readers as draw their principles of judgement rather from books than from reason. Milton, though he intituled *Paradise Lost* only a *poem*, yet calls it himself *heroick song*.[11] Dryden, petulantly and indecently, denies the heroism of Adam, because he was overcome;[12] but there is no reason why the hero should not be unfortunate, except established practice, since success and virtue do not go necessarily together. Cato is the hero of Lucan; but Lucan's authority will not be suffered by Quintilian to decide. However, if success be necessary, Adam's deceiver was at last crushed; Adam was restored to his Maker's favour, and therefore may securely resume his human rank.

After the scheme and fabrick of the poem, must be considered its component parts, the sentiments and the diction.

The *sentiments*, as expressive of manners, or appropriated to characters, are, for the greater part, unexceptionably just.

Splendid passages, containing lessons of morality, or precepts of prudence, occur seldom. Such is the original formation of this poem, that as it admits no human manners till the Fall, it can give little assistance to human conduct. Its end is to raise the thoughts above sublunary cares or pleasures. Yet the praise of that fortitude with which Abdiel maintained his singularity of virtue against the scorn of multitudes, may be accommodated to all times; and Raphael's reproof of Adam's curiosity after the planetary motions, with the answer returned by Adam, may be confidently opposed to any rule of life which any poet has delivered.

The thoughts which are occasionally called forth in the progress, are such as could only be produced by an imagination in the highest degree fervid and active, to which materials were supplied by incessant study and unlimited curiosity. The heat of Milton's mind might be said to sublimate his learning, to throw off into his work the spirit of science, unmingled with its grosser parts.

He had considered creation in its whole extent, and his descriptions are therefore learned. He had accustomed his imagination to unrestrained indulgence, and his conceptions therefore were extensive. The characteristick quality of his poem is sublimity. He sometimes descends to the elegant, but his element is the great. He can occasionally invest himself with grace; but his natural port is gigantick loftiness. He can please when pleasure is required; but it is his peculiar power to astonish.

He seems to have been well acquainted with his own genius, and to know what it was that Nature had bestowed upon him more bountifully than upon others; the power of displaying the vast, illuminating the splendid, enforcing the awful, darkening the gloomy, and aggravating the dreadful: he therefore chose a subject on which too much could not be said, on which he might tire his fancy without the censure of extravagance.

The appearances of nature, and the occurrences of life, did not satiate his appetite of greatness. To paint things as they are, requires a minute attention, and employs the memory rather than the fancy. Milton's delight was to sport in the wide regions of possibility; reality was a scene too narrow for his mind. He sent his faculties out upon discovery, into worlds where only imagination can travel, and delighted to form new modes of existence, and furnish sentiment and action to superior beings, to trace the counsels of hell, or accompany the choirs of heaven.

Whatever be his subject, he never fails to fill the imagination. But his images and descriptions of the scenes or operations of Nature do not seem to be always copied from original form, nor to have the freshness, raciness, and energy of immediate observation. He saw Nature, as Dryden expresses it, *through the spectacles of books*;[13] and on most occasions calls learning to his assistance. The garden of Eden brings to his mind the vale of *Enna*, where Proserpine was gathering flowers. Satan makes his way through fighting elements, like *Argo* between the *Cyanean* rocks, or *Ulysses* between the two *Sicilian* whirlpools, when he shunned *Charybdis* on the *larboard*. The mythological allusions have been justly censured, as not being always used with notice of their vanity; but they contribute variety to the narration, and produce an alternate exercise of the memory and the fancy.

But he could not be always in other worlds: he must sometimes revisit earth, and tell of things visible and known. When he cannot raise wonder by the sublimity of his mind, he gives delight by its fertility.

His similies are less numerous, and more various, than those of his predecessors. But he does not confine himself within the limits of rigorous comparison: his great excellence is amplitude, and he expands the adventitious image beyond the dimensions which the occasion required. Thus, comparing the shield of Satan to the orb of the Moon, he crouds the imagination with the discovery of the telescope, and all the wonders which the telescope discovers.

Of his moral sentiments it is hardly praise to affirm that they excel those of all other poets; for this superiority he was indebted to his acquaintance with the sacred writings. The ancient epick poets, wanting the light of Revelation, were very unskilful teachers of virtue: their principal characters may be great, but they are not amiable. The reader may rise from their works with a greater degree of active or passive fortitude, and sometimes of prudence; but he will be able to carry away few precepts of justice, and none of mercy.

From the Italian writers it appears, that the advantages of even Christian knowledge may be supposed in vain. Ariosto's pravity is generally known; and though the *Deliverance of Jerusalem* may be considered as a sacred subject, the poet[14] has been very sparing of moral instruction.

In Milton every line breathes sanctity of thought, and purity of manners, except when the train of the narration requires the introduction of the rebellious spirits; and even they are compelled to acknowledge their subjection to God, in such a manner as excites reverence, and confirms piety.

Of human beings there are but two; but those two are the

parents of mankind, venerable before their fall for dignity and innocence, and amiable after it for repentance and submission. In their first state their affection is tender without weakness, and their piety sublime without presumption. When they have sinned, they shew how discord begins in mutual frailty, and how it ought to cease in mutual forbearance; how confidence of the divine favour is forfeited by sin, and how hope of pardon may be obtained by penitence and prayer. A state of innocence we can only conceive, if indeed, in our present misery, it be possible to conceive it; but the sentiments and worship proper to a fallen and offending being, we have all to learn, as we have all to practise.

The poet, whatever be done, is always great. Our progenitors, in their first state, conversed with angels; even when folly and sin had degraded them, they had not in their humiliation *the port of mean suitors*;[15] and they rise again to reverential regard, when we find that their prayers were heard.

As human passions did not enter the world before the Fall, there is in the *Paradise Lost* little opportunity for the pathetick; but what little there is has not been lost. That passion which is peculiar to rational nature, the anguish arising from the consciousness of transgression, and the horrours attending the sense of the Divine Displeasure, are very justly described and forcibly impressed. But the passions are moved only on one occasion; sublimity is the general and prevailing quality in this poem; sublimity variously modified, sometimes descriptive, sometimes argumentative.

The defects and faults of *Paradise Lost*, for faults and defects every work of man must have, it is the business of impartial criticism to discover. As, in displaying the excellence of Milton, I have not made long quotations, because of selecting beauties there had been no end, I shall in the same general manner mention that which seems to deserve censure; for what Englishman can take delight in transcribing passages, which, if they lessen the reputation of Milton, diminish in some degree the honour of our country?

The generality of my scheme does not admit the frequent notice of verbal inaccuracies; which Bentley, perhaps better skilled in grammar than in poetry, has often found, though he sometimes made them, and which he imputed to the obtrusions of a reviser whom the author's blindness obliged him to employ.[16] A supposition rash and groundless, if he thought it true; and vile and pernicious, if, as is said, he in private allowed it to be false.

The plan of *Paradise Lost* has this inconvenience, that it comprises neither human actions nor human manners. The man and woman who act and suffer, are in a state which no other man or woman can ever know. The reader finds no transaction in which he can be engaged; beholds no condition in which he can by any effort of imagination place himself; he has, therefore, little natural curiosity or sympathy.

We all, indeed, feel the effects of Adam's disobedience; we all sin like Adam, and like him must all bewail our offences; we have restless and insidious enemies in the fallen angels, and in the blessed spirits we have guardians and friends; in the Redemption of mankind we hope to be included: in the description of heaven and hell we are surely interested, as we are all to reside hereafter either in the regions of horrour or of bliss.

But these truths are too important to be new; they have been taught to our infancy; they have mingled with our solitary thoughts and familiar conversation, and are habitually interwoven with the whole texture of life. Being therefore not new, they raise no unaccustomed emotion in the mind; what we knew before, we cannot learn; what is not unexpected, cannot surprise.

Of the ideas suggested by these awful scenes, from some we recede with reverence, except when stated hours require their association; and from others we shrink with horrour, or admit them only as salutary inflictions, as counterpoises to our interests and passions. Such images rather obstruct the career of fancy than incite it.

Pleasure and terrour are indeed the genuine sources of poetry; but poetical pleasure must be such as human imagination can at least conceive, and poetical terrour such as human strength and fortitude may combat. The good and evil of Eternity are too ponderous for the wings of wit; the mind sinks under them in passive helplessness, content with calm belief and humble adoration.

Known truths, however, may take a different appearance, and be conveyed to the mind by a new train of intermediate images. This Milton has undertaken, and performed with pregnancy and vigour of mind peculiar to himself. Whoever considers the few radical positions which the Scriptures afforded him, will wonder by what energetick operation he expanded them to such extent, and ramified them to so much variety, restrained as he was by religious reverence from licentiousness of fiction.

Here is a full display of the united force of study and genius; of a great accumulation of materials, with judgement to digest, and fancy to combine them: Milton was able to select from nature, or from story, from ancient fable, or from modern science, whatever could illustrate or adorn his thoughts. An accumulation of knowledge impregnated his mind, fermented by study, and exalted by imagination.

It has been therefore said, without an indecent hyperbole, by one of his encomiasts, that in reading *Paradise Lost* we read a book of universal knowledge.

But original deficience cannot be supplied. The want of human interest is always felt. *Paradise Lost* is one of the books which the reader admires and lays down, and forgets to take up again. None ever wished it longer than it is. Its perusal is a duty rather than a pleasure. We read Milton for instruction, retire harrassed and overburdened, and look elsewhere for recreation; we desert our master, and seek for companions.

Another inconvenience of Milton's design is, that it requires the description of what cannot be described, the agency of spirits. He saw that immateriality supplied no images, and that he could not show angels acting but by instruments of action; he therefore invested them with form and matter. This, being necessary, was therefore defensible; and he should have secured the consistency of his system, by keeping immateriality out of sight, and enticing his reader to drop it from his thoughts. But he has unhappily perplexed his poetry with his philosophy. His infernal and celestial powers are sometimes pure spirit, and sometimes animated body. When Satan walks with his lance upon the *burning marle*, he has a body; when, in his passage between hell and the new world, he is in danger of sinking in the vacuity, and is supported by a gust of rising vapours, he has a body; when he animates the toad, he seems to be mere spirit, that can penetrate matter at pleasure; when he *starts up in his own shape*, he has at least a determined form; and when he is brought before Gabriel, he has *a spear and a shield*, which he had the power of hiding in the toad, though the arms of the contending angels are evidently material.

The vulgar inhabitants of Pandaemonium, being *incorporeal spirits*, are *at large, though without number*, in a limited space; yet in the battle, when they were overwhelmed by mountains, their armour hurt them, *crushed in upon their substance, now grown gross by sinning*. This likewise happened to the uncorrupted angels, who were overthrown *the sooner for their arms, for unarmed they might easily as spirits have evaded by contraction or remove*. Even as spirits they are hardly spiritual; for *contraction* and *remove* are images of matter; but if they could have escaped without their armour, they might have escaped from it, and left only the empty cover to be battered. Uriel, when he rides on a sun-beam, is material; Satan is material when he is afraid of the prowess of Adam.

The confusion of spirit and matter which pervades the whole narration of the war of heaven fills it with incongruity; and the book, in which it is related, is, I believe, the favourite of children, and gradually neglected as knowledge is increased.

After the operation of immaterial agents, which cannot be explained, may be considered that of allegorical persons, which have no real existence. To exalt causes into agents, to invest abstract ideas with form, and animate them with activity, has always been the right of poetry. But such airy beings are, for the most part, suffered only to do their natural office, and retire. Thus Fame tells a tale, and Victory hovers over a general, or perches on a standard; but Fame and Victory can do no more. To give them any real employment, or ascribe to them any material agency, is to make them allegorical no longer, but to shock the mind by ascribing effects to non-entity. In the *Prometheus* of Aeschylus, we see *Violence* and *Strength*, and in the *Alcestis* of Euripides, we see *Death*, brought upon the stage, all as active persons of the drama; but no precedents can justify absurdity.

Milton's allegory of Sin and Death is undoubtedly faulty. Sin is indeed the mother of Death, and may be allowed to be the portress of hell; but when they stop the journey of Satan, a journey described as real, and when Death offers him battle, the allegory is broken. That Sin and Death should have shewn the way to hell, might have been allowed; but they cannot facilitate the passage by building a bridge, because the difficulty of Satan's passage is described as real and sensible, and the bridge ought to be only figurative. The hell assigned to the rebellious spirits is described as not less local than the residence of man. It is placed in some distant part of space, separated from the regions of harmony and order by a chaotick waste and an unoccupied vacuity; but *Sin* and *Death* worked up a *mole* of *aggregated soil*, cemented with *asphaltus*; a work too bulky for ideal architects.

This unskilful allegory appears to me one of the greatest faults of the poem; and to this there was no temptation, but the author's opinion of its beauty.

To the conduct of the narrative some objections may be made. Satan is with great expectation brought before Gabriel in Paradise, and is suffered to go away unmolested. The creation of man is represented as the consequence of the vacuity left in heaven by the expulsion of the rebels; yet Satan mentions it as a report *rife in heaven* before his departure.

To find sentiments for the state of innocence, was very difficult; and something of anticipation perhaps is now and then discovered. Adam's discourse of dreams seems not to be the speculation of a new-created being. I know not whether his answer to the angel's reproof for curiosity does not want something of propriety: it is the speech of a man acquainted with many other men. Some philosophical notions, especially when the philosophy is false, might have been better omitted. The angel, in a comparison, speaks of *timorous deer*, before deer were yet timorous, and before Adam could understand the comparison.

Dryden remarks, that Milton has some flats among his elevations.[17] This is only to say, that all the parts are not equal. In every work, one part must be for the sake of others; a palace must have passages; a poem must have transitions. It is no more to be required that wit should always be blazing, than that the sun should always stand at noon. In a great work there is a vicissitude of luminous and opaque parts, as there is in the world a succession of day and night. Milton, when he has expatiated in the sky, may be allowed sometimes to revisit earth; for what other author ever soared so high, or sustained his flight so long?

Milton, being well versed in the Italian poets, appears to have borrowed often from them; and, as every man catches something from his companions, his desire of imitating Ariosto's levity has disgraced his work with the *Paradise of Fools*; a fiction not in itself ill-imagined, but too ludicrous for its place.

His play on words, in which he delights too often; his equivocations, which Bentley endeavours to defend by the example of the ancients; his unnecessary and ungraceful use of terms of art; it is not necessary to mention, because they are easily remarked, and generally censured, and at last bear so little proportion to the whole, that they scarcely deserve the attention of a critick.

Such are the faults of that wonderful performance *Paradise Lost*; which he who can put in balance with its beauties must be considered not as nice but as dull, as less to be censured for want of candour, than pitied for want of sensibility.

Of *Paradise Regained*, the general judgement seems now to be right, that it is in many parts elegant, and every-where instructive. It was not to be supposed that the writer of *Paradise Lost* could ever write without great effusions of fancy, and exalted precepts of wisdom. The basis of *Paradise Regained* is narrow; a dialogue without action can never please like an union of the narrative and dramatic powers. Had this poem been written not by Milton, but by some imitator, it would have claimed and received universal praise.

If *Paradise Regained* has been too much depreciated, *Sampson Agonistes* has in requital been too much admired. It could only be by long prejudice, and the bigotry of learning, that Milton could prefer the ancient tragedies, with their encumbrance of a chorus, to the exhibitions of the French and English stages; and it is only by a blind confidence in the reputation of Milton, that a drama can be praised in which the intermediate parts have neither cause nor consequence, neither hasten nor retard the catastrophe.

In this tragedy are however many particular beauties, many just sentiments and striking lines; but it wants that power of attracting the attention which a well-connected plan produces.

Milton would not have excelled in dramatick writing; he knew human nature only in the gross, and had never studied the shades of character, nor the combinations of concurring, or the perplexity of contending passions. He had read much, and knew what books could teach; but had mingled little in the world, and was deficient in the knowledge which experience must confer.

Through all his greater works there prevails an uniform peculiarity of *Diction*, a mode and cast of expression which bears little resemblance to that of any former writer, and which is so far removed from common use, that an unlearned reader, when he first opens his book, finds himself surprised by a new language.

This novelty has been, by those who can find nothing wrong in Milton, imputed to his laborious endeavours after words suitable to the grandeur of his ideas. *Our language,* says Addison, *sunk under him.*[18] But the truth is, that, both in prose and verse, he had formed his style by a perverse and pedantick principle. He was desirous to use English words with a foreign idiom. This in all his prose is discovered and condemned; for there judgment operates freely, neither softened by the beauty, nor awed by the dignity of his thoughts; but such is the power of his poetry, that his call is obeyed without resistance, the reader feels himself in captivity to a higher and nobler mind, and criticism sinks in admiration.

* * *

Rhyme, he says, and says truly, *is no necessary adjunct of true poetry.*[19] But perhaps, of poetry as a mental operation, metre or musick is no necessary adjunct: it is however by the musick of metre that poetry has been discriminated in all languages; and in languages melodiously constructed with a due proportion of long and short syllables, metre is sufficient. But one language cannot communicate its rules to another: where metre is scanty and imperfect, some help is necessary. The musick of the English heroick line strikes the ear so faintly that it is easily lost, unless all the syllables of every line co-operate together: this co-operation can be only obtained by the preservation of every verse unmingled with another, as a distinct system of sounds; and this distinctness is obtained and preserved by the artifice of rhyme. The variety of pauses, so much boasted by the lovers of blank verse, changes the measures of an English poet to the periods of a declaimer; and there are only a few skilful and happy readers of Milton, who enable their audience to perceive where the lines end or begin. *Blank verse,* said an ingenious critick,[20] *seems to be verse only to the eye.*

Poetry may subsist without rhyme, but English poetry will not often please; nor can rhyme ever be safely spared but where the subject is able to support itself. Blank verse makes some approach to that which is called the *lapidary style*; has neither the easiness of prose, nor the melody of numbers, and therefore tires by long continuance. Of the Italian writers without rhyme, whom Milton alleges as precedents, not one is popular; what reason could urge in its defence, has been confuted by the ear.

But, whatever be the advantage of rhyme, I cannot prevail on myself to wish that Milton had been a rhymer; for I cannot wish his work to be other than it is; yet, like other heroes, he is to be admired rather than imitated. He that thinks himself capable of astonishing, may write blank verse; but those that hope only to please, must condescend to rhyme.

The highest praise of genius is original invention. Milton cannot be said to have contrived the structure of an epick poem, and therefore owes reverence to that vigour and amplitude of mind to which all generations must be indebted for the art of poetical narration, for the texture of the fable, the variation of incidents, the interposition of dialogue, and all the stratagems that surprise and enchain attention. But, of all the borrowers from Homer, Milton is perhaps the least indebted. He was naturally a thinker for himself, confident of his own abilities, and disdainful of help or hindrance: he did not refuse admission to the thoughts or images of his predecessors, but he did not seek them. From his contemporaries he neither courted nor received support; there is in his writings nothing by which the pride of other authors might be gratified, or favour gained; no exchange of praise, nor solicitation of support. His great works were performed under discountenance, and in blindness, but difficulties vanished at his touch; he was born for whatever is arduous; and his work is not the greatest of heroick poems, only because it is not the first.

WALLER[21]

Let no pious ear be offended if I advance, in opposition to many authorities, that poetical devotion cannot often please. The doctrines of religion may indeed be defended in a didactick poem; and he who has the happy power of arguing in verse, will not lose it because his subject is sacred. A poet may describe the beauty and the grandeur of Nature, the flowers of the spring, and the harvests of Autumn, the vicissitudes of the Tide, and the revolutions of the Sky, and praise the Maker for his works in lines which no reader shall lay aside. The subject of the disputation is not piety, but the motives to piety; that of the description is not God, but the works of God.

Contemplative piety, or the intercourse between God and the human soul, cannot be poetical. Man admitted to implore the mercy of his Creator, and plead the merits of his Redeemer, is already in a higher state than poetry can confer.

The essence of poetry is invention; such invention as, by producing something unexpected, surprises and delights. The topicks of devotion are few, and being few are universally known; but, few as they are, they can be made no more; they can receive no grace from novelty of sentiment, and very little from novelty of expression.

Poetry pleases by exhibiting an idea more grateful to the mind than things themselves afford. This effect proceeds from the display of those parts of nature which attract, and the concealment of those which repel the imagination: but religion must be shewn as it is; suppression and addition equally corrupt it; and such as it is, it is known already.

From poetry the reader justly expects, and from good poetry

always obtains, the enlargement of his comprehension and elevation of his fancy; but this is rarely to be hoped by Christians from
metrical devotion. Whatever is great, desireable, or tremendous,
is comprised in the name of the Supreme Being. Omnipotence
cannot be exalted; Infinity cannot be amplified; Perfection cannot be improved.

The employments of pious meditation are Faith, Thanksgiving, Repentance, and Supplication. Faith, invariably uniform,
cannot be invested by fancy with decorations. Thanksgiving, the
most joyful of all holy effusions, yet addressed to a Being without
passions, is confined to a few modes, and is to be felt rather than
expressed. Repentance trembling in the presence of the judge, is
not at leisure for cadences and epithets. Supplication of man to
man may diffuse itself through many topicks of persuasion; but
supplication to God can only cry for mercy.

Of sentiments purely religious, it will be found that the most
simple expression is the most sublime. Poetry loses its lustre and
its power, because it is applied to the decoration of something
more excellent than itself. All that pious verse can do is to help the
memory, and delight the ear, and for these purposes it may be
very useful; but it supplies nothing to the mind. The ideas of
Christian Theology are too simple for eloquence, too sacred for
fiction, and too majestick for ornament; to recommend them by
tropes and figures, is to magnify by a concave mirror the sidereal
hemisphere.

DRYDEN

Dryden may be properly considered as the father of English
criticism, as the writer who first taught us to determine upon
principles the merit of composition. Of our former poets, the
greatest dramatist wrote without rules, conducted through life
and nature by a genius that rarely misled, and rarely deserted
him. Of the rest, those who knew the laws of propriety had
neglected to teach them.

Two *Arts of English Poetry* were written in the days of Elizabeth
by Webb and Puttenham, from which something might be

learned, and a few hints had been given by Jonson and Cowley; but Dryden's *Essay on Dramatick Poetry* was the first regular and valuable treatise on the art of writing.[22]

He who, having formed his opinions in the present age of English literature, turns back to peruse this dialogue, will not perhaps find much increase of knowledge, or much novelty of instruction; but he is to remember that critical principles were then in the hands of a few, who had gathered them partly from the Ancients, and partly from the Italians and French. The structure of dramatick poems was not then generally understood. Audiences applauded by instinct, and poets perhaps often pleased by chance.

A writer who obtains his full purpose loses himself in his own lustre. Of an opinion which is no longer doubted, the evidence ceases to be examined. Of an art universally practised, the first teacher is forgotten. Learning once made popular is no longer learning; it has the appearance of something which we have bestowed upon ourselves, as the dew appears to rise from the field which it refreshes.

To judge rightly of an author, we must transport ourselves to his time, and examine what were the wants of his contemporaries, and what were his means of supplying them. That which is easy at one time was difficult at another. Dryden at least imported his science, and gave his country what it wanted before; or rather, he imported only the materials, and manufactured them by his own skill.

The dialogue on the Drama was one of his first essays of criticism, written when he was yet a timorous candidate for reputation, and therefore laboured with that diligence which he might allow himself somewhat to remit, when his name gave sanction to his positions, and his awe of the public was abated, partly by custom, and partly by success. It will not be easy to find, in all the opulence of our language, a treatise so artfully variegated with successive representations of opposite probabilities, so enlivened with imagery, so brightned with illustrations. His portraits of the English dramatists are wrought with great spirit and diligence. The account of Shakespeare may stand as a perpetual model of encomiastick criticism; exact without minuteness, and lofty without exaggeration. The praise lavished by Longinus, on the attestation of the heroes of Marathon, by Demosthenes,[23] fades away before it. In a few lines is exhibited a character, so extensive in its comprehension, and so curious in its limitations, that nothing can be added, diminished, or reformed; nor can the editors and admirers of Shakespeare, in all their emulation of reverence, boast of much more than of having diffused and paraphrased this epitome of excellence, of having changed Dryden's gold for baser metal, of lower value though of greater bulk.

In this, and in all his other essays on the same subject, the criticism of Dryden is the criticism of a poet; not a dull collection of theorems, nor a rude detection of faults, which perhaps the censor was not able to have committed; but a gay and vigorous dissertation, where delight is mingled with instruction, and where the author proves his right of judgement, by his power of performance.

The different manner and effect with which critical knowledge may be conveyed, was perhaps never more clearly exemplified than in the performances of Rymer and Dryden. It was said of a dispute between two mathematicians, "malim cum Scaligero errare, quam cum Clavio recte sapere;" that *it was more eligible to go wrong with one than right with the other.* A tendency of the same kind every mind must feel at the perusal of Dryden's prefaces and Rymer's discourses. With Dryden we are wandering in quest of Truth; whom we find, if we find her at all, drest in the graces of elegance; and if we miss her, the labour of the pursuit rewards itself; we are led only through fragrance and flowers: Rymer, without taking a nearer, takes a rougher way; every step is to be made through thorns and brambles; and Truth, if we meet her, appears repulsive by her mien, and ungraceful by her habit. Dryden's criticism has the majesty of a queen; Rymer's has the ferocity of a tyrant.

As he had studied with great diligence the art of poetry, and enlarged or rectified his notions, by experience perpetually increasing, he had his mind stored with principles and observations; he poured out his knowledge with little labour; for of labour, notwithstanding the multiplicity of his productions, there is sufficient reason to suspect that he was not a lover. To write *con amore,* with fondness for the employment, with perpetual touches and retouches, with unwillingness to take leave of his own idea, and an unwearied pursuit of unattainable perfection, was, I think, no part of his character.

His Criticism may be considered as general or occasional. In his general precepts, which depend upon the nature of things, and the structure of the human mind, he may doubtless be safely recommended to the confidence of the reader; but his occasional and particular positions were sometimes interested, sometimes negligent, and sometimes capricious. It is not without reason that Trapp, speaking of the praises which he bestows on Palamon and Arcite, says, "Novimus judicium Drydeni de poemate quodam *Chauceri,* pulchro sane illo, et admodum laudando, nimirum quod non modo vere epicum sit, sed Iliada etiam atque Aeneada aequet, imo superet. Sed novimus eodem tempore viri illius maximi non semper accuratissimas esse censuras, nec ad severissimam critices normam exactas: illo judice id plerumque optimum est, quod nunc prae manibus habet, & in quo nunc occupatur." [We know our countryman Mr. Dryden's judgment about a poem of Chaucer's, truly beautiful indeed and worthy of praise; namely that it was not only equal, but even superior to the *Iliad* and *Aeneid.* But we know likewise that his opinion was not always the most accurate, nor formed upon the severest rules of criticism. What was in hand was generally most in esteem; if it was uppermost in his thoughts it was so in his judgment too.] [24]

He is therefore by no means constant to himself. His defence and desertion of dramatick rhyme is generally known. *Spence,* [25] in his remarks on Pope's Odyssey, produces what he thinks an unconquerable quotation from Dryden's preface to the Eneid, in favour of translating an epic poem into blank verse; but he forgets that when his author attempted the Iliad, some years afterwards, he departed from his own decision, and translated into rhyme.

When he has any objection to obviate, or any license to defend, he is not very scrupulous about what he asserts, nor very cautious, if the present purpose be served, not to entangle himself in his own sophistries. But, when all arts are exhausted, like other hunted animals, he sometimes stands at bay; when he cannot disown the grossness of one of his plays, he declares that he knows not any law that prescribes morality to a comick poet.

His remarks on ancient or modern writers are not always to be trusted. His parallel of the versification of Ovid with that of Claudian has been very justly censured by *Sewel*.[26] His comparison of the first line of Virgil with the first of Statius is not happier. Virgil, he says, is soft and gentle, and would have thought Statius mad if he had heard him thundering out

> Quae superimposito moles geminata colosso.
> [What great mass, doubled by the colossus placed upon it.][27]

Statius perhaps heats himself, as he proceeds, to exaggerations somewhat hyperbolical; but undoubtedly Virgil would have been too hasty, if he had condemned him to straw for one sounding line. Dryden wanted an instance, and the first that occurred was imprest into the service.

What he wishes to say, he says at hazard; he cited *Gorbuduc,* which he had never seen; gives a false account of *Chapman's* versification; and discovers, in the preface to his Fables, that he translated the first book of the Iliad, without knowing what was in the second.

It will be difficult to prove that Dryden ever made any great advances in literature. As having distinguished himself at Westminster under the tuition of Busby, who advanced his scholars to a height of knowledge very rarely attained in grammar-schools, he resided afterwards at Cambridge, it is not to be supposed, that his skill in the ancient languages was deficient, compared with that of common students; but his scholastick acquisitions seem not proportionate to his opportunities and abilities. He could not, like Milton or Cowley, have made his name illustrious merely by his learning. He mentions but few books, and those such as lie in the beaten track of regular study; from which if ever he departs, he is in danger of losing himself in unknown regions.

In his Dialogue on the Drama, he pronounces with great confidence that the Latin tragedy of Medea is not Ovid's, because it is not sufficiently interesting and pathetick. He might have determined the question upon surer evidence; for it is quoted by Quintilian as the work of Seneca; and the only line which remains of Ovid's play, for one line is left us, is not there to be found. There was therefore no need of the gravity of conjecture, or the discussion of plot or sentiment, to find what was already known upon higher authority than such discussions can ever reach.

His literature, though not always free from ostentation, will be commonly found either obvious, and made his own by the art of dressing it; or superficial, which, by what he gives, shews what he wanted; or erroneous, hastily collected, and negligently scattered.

Yet it cannot be said that his genius is ever unprovided of matter, or that his fancy languishes in penury of ideas. His works abound with knowledge, and sparkle with illustrations. There is scarcely any science or faculty that does not supply him with occasional images and lucky similitudes; every page discovers a mind very widely acquainted both with art and nature, and in full possession of great stores of intellectual wealth. Of him that knows much, it is natural to suppose that he has read with diligence; yet I rather believe that the knowledge of Dryden was gleaned from accidental intelligence and various conversation, by a quick apprehension, a judicious selection, and a happy memory, a keen appetite of knowledge, and a powerful digestion; by vigilance that permitted nothing to pass without notice, and a habit of reflection that suffered nothing useful to be lost. A mind like Dryden's, always curious, always active, to which every understanding was proud to be associated, and of which every one solicited the regard, by an ambitious display of himself, had a more pleasant, perhaps a nearer way, to knowledge than by the silent progress of solitary reading. I do not suppose that he despised books, or intentionally neglected them; but that he was carried out, by the impetuosity of his genius, to more vivid and speedy instructors; and that his studies were rather desultory and fortuitous than constant and systematical.

It must be confessed that he scarcely ever appears to want book-learning but when he mentions books; and to him may be transferred the praise which he gives his master Charles.

> His conversation, wit, and parts,
> His knowledge in the noblest useful arts,
> Were such, dead authors could not give,

But habitudes of those that live;
Who, lighting him, did greater lights receive:
He drain'd from all, and all they knew,
His apprehension quick, his judgement true:
That the most learn'd with shame confess
His knowledge more, his reading only less.[28]

Of all this, however, if the proof be demanded, I will not undertake to give it; the atoms of probability, of which my opinion has been formed, lie scattered over all his works; and by him who thinks the question worth his notice, his works must be perused with very close attention.

Criticism, either didactick or defensive, occupies almost all his prose, except those pages which he has devoted to his patrons; but none of his prefaces, were ever thought tedious. They have not the formality of a settled style, in which the first half of the sentence betrays the other. The clauses are never balanced, nor the periods modelled; every word seems to drop by chance, though it falls into its proper place. Nothing is cold or languid; the whole is airy, animated, and vigorous; what is little, is gay; what is great, is splendid. He may be thought to mention himself too frequently; but while he forces himself upon our esteem, we cannot refuse him to stand high in his own. Every thing is excused by the play of images and the spriteliness of expression. Though all is easy, nothing is feeble; though all seems careless, there is nothing harsh; and though, since his earlier works, more than a century has passed, they have nothing yet uncouth or obsolete.

He who writes much, will not easily escape a manner, such a recurrence of particular modes as may be easily noted. Dryden is always *another and the same,* he does not exhibit a second time the same elegances in the same form, nor appears to have any art other than that of expressing with clearness what he thinks with vigour. His style could not easily be imitated, either seriously or ludicrously; for, being always equable and always varied, it has no prominent or discriminative characters. The beauty who is totally free from disproportion of parts and features, cannot be ridiculed by an overcharged resemblance.

From his prose, however, Dryden derives only his accidental and secondary praise; the veneration with which his name is pronounced by every cultivator of English literature, is paid to him as he refined the language, improved the sentiments, and tuned the numbers of English Poetry.

After about half a century of forced thoughts, and rugged metre, some advances towards nature and harmony had been already made by Waller and Denham; they had shewn that long discourses in rhyme grew more pleasing when they were broken into couplets, and that verse consisted not only in the number but the arrangement of syllables.

But though they did much, who can deny that they left much to do? Their works were not many, nor were their minds of very ample comprehension. More examples of more modes of composition were necessary for the establishment of regularity, and the introduction of propriety in word and thought.

Every language of a learned nation necessarily divides itself into diction scholastick and popular, grave and familiar, elegant and gross; and from a nice distinction of these different parts, arises a great part of the beauty of style. But if we except a few minds, the favourites of nature, to whom their own original rectitude was in the place of rules, this delicacy of selection was little known to our authors; our speech lay before them in a heap of confusion, and every man took for every purpose what chance might offer him.

There was therefore before the time of Dryden no poetical diction, no system of words at once refined from the grossness of domestick use, and free from the harshness of terms appropriated to particular arts. Words too familiar, or too remote, defeat the purpose of a poet. From those sounds which we hear on small or on coarse occasions, we do not easily receive strong impressions, or delightful images; and words to which we are nearly strangers, whenever they occur, draw that attention on themselves which they should transmit to things.

Those happy combinations of words which distinguish poetry from prose, had been rarely attempted; we had few elegances or flowers of speech, the roses had not yet been plucked from the bramble, or different colours had not been joined to enliven one another.

It may be doubted whether Waller and Denham could have over-born the prejudices which had long prevailed, and which even then were sheltered by the protection of Cowley. The new versification, as it was called, may be considered as owing its establishment to Dryden; from whose time it is apparent that English poetry has had no tendency to relapse to its former savageness.

The affluence and comprehension of our language is very illustriously displayed in our poetical translations of Ancient Writers; a work which the French seem to relinquish in despair, and which we were long unable to perform with dexterity. Ben Jonson thought it necessary to copy Horace almost word by word; Feltham, his contemporary and adversary, considers it as indispensably requisite in a translation to give line for line. It is said that Sandys, whom Dryden calls the best versifier of the last age, has struggled hard to comprise every book of his English Metamorphoses in the same number of verses with the original. Holyday had nothing in view but to shew that he understood his author, with so little regard to the grandeur of his diction, or the volubility of his numbers, that his metres can hardly be called verses; they cannot be read without reluctance, nor will the labour always be rewarded by understanding them. Cowley saw that such *copyers* were a *servile race*; he asserted his liberty, and spread his wings so boldly that he left his authors. It was reserved for Dryden to fix the limits of poetical liberty, and give us just rules and examples of translation.[29]

When languages are formed upon different principles, it is impossible that the same modes of expression should always be elegant in both. While they run on together, the closest translation may be considered as the best; but when they divaricate, each must take its natural course. Where correspondence cannot be obtained, it is necessary to be content with something equivalent. *Translation therefore*, says Dryden, *is not so loose as paraphrase, nor so close as metaphrase.*[30]

* * *

Absalom and Achitophel is a work so well known, that particular criticism is superfluous. If it be considered as a poem political and controversial, it will be found to comprise all the excellences of which the subject is susceptible; acrimony of censure, elegance of praise, artful delineation of characters, variety and vigour of sentiment, happy turns of language, and pleasing harmony of numbers; and all these raised to such a height as can scarcely be found in any other English composition.

It is not, however, without faults; some lines are inelegant or improper, and too many are irreligiously licentious. The original structure of the poem was defective; allegories drawn to great length will always break; Charles could not run continually parallel with David.

The subject had likewise another inconvenience: it admitted little imagery or description, and a long poem of mere sentiments easily becomes tedious; though all the parts are forcible, and every line kindles new rapture, the reader, if not relieved by interposition of something that sooths the fancy, grows weary of admiration, and defers the rest.

As an approach to historical truth was necessary, the action and catastrophe were not in the poet's power; there is therefore an unpleasing disproportion between the beginning and the end. We are alarmed by a faction formed out of many sects various in their principles, but agreeing in their purpose of mischief, formidable for their numbers, and strong by their supports, while the king's friends are few and weak. The chiefs on either part are set forth to view; but when expectation is at the height, the king makes a speech, and

> Henceforth a series of new times began.[31]

Who can forbear to think of an enchanted castle, with a wide moat and lofty battlements, walls of marble and gates of brass, which vanishes at once into air, when the destined knight blows his horn before it?

* * *

In a general survey of Dryden's labours, he appears to have had a mind very comprehensive by nature, and much enriched with acquired knowledge. His compositions are the effects of a vigourous genius operating upon large materials.

The power that predominated in his intellectual operations, was rather strong reason than quick sensibility. Upon all occasions that were presented, he studied rather than felt, and produced sentiments not such as Nature enforces, but meditation supplies. With the simple and elemental passions, as they spring separate in the mind, he seems not much acquainted; and seldom describes them but as they are complicated by the various relations of society, and confused in the tumults and agitations of life.

What he says of love may contribute to the explanation of his character:

> Love various minds does variously inspire;
> It stirs in gentle bosoms gentle fire,
> Like that of incense on the altar laid;
> But raging flames tempestuous souls invade,
> A fire which every windy passion blows;
> With pride it mounts, or with revenge it glows.[32]

Dryden's was not one of the *gentle bosoms*: Love, as it subsists in itself, with no tendency but to the person loved, and wishing only for correspondent kindness; such love as shuts out all other interest; the Love of the Golden Age, was too soft and subtle to put his faculties in motion. He hardly conceived it but in its turbulent effervescence with some other desires; when it was inflamed by rivalry, or obstructed by difficulties: when it invigorated ambition, or exasperated revenge.

He is therefore, with all his variety of excellence, not often pathetick; and had so little sensibility of the power of effusions purely natural, that he did not esteem them in others. Simplicity gave him no pleasure; and for the first part of his life he looked on *Otway* with contempt, though at last, indeed very late, he confessed that in his play *there was Nature, which is the chief beauty.*[33]

We do not always know our own motives. I am not certain whether it was not rather the difficulty which he found in exhibiting the genuine operations of the heart, than a servile submission to an injudicious audience that filled his plays with false magnificence. It was necessary to fix attention; and the mind can be captivated only by recollection, or by curiosity; by reviving natural sentiments, or impressing new appearances of things: sentences were readier at his call than images; he could more easily fill the ear with some splendid novelty, than awaken those ideas that slumber in the heart.

* * *

Of Dryden's works it was said by Pope, that *he could select from them better specimens of every mode of poetry than any other English writer could supply.* Perhaps no nation ever produced a writer that enriched his language with such variety of models. To him we owe the improvement, perhaps the completion of our metre, the refinement of our language, and much of the correctness of our sentiments. By him we were taught *sapere & fari*, to think naturally and express forcibly. Though Davies has reasoned in rhyme before him,[34] it may be perhaps maintained that he was the first who joined argument with poetry. He shewed us the true bounds of a translator's liberty. What was said of Rome, adorned by Augustus, may be applied by an easy metaphor to English poetry embellished by Dryden, *lateritiam invenit, marmoream reliquit,*[35] he found it brick, and he left it marble.

ROWE

The *Fair Penitent*, his next production (1703), is one of the most pleasing tragedies on the stage, where it still keeps its turns of appearing, and probably will long keep them, for there is scarcely any work of any poet at once so interesting by the fable, and so delightful by the language. The story is domestick, and therefore easily received by the imagination, and assimilated to common life; the diction is exquisitely harmonious, and soft or spritely as occasion requires.

The character of *Lothario* seems to have been expanded by Richardson into *Lovelace,*[36] but he has excelled his original in the moral effect of the fiction. Lothario, with gaiety which cannot be hated, and bravery which cannot be despised, retains too much of the spectator's kindness. It was in the power of Richardson alone to teach us at once esteem and detestation, to make virtuous resentment overpower all the benevolence which wit, elegance, and courage, naturally excite; and to lose at last the hero in the villain.

The fifth act is not equal to the former; the events of the drama are exhausted, and little remains but to talk of what is past. It has been observed, that the title of the play does not sufficiently correspond with the behaviour of Calista, who at last shews no evident signs of repentance, but may be reasonably suspected of feeling pain from detection rather than from guilt, and expresses more shame than sorrow, and more rage than shame.

* * *

In the construction of his dramas, there is not much art; he is not a nice observer of the Unities. He extends time and varies place as his convenience requires. To vary the place is not, in my opinion, any violation of Nature, if the change be made between the acts; for it is no less easy for the spectator to suppose himself at Athens in the second act, than at Thebes in the first; but to change the scene, as is done by Rowe, in the middle of an act, is to add more acts to the play, since an act is so much of the business as is transacted without interruption. Rowe, by this licence, easily extricates himself from difficulties; as in *Jane Grey*, when we have been terrified with all the dreadful pomp of publick execution, and are wondering how the heroine or the poet will proceed, no sooner has *Jane* pronounced some prophetick rhymes, than—pass and be gone—the scene closes, and *Pembroke* and *Gardiner* are turned out upon the stage.

I know not that there can be found in his plays any deep search into nature, any accurate discriminations of kindred qualities, or nice display of passion in its progress; all is general and undefined. Nor does he much interest or affect the auditor, except in *Jane Shore*, who is always seen and heard with pity. *Alicia* is a character of empty noise, with no resemblance to real sorrow or to natural madness.

Whence, then, has Rowe his reputation? From the reasonableness and propriety of some of his scenes, from the elegance of his diction, and the suavity of his verse. He seldom moves either pity or terror, but he often elevates the sentiments; he seldom pierces the breast, but he always delights the ear, and often improves the understanding.

ADDISON

It is recorded by Budgell, that of the characters feigned or exhibited in the Spectator, the favourite of Addison was Sir Roger de Coverley, of whom he had formed a very delicate and discriminated idea, which he would not suffer to be violated; and therefore when Steele had shewn him innocently picking up a girl in the Temple, and taking her to a tavern, he drew upon himself so much of his friend's indignation, that he was forced to appease him by a promise of forbearing Sir Roger for the time to come.

The reason which induced Cervantes to bring his hero to the grave, *para mi sola nacio Don Quixote, y yo para el* [Don Quixote was born for me alone, and I for him],[37] made Addison declare, with an undue vehemence of expression, that he would kill Sir Roger; being of opinion that they were born for one another, and that any other hand would do him wrong.

It may be doubted whether Addison ever filled up his original delineation. He describes his Knight as having his imagination somewhat warped; but of this perversion he has made very little use. The irregularities in Sir Roger's conduct, seem not so much the effects of a mind deviating from the beaten track of life, by the perpetual pressure of some overwhelming idea, as of habitual rusticity, and that negligence which solitary grandeur naturally generates.

The variable weather of the mind, the flying vapours of incipient madness, which from time to time cloud reason, without eclipsing it, it requires so much nicety to exhibit, that Addison seems to have been deterred from prosecuting his own design.

To Sir Roger, who, as a country gentleman, appears to be a Tory, or, as it is gently expressed, an adherent to the landed interest, is opposed Sir Andrew Freeport, a new man, a wealthy merchant, zealous for the moneyed interest, and a Whig. Of this contrariety of opinions, it is probable more consequences were at

first intended, than could be produced when the resolution was
taken to exclude party from the paper. Sir Andrew does but little,
and that little seems not to have pleased Addison, who, when he
dismissed him from the club, changed his opinions. Steele had
made him, in the true spirit of unfeeling commerce, declare that
he *would not build an hospital for idle people*;[38] but at last he buys
land, settles in the country, and builds not a manufactory, but an
hospital for twelve old husbandmen, for men with whom a merchant has little acquaintance, and whom he commonly considers
with little kindness.

* * *

The tragedy of Cato, which, contrary to the rule observed in
selecting the works of other poets, has by the weight of its character forced its way into the late collection, is unquestionably the
noblest production of Addison's genius. Of a work so much read,
it is difficult to say any thing new. About things on which the
public thinks long, it commonly attains to think right; and of Cato
it has been not unjustly determined, that it is rather a poem in
dialogue than a drama, rather a succession of just sentiments in
elegant language, than a representation of natural affections, or
of any state probable or possible in human life. Nothing here
excites or asswages emotion; here is *no magical power of raising phan-
tastick terror or wild anxiety*. The events are expected without solicitude, and are remembered without joy or sorrow. Of the agents
we have no care: we consider not what they are doing, or what
they are suffering; we wish only to know what they have to say.
Cato is a being above our solicitude; a man of whom the gods take
care, and whom we leave to their care with heedless confidence.
To the rest, neither gods nor men can have much attention; for
there is not one amongst them that strongly attracts either affection or esteem. But they are made the vehicles of such sentiments
and such expression, that there is scarcely a scene in the play
which the reader does not wish to impress upon his memory.

* * *

Addison is now to be considered as a critick; a name which the
present generation is scarcely willing to allow him. His criticism is

condemned as tentative or experimental, rather than scientifick, and he is considered as deciding by taste rather than by principles.

It is not uncommon for those who have grown wise by the labour of others, to add a little of their own, and overlook their masters. Addison is now despised by some who perhaps would never have seen his defects, but by the lights which he afforded them. That he always wrote as he would think it necessary to write now, cannot be affirmed; his instructions were such as the character of his readers made proper. That general knowledge which now circulates in common talk, was in his time rarely to be found. Men not professing learning were not ashamed of ignorance; and in the female world, any acquaintance with books was distinguished only to be censured. His purpose was to infuse literary curiosity, by gentle and unsuspected conveyance, into the gay, the idle, and the wealthy; he therefore presented knowledge in the most alluring form, not lofty and austere, but accessible and familiar. When he shewed them their defects, he shewed them likewise that they might be easily supplied. His attempt succeeded; enquiry was awakened, and comprehension expanded. An emulation of intellectual elegance was excited, and from his time to our own, life has been gradually exalted, and conversation purified and enlarged.

Dryden had not many years before, scattered criticism over his Prefaces with very little parcimony; but, though he sometimes condescended to be somewhat familiar, his manner was in general too scholastick for those who had yet their rudiments to learn, and found it not easy to understand their master. His observations were framed rather for those that were learning to write, than for those that read only to talk.

An instructor like Addison was now wanting, whose remarks being superficial, might be easily understood, and being just, might prepare the mind for more attainments. Had he presented *Paradise Lost* to the publick with all the pomp of system and severity of science, the criticism would perhaps have been admired, and the poem still have been neglected; but by the blandishments of gentleness and facility he has made Milton an universal favourite, with whom readers of every class think it necessary to be pleased.[39]

* * *

As a describer of life and manners, he must be allowed to stand perhaps the first of the first rank. His humour, which, as Steele observes, is peculiar to himself, is so happily diffused as to give the grace of novelty to domestick scenes and daily occurrences. He never *outsteps the modesty of nature,* nor raises merriment or wonder by the violation of truth. His figures neither divert by distortion, nor amaze by aggravation. He copies life with so much fidelity, that he can be hardly said to invent; yet his exhibitions have an air so much original, that it is difficult to suppose them not merely the product of imagination.

As a teacher of wisdom, he may be confidently followed. His religion has nothing in it enthusiastick or superstitious: he appears neither weakly credulous nor wantonly sceptical; his morality is neither dangerously lax, nor impracticably rigid. All the enchantment of fancy, and all the cogency of argument, are employed to recommend to the reader his real interest, the care of pleasing the Author of his being. Truth is shewn sometimes as the phantom of a vision, sometimes appears half-veiled in an allegory; sometimes attracts regard in the robes of fancy, and sometimes steps forth in the confidence of reason. She wears a thousand dresses, and in all is pleasing.

> Mille habet ornatus, mille decenter habet.[40]

His prose is the model of the middle style; on grave subjects not formal, on light occasions not groveling; pure without scrupulosity, and exact without apparent elaboration; always equable, and always easy, without glowing words or pointed sentences. Addison never deviates from his track to snatch a grace;[41] he seeks no ambitious ornaments, and tries no hazardous innovations. His page is always luminous, but never blazes in unexpected splendour.

It was apparently his principal endeavour to avoid all harshness and severity of diction; he is therefore sometimes verbose in his transitions and connections, and sometimes descends too much to the language of conversation; yet if his language had been less idiomatical, it might have lost somewhat of its genuine Anglicism. What he attempted, he performed; he is never feeble, and he did not wish to be energetick; he is never rapid, and he never stagnates. His sentences have neither studied amplitude, nor affected brevity; his periods, though not diligently rounded, are voluble and easy. Whoever wishes to attain an English style, familiar but not coarse, and elegant but not ostentatious, must give his days and nights to the volumes of Addison.

GAY

Of this performance [*The Beggar's Opera*], when it was printed, the reception was different, according to the different opinion of its readers. Swift commended it for the excellence of its morality, as a piece that *placed all kinds of vice in the strongest and most odious light*; but others, and among them Dr. Herring, afterwards archbishop of Canterbury, censured it as giving encouragement not only to vice but to crimes, by making a highwayman the hero, and dismissing him at last unpunished. It has been even said, that after the exhibition of the *Beggar's Opera* the gangs of robbers were evidently multiplied.

Both these decisions are surely exaggerated. The play, like many others, was plainly written only to divert, without any moral purpose, and is therefore not likely to do good; nor can it be conceived, without more speculation than life requires or admits, to be productive of much evil. Highwaymen and house-breakers seldom frequent the play-house, or mingle in any elegant diversion; nor is it possible for any one to imagine that he may rob with safety, because he sees Macheath reprieved upon the stage.

* * *

As a poet, he cannot be rated very high. He was, as I once heard a female critick remark, *of a lower order*. He had not in any great degree the *mens divinior*, the dignity of genius. Much however must be allowed to the author of a new species of composition, though it be not of the highest kind. We owe to Gay the Ballad Opera; a mode of comedy which at first was supposed to delight only by its novelty, but has now by the experience of half a century been found so well accommodated to the disposition of a popular audience, that it is likely to keep long possession of the stage. Whether this new drama was the product of judgement or of luck, the praise of it must be given to the inventor; and there are many writers read with more reverence, to whom such merit of originality cannot be attributed.

SWIFT

This important year [1727 according to Johnson, but actually November, 1726] sent likewise into the world *Gulliver's Travels*, a production so new and strange, that it filled the reader with a mingled emotion of merriment and amazement. It was received with such avidity, that the price of the first edition was raised before the second could be made; it was read by the high and the low, the learned and illiterate. Criticism was for a while lost in wonder; no rules of judgement were applied to a book written in open defiance of truth and regularity. But when distinctions came to be made, the part which gave least pleasure was that which describes the *Flying Island*, and that which gave most disgust must be the history of the *Houyhnhnms*.

* * *

When Swift is considered as an author, it is just to estimate his powers by their effects. In the reign of Queen Anne he turned the stream of popularity against the Whigs, and must be confessed to have dictated for a time the political opinions of the English nation. In the succeeding reign he delivered Ireland from plunder and oppression; and shewed that wit, confederated with truth, had such force as authority was unable to resist. He said truly of himself, that Ireland *was his debtor*.[42] It was from the time when he first began to patronize the Irish, that they may date their riches and prosperity. He taught them first to know their own interest, their weight, and their strength, and gave them spirit to assert that equality with their fellow-subjects to which they have ever since been making vigorous advances, and to claim those rights which they have at last established. Nor can they be charged with ingratitude to their benefactor; for they reverenced him as a guardian, and obeyed him as a dictator.

In his works, he has given very different specimens both of sentiment and expression. His *Tale of a Tub* has little resemblance to his other pieces. It exhibits a vehemence and rapidity of mind, a copiousness of images, and vivacity of diction, such as he afterwards never possessed, or never exerted. It is of a mode so distinct and peculiar, that it must be considered by itself; what is true of that, is not true of any thing else which he has written.

In his other works is found an equable tenour of easy language, which rather trickles than flows. His delight was simplicity. That he has in his works no metaphor, as has been said, is not true; but his few metaphors seem to be received rather by necessity than choice. He studied purity; and though perhaps all his strictures are not exact, yet it is not often that solecisms can be found; and whoever depends on his authority may generally conclude himself safe. His sentences are never too much dilated or contracted; and it will not be easy to find any embarrassment in the complication of his clauses, any inconsequence in his connections, or abruptness in his transitions.

His style was well suited to his thoughts, which are never subtilised by nice disquisitions, decorated by sparkling conceits, elevated by ambitious sentences, or variegated by far-sought learning. He pays no court to the passions; he excites neither surprise nor admiration; he always understands himself: and his reader always understands him: the peruser of Swift wants little previous knowledge; it will be sufficient that he is acquainted with common words and common things; he is neither required to mount elevations, nor to explore profundities; his passage is always on a level, along solid ground, without asperities, without obstruction.

This easy and safe conveyance of meaning it was Swift's desire to attain, and for having attained he deserves praise, though perhaps not the highest praise. For purposes merely didactick, when something is to be told that was not known before, it is the best mode, but against that inattention by which known truths are suffered to lie neglected, it makes no provision; it instructs, but does not persuade.

POPE

[Comparison of Pope and Dryden.]

In acquired knowledge, the superiority must be allowed to Dryden, whose education was more scholastick, and who before he became an author had been allowed more time for study, with better means of information. His mind has a larger range, and he collects his images and illustrations from a more extensive circumference of science. Dryden knew more of man in his general nature, and Pope in his local manners. The notions of Dryden were formed by comprehensive speculation, and those of Pope by minute attention. There is more dignity in the knowledge of Dryden, and more certainty in that of Pope.

Poetry was not the sole praise of either; for both excelled likewise in prose; but Pope did not borrow his prose from his predecessor. The style of Dryden is capricious and varied, that of Pope is cautious and uniform; Dryden obeys the motions of his own mind, Pope constrains his mind to his own rules of composition. Dryden is sometimes vehement and rapid; Pope is always smooth, uniform, and gentle. Dryden's page is a natural field, rising into inequalities, and diversified by the varied exuberance of abundant vegetation; Pope's is a velvet lawn, shaven by the scythe, and levelled by the roller.

Of genius, that power which constitutes a poet; that quality without which judgement is cold and knowledge is inert; that energy which collects, combines, amplifies, and animates; the superiority must, with some hesitation, be allowed to Dryden. It is not to be inferred that of this poetical vigour Pope had only a little, because Dryden had more; for every other writer since Milton must give place to Pope; and even of Dryden it must be said, that if he has brighter paragraphs, he has not better poems. Dryden's performances were always hasty, either excited by some external occasion, or extorted by domestick necessity; he composed without consideration, and published without correction. What his mind could supply at call, or gather in one excursion, was all that he sought, and all that he gave. The dilatory caution of Pope enabled him to condense his sentiments, to multiply his images, and to accumulate all that study might produce, or chance might supply. If the flights of Dryden therefore are higher, Pope continues longer on the wing. If of Dryden's fire the blaze is brighter, of Pope's the heat is more regular and constant. Dryden often surpasses expectation, and Pope never falls below it. Dryden is read with frequent astonishment, and Pope with perpetual delight.

This parallel will, I hope, when it is well considered, be found just; and if the reader should suspect me, as I suspect myself, of some partial fondness for the memory of Dryden, let him not too hastily condemn me; for meditation and enquiry may, perhaps, shew him the reasonableness of my determination.

The Works of Pope are now to be distinctly examined, not so much with attention to slight faults or petty beauties, as to the general character and effect of each performance.

It seems natural for a young poet to initiate himself by Pastorals, which, not professing to imitate real life, require no experience, and, exhibiting only the simple operation of unmingled passions, admit no subtle reasoning or deep enquiry. Pope's Pastorals are not however composed but with close thought; they have reference to the times of the day, the seasons of the year, and the periods of human life. The last, that which turns the attention upon age and death, was the author's favourite. To tell of disappointment and misery, to thicken the darkness of futurity, and perplex the labyrinth of uncertainty, has been always a delicious employment of the poets. His preference was probably just. I wish, however, that his fondness had not overlooked a line in which the *Zephyrs* are made *to lament in silence*.[43]

To charge these Pastorals with want of invention, is to require what never was intended. The imitations are so ambitiously frequent, that the writer evidently means rather to shew his literature than his wit. It is surely sufficient for an author of sixteen not only to be able to copy the poems of antiquity with judicious selection, but to have obtained sufficient power of language, and skill in metre, to exhibit a series of versification, which had in English poetry no precedent, nor has since had an imitation.

The design of *Windsor Forest* is evidently derived from *Cooper's*

Hill, with some attention to Waller's poem on *The Park*; but Pope cannot be denied to excel his masters in variety and elegance, and the art of interchanging description, narrative, and morality. The objection made by Dennis is the want of plan, of a regular subordination of parts terminating in the principal and original design.[44] There is this want in most descriptive poems, because as the scenes, which they must exhibit successively, are all subsisting at the same time, the order in which they are shewn must by necessity be arbitrary, and more is not to be expected from the last part than from the first. The attention, therefore, which cannot be detained by suspense, must be excited by diversity, such as his poem offers to its reader.

But the desire of diversity may be too much indulged; the parts of *Windsor Forest* which deserve least praise, are those which were added to enliven the stillness of the scene, the appearance of Father Thames, and the transformation of *Lodona*. Addison had in his *Campaign* derided the *rivers* that *rise from their oozy beds* to tell stories of heroes,[45] and it is therefore strange that Pope should adopt a fiction not only unnatural but lately censured. The story of *Lodona* is told with sweetness; but a new metamorphosis is a ready and puerile expedient; nothing is easier than to tell how a flower was once a blooming virgin, or a rock an obdurate tyrant.

The *Temple of Fame* has, as Steele warmly declared, *a thousand beauties*. Every part is splendid; there is great luxuriance of ornaments; the original vision of Chaucer was never denied to be much improved; the allegory is very skilfully continued, the imagery is properly selected, and learnedly displayed: yet, with all this comprehension of excellence, as its scene is laid in remote ages, and its sentiments, if the concluding paragraph be excepted, have little relation to general manners or common life, it never obtained much notice, but is turned silently over, and seldom quoted or mentioned with either praise or blame.

That the *Messiah* excels the *Pollio* is no great praise, if it be considered from what original the improvements are derived.[46]

The *Verses on the unfortunate Lady* have drawn much attention by the illaudable singularity of treating suicide with respect; and they must be allowed to be written in some parts with vigorous animation, and in others with gentle tenderness; nor has Pope produced any poem in which the sense predominates more over the diction. But the tale is not skilfully told; it is not easy to discover the character of either the Lady or her Guardian. History relates that she was about to disparage herself by a marriage with an inferior; Pope praises her for the dignity of ambition, and yet condemns the unkle to detestation for his pride; the ambitious love of a niece may be opposed by the interest, malice, or envy of an unkle, but never by his pride. On such an occasion a poet may be allowed to be obscure, but inconsistency never can be right.

The *Ode for St. Cecilia's Day* was undertaken at the desire of Steele: in this the author is generally confessed to have miscarried, yet he has miscarried only as compared with Dryden; for he has far outgone other competitors. Dryden's plan is better chosen; history will always take stronger hold of the attention than fable: the passions excited by Dryden are the pleasures and pains of real life, the scene of Pope is laid in imaginary existence; Pope is read with calm acquiescence, Dryden with turbulent delight; Pope hangs upon the ear, and Dryden finds the passes of the mind.

Both the odes want the essential constituent of metrical compositions, the stated recurrence of settled numbers. It may be alleged, that Pindar is said by Horace to have written *numeris lege solutis* [in free verse]:[47] but as no such lax performances have been transmitted to us, the meaning of that expression cannot be fixed; and perhaps the like return might properly be made to a modern Pindarist, as Mr. Cobb received from Bentley, who, when he found his criticisms upon a Greek Exercise, which Cobb had presented, refuted one after another by Pindar's authority, cried out at last, *Pindar was a bold fellow, but thou art an impudent one.*

If Pope's ode be particularly inspected, it will be found that the first stanza consists of sounds well chosén indeed, but only sounds.

The second consists of hyperbolical common-places, easily to be found, and perhaps without much difficulty to be as well expressed.

In the third, however, there are numbers, images, harmony, and vigour, not unworthy the antagonist of Dryden. Had all been like this—but every part cannot be the best.

The next stanzas place and detain us in the dark and dismal regions of mythology, where neither hope nor fear, neither joy nor sorrow can be found: the poet however faithfully attends us; we have all that can be performed by elegance of diction, or sweetness of versification; but what can form avail without better matter?

The last stanza recurs again to common-places. The conclusion is too evidently modelled by that of Dryden; and it may be remarked that both end with the same fault, the comparison of each is literal on one side, and metaphorical on the other.

Poets do not always express their own thoughts; Pope, with all this labour in the praise of Musick, was ignorant of its principles, and insensible of its effects.

One of his greatest though of his earliest works is the *Essay on Criticism*, which, if he had written nothing else, would have placed him among the first criticks and the first poets, as it exhibits every mode of excellence that can embellish or dignify didactick composition, selection of matter, novelty of arrangement, justness of precept, splendour of illustration, and propriety of digression. I know not whether it be pleasing to consider that he produced this piece at twenty, and never afterwards excelled it: he that delights himself with observing that such powers may be so soon attained, cannot but grieve to think that life was ever after at a stand.

To·mention the particular beauties of the Essay would be unprofitably tedious; but I cannot forbear to observe, that the comparison of a student's progress in the sciences with the journey of a traveller in the Alps, is perhaps the best that English poetry can shew.[48] A simile, to be perfect, must both illustrate and ennoble the subject; must shew it to the understanding in a clearer view, and display it to the fancy with greater dignity; but either of these qualities may be sufficient to recommend it. In didactick poetry, of which the great purpose is instruction, a simile may be praised which illustrates, though it does not ennoble; in heroicks, that may be admitted which ennobles, though it does not illustrate. That it may be complete, it is required to exhibit, independently of its references, a pleasing image; for a simile is said to be a short episode. To this antiquity was so attentive, that circumstances were sometimes added, which, having no parallels, served only to fill the imagination, and produced what Perrault ludicrously called *comparisons with a long tail*. In their similies the greatest writers have sometimes failed; the ship-race, compared with the chariot-race, is neither illustrated nor aggrandised;[49] land and water make all the difference: when Apollo, running after Daphne, is likened to a greyhound chasing a hare, there is nothing gained;[50] the ideas of pursuit and flight are too plain to be made plainer, and a god and the daughter of a god are not represented much to their advantage, by a hare and dog. The simile of the Alps has no useless parts, yet affords a striking picture by itself; it makes the foregoing position better understood, and enables it to take faster hold on the attention; it assists the apprehension, and elevates the fancy.

Let me likewise dwell a little on the celebrated paragraph, in which it is directed that *the sound should seem an echo to the sense*;[51] a precept which Pope is allowed to have observed beyond any other English poet.

This notion of representative metre, and the desire of discovering frequent adaptations of the sound to the sense, have produced, in my opinion, many wild conceits and imaginary beauties. All that can furnish this representation are the sounds of the words considered singly, and the time in which they are pronounced. Every language has some words framed to exhibit the noises which they express, as *thump, rattle, growl, hiss*. These however are but few, and the poet cannot make them more, nor can they be of any use but when sound is to be mentioned. The time of pronunciation was in the dactylick measures of the learned languages capable of considerable variety; but that variety could be accommodated only to motion or duration, and different degrees of motion were perhaps expressed by verses rapid or slow, without much attention of the writer, when the image had full possession of his fancy; but our language having little flexibility, our verses can differ very little in their cadence. The fancied resemblances, I fear, arise sometimes merely from the ambiguity of words; there is supposed to be some relation between a *soft* line and a *soft* couch, or between *hard* syllables and *hard* fortune.

Motion, however, may be in some sort exemplified; and yet it may be suspected that even in such resemblances the mind often governs the ear, and the sounds are estimated by their meaning. One of the most successful attempts has been to describe the labour of Sisyphus:

> With many a weary step, and many a groan,
> Up a high hill he heaves a huge round stone;
> The huge round stone, resulting with a bound,
> Thunders impetuous down, and smoaks along the ground.[52]

Who does not perceive the stone to move slowly upward, and roll violently back? But set the same numbers to another sense:

> While many a merry tale, and many a song,
> Chear'd the rough road, we wish'd the rough road long.
> The rough road then, returning in a round,
> Mock'd our impatient steps, for all was fairy ground.

We have now surely lost much of the delay, and much of the rapidity.

But to shew how little the greatest master of numbers can fix the principles of representative harmony, it will be sufficient to remark that the poet, who tells us, that

> When Ajax strives—the words move slow.
> Not so when swift Camilla scours the plain,
> Flies o'er th' unbending corn, and skims along the main;[53]

when he had enjoyed for about thirty years the praise of Camilla's lightness of foot, tried another experiment upon *sound* and *time*, and produced this memorable triplet:

> Waller was smooth; but Dryden taught to join
> The varying verse, the full resounding line,
> The long majestick march, and energy divine.[54]

Here are the swiftness of the rapid race, and the march of slow-paced majesty, exhibited by the same poet in the same sequence of syllables, except that the exact prosodist will find the line of *swiftness* by one time longer than that of *tardiness*.

Beauties of this kind are commonly fancied; and when real, are technical and nugatory, not to be rejected, and not to be solicited.

To the praises which have been accumulated on *The Rape of the Lock* by readers of every class, from the critick to the waiting-maid, it is difficult to make any addition. Of that which is universally allowed to be the most attractive of all ludicrous[55] compositions, let it rather be now enquired from what sources the power of pleasing is derived.

Dr. Warburton, who excelled in critical perspicacity, has remarked that the preternatural agents are very happily adapted to the purposes of the poem. The heathen deities can no longer gain attention: we should have turned away from a contest between Venus and Diana. The employment of allegorical persons always excites conviction of its own absurdity; they may produce effects, but cannot conduct actions; when the phantom is put in motion, it dissolves; thus *Discord* may raise a mutiny, but *Discord* cannot conduct a march, nor besiege a town. Pope brought into view a new race of Beings, with powers and passions proportionate to their operation. The sylphs and gnomes act at the toilet and the tea-table, what more terrifick and more powerful phantoms perform on the stormy ocean, or the field of battle; they give their proper help, and do their proper mischief.

Pope is said, by an objector,[56] not to have been the inventer of this petty nation; a charge which might with more justice have been brought against the author of the *Iliad*, who doubtless adopted the religious system of his country; for what is there but the names of his agents which Pope has not invented? Has he not assigned them characters and operations never heard of before? Has he not, at least, given them their first poetical existence? If this is not sufficient to denominate his work original, nothing original ever can be written.

In this work are exhibited, in a very high degree, the two most engaging powers of an author. New things are made familiar, and familiar things are made new. A race of aerial people, never heard of before, is presented to us in a manner so clear and easy, that the reader seeks for no further information, but immediately mingles with his new acquaintance, adopts their interest, and attends their pursuits, loves a sylph, and detests a gnome.

That familiar things are made new, every paragraph will prove. The subject of the poem is an event below the common incidents of common life; nothing real is introduced that is not seen so often as to be no longer regarded, yet the whole detail of a female-day is here brought before us invested with so much art of decoration, that, though nothing is disguised, every thing is striking, and we feel all the appetite of curiosity for that from which we have a thousand times turned fastidiously away.

The purpose of the Poet is, as he tells us, to laugh at *the little unguarded follies of the female sex*. It is therefore without justice that Dennis charges the *Rape of the Lock* with the want of a moral, and for that reason sets it below the *Lutrin*, which exposes the pride and discord of the clergy.[57] Perhaps neither Pope nor Boileau has made the world much better than he found it; but if they had both succeeded, it were easy to tell who would have deserved most from publick gratitude. The freaks, and humours, and spleen, and vanity of women, as they embroil families in discord, and fill houses with disquiet, do more to obstruct the happiness of life in a year than the ambition of the clergy in many centuries. It has been well observed, that the misery of man proceeds not from any single crush of overwhelming evil, but from small vexations continually repeated.

It is remarked by Dennis likewise, that the machinery is superfluous; that, by all the bustle of preternatural operation, the main event is neither hastened nor retarded. To this charge an efficacious answer is not easily made. The sylphs cannot be said to help or to oppose, and it must be allowed to imply some want of art, that their power has not been sufficiently intermingled with the action. Other parts may likewise be charged with want of connection; the game at *ombre* might be spared, but if the Lady had lost her hair while she was intent upon her cards, it might have been inferred that those who are too fond of play will be in danger of neglecting more important interests. Those perhaps are faults; but what are such faults to so much excellence!

The Epistle of *Eloise to Abelard* is one of the most happy productions of human wit: the subject is so judiciously chosen, that it would be difficult, in turning over the annals of the world, to find another which so many circumstances concur to recommend. We regularly interest ourselves most in the fortune of those who most deserve our notice. Abelard and Eloise were conspicuous in their days for eminence of merit. The heart naturally loves truth. The adventures and misfortunes of this illustrious pair are known from undisputed history. Their fate does not leave the mind in hopeless dejection; for they both found quiet and consolation in retirement and piety. So new and so affecting is their story, that it supersedes invention, and imagination ranges at full liberty without straggling into scenes of fable.

The story, thus skilfully adopted, has been diligently improved. Pope has left nothing behind him, which seems more the effect of studious perseverance and laborious revisal. Here is particularly observable the *curiosa felicitas*, a fruitful soil, and careful cultivation. Here is no crudeness of sense, nor asperity of language.

The sources from which sentiments, which have so much vigour and efficacy, have been drawn, are shewn to be the mystick writers by the learned author[58] of the *Essay on the Life and Writings of Pope*; a book which teaches how the brow of Criticism may be smoothed, and how she may be enabled, with all her severity, to attract and to delight.

The train of my disquisition has now conducted me to that poetical wonder, the translation of the *Iliad*; a performance which no age or nation can pretend to equal. To the Greeks translation was almost unknown; it was totally unknown to the inhabitants of Greece. They had no recourse to the Barbarians for poetical beauties, but sought for every thing in Homer, where, indeed, there is but little which they might not find.

The Italians have been very diligent translators; but I can hear of no version, unless perhaps Anguillara's Ovid may be excepted, which is read with eagerness. The *Iliad* of Salvini every reader may discover to be punctiliously exact; but it seems to be the work of a linguist skilfully pedantick, and his countrymen, the proper judges of its power to please, reject it with disgust.[59]

Their predecessors the Romans have left some specimens of

translation behind them, and that employment must have had some credit in which Tully and Germanicus engaged; but unless we suppose, what is perhaps true, that the plays of Terence were versions of Menander, nothing translated seems ever to have risen to high reputation. The French, in the meridian hour of their learning, were very laudably industrious to enrich their own language with the wisdom of the ancients; but found themselves reduced, by whatever necessity, to turn the Greek and Roman poetry into prose. Whoever could read an author, could translate him. From such rivals little can be feared.

The chief help of Pope in this arduous undertaking was drawn from the versions of Dryden. Virgil had borrowed much of his imagery from Homer, and part of the debt was now paid by his translator. Pope searched the pages of Dryden for happy combinations of heroic diction; but it will not be denied that he added much to what he found. He cultivated our language with so much diligence and art, that he has left in his *Homer* a treasure of poetical elegances to posterity. His version may be said to have tuned the English tongue; for since its appearance no writer, however deficient in other powers, has wanted melody. Such a series of lines so elaborately corrected, and so sweetly modulated, took possession of the publick ear; the vulgar was enamoured of the poem, and the learned wondered at the translation.

But in the most general applause discordant voices will always be heard. It has been objected by some, who wish to be numbered among the sons of learning, that Pope's version of Homer is not Homerical; that it exhibits no resemblance of the original and characteristick manner of the Father of Poetry, as it wants his awful simplicity, his artless grandeur, his unaffected majesty. This cannot be totally denied; but it must be remembered that *necessitas quod cogit defendit*; that may be lawfully done which cannot be forborn. Time and place will always enforce regard. In estimating this translation, consideration must be had of the nature of our language, the form of our metre, and, above all, of the change which two thousand years have made in the modes of life and the habits of thought. Virgil wrote in a language of the same general fabrick with that of Homer, in verses of the same measure, and in an age nearer to Homer's time by eighteen hundred years; yet he found, even then, the state of the world so much altered, and the demand for elegance so much increased, that mere nature would be endured no longer; and perhaps, in the multitude of borrowed passages, very few can be shewn which he has not embellished.

There is a time when nations emerging from barbarity, and falling into regular subordination, gain leisure to grow wise, and feel the shame of ignorance and the craving pain of unsatisfied curiosity. To this hunger of the mind plain sense is grateful; that which fills the void removes uneasiness, and to be free from pain for a while is pleasure; but repletion generates fastidiousness; a saturated intellect soon becomes luxurious, and knowledge finds no willing reception till it is recommended by artificial diction. Thus it will be found, in the progress of learning, that in all nations the first writers are simple, and that every age improves in elegance. One refinement always makes way for another, and what was expedient to Virgil was necessary to Pope.

I suppose many readers of the English *Iliad*, when they have been touched with some unexpected beauty of the lighter kind, have tried to enjoy it in the original, where, alas! it was not to be found. Homer doubtless owes to his translator many *Ovidian* graces not exactly suitable to his character; but to have added can be no great crime, if nothing be taken away. Elegance is surely to be desired, if it be not gained at the expence of dignity. A hero would wish to be loved, as well as to be reverenced.

To a thousand cavils one answer is sufficient; the purpose of a writer is to be read, and the criticism which would destroy the power of pleasing must be blown aside. Pope wrote for his own age and his own nation: he knew that it was necessary to colour the images and point the sentiments of his author; he therefore made him graceful, but lost him some of his sublimity.

The copious notes with which the version is accompanied, and by which it is recommended to many readers, though they were undoubtedly written to swell the volumes, ought not to pass without praise: commentaries which attract the reader by the pleasure of perusal have not often appeared; the notes of others are read to clear difficulties, those of Pope to vary entertainment.

It has however been objected, with sufficient reason, that there is in the commentary too much of unseasonable levity and affected gaiety; that too many appeals are made to the Ladies, and the ease which is so carefully preserved is sometimes the ease of a trifler. Every art has its terms, and every kind of instruction its proper style; the gravity of common criticks may be tedious, but is less despicable than childish merriment.

Of the *Odyssey* nothing remains to be observed: the same general praise may be given to both translations, and a particular examination of either would require a large volume. The notes were written by Broome, who endeavoured not unsuccessfully to imitate his master.

Of the *Dunciad* the hint is confessedly taken from Dryden's *Mac Flecknoe*; but the plan is so enlarged and diversified as justly to claim the praise of an original, and affords perhaps the best specimen that has yet appeared of personal satire ludicrously pompous.

That the design was moral, whatever the author might tell either his readers or himself, I am not convinced. The first motive was the desire of revenging the contempt with which Theobald had treated his *Shakspeare*, and regaining the honour which he had lost, by crushing his opponent. Theobald was not of bulk enough to fill a poem, and therefore it was necessary to find other enemies with other names, at whose expence he might divert the publick.

In this design there was petulance and malignity enough; but I cannot think it very criminal. An author places himself uncalled before the tribunal of Criticism, and solicits fame at the hazard of disgrace. Dulness or deformity are not culpable in themselves, but may be very justly reproached when they pretend to the honour of wit or the influence of beauty. If bad writers were to pass without reprehension, what should restrain them? *impune diem consumpserit ingens Telephus* [Shall some huge *Telephus*, immune from revenge, eat up a whole day?];[60] and upon bad writers only will censure have much effect. The satire which brought Theobald and Moore into contempt, dropped impotent from Bentley, like the javelin of Priam.[61]

All truth is valuable, and satirical criticism may be considered as useful when it rectifies error and improves judgement; he that refines the publick taste is a publick benefactor.

The beauties of this poem are well known; its chief fault is the grossness of its images. Pope and Swift had an unnatural delight in ideas physically impure, such as every other tongue utters with unwillingness, and of which every ear shrinks from the mention.

But even this fault, offensive as it is, may be forgiven for the excellence of other passages; such as the formation and dissolution of Moore, the account of the Traveller, the misfortune of the Florist, and the crouded thoughts and stately numbers which dignify the concluding paragraph.[62]

The alterations which have been made in the *Dunciad*, not always for the better, require that it should be published, as in the last collection, with all its variations.

The *Essay on Man* was a work of great labour and long consideration, but certainly not the happiest of Pope's performances. The subject is perhaps not very proper for poetry, and the poet was not sufficiently master of his subject; metaphysical morality was to him a new study, he was proud of his acquisitions, and, supposing himself master of great secrets, was in haste to teach what he had not learned. Thus he tells us, in the first Epistle, that from the nature of the Supreme Being may be deduced an order of beings such as mankind, because Infinite Excellence can do only what is best. He finds out that these beings must be *somewhere,* and *all the question is whether man be in a wrong place.* Surely if, according to the poet's Leibnitian reasoning, we may infer that man ought to be, only because he is, we may allow that his place is the right place, because he has it. Supreme Wisdom is not less infallible in disposing than in creating. But what is meant by *somewhere* and *place*, and *wrong place*, it had been vain to ask Pope, who probably had never asked himself.

Having exalted himself into the chair of wisdom, he tells us much that every man knows, and much that he does not know himself; that we see but little, and that the order of the universe is beyond our comprehension; an opinion not very uncommon; and that there is a chain of subordinate beings *from infinite to nothing*, of which himself and his readers are equally ignorant.

But he gives us one comfort, which, without his help, he supposes unattainable, in the position *that though we are fools, yet God is wise.*[63]

This Essay affords an egregious instance of the predominance of genius, the dazzling splendour of imagery, and the seductive powers of eloquence. Never were penury of knowledge and vulgarity of sentiment so happily disguised. The reader feels his mind full, though he learns nothing; and when he meets it in its new array, no longer knows the talk of his mother and his nurse. When these wonder-working sounds sink into sense, and the doctrine of the Essay, disrobed of its ornaments, is left to the powers of its naked excellence, what shall we discover? That we are, in comparison with our Creator, very weak and ignorant; that we do not uphold the chain of existence, and that we could not make one another with more skill than we are made. We may learn yet more; that the arts of human life were copied from the instinctive operations of other animals; that if the world be made for man, it may be said that man was made for geese. To these profound principles of natural knowledge are added some moral instructions equally new; that self-interest, well understood, will produce social concord; that men are mutual gainers by mutual benefits; that evil is sometimes balanced by good; that human advantages are unstable and fallacious, of uncertain duration, and doubtful effect; that our true honour is, not to have a great part, but to act it well: that virtue only is our own; and that happiness is always in our power.

Surely a man of no very comprehensive search may venture to say that he has heard all this before; but it was never till now recommended by such a blaze of embellishment, or such sweetness of melody. The vigorous contraction of some thoughts, the luxuriant amplification of others, the incidental illustrations, and sometimes the dignity, sometimes the softness of the verses, enchain philosophy, suspend criticism, and oppress judgement by overpowering pleasure.

This is true of many paragraphs; yet if I had undertaken to exemplify Pope's felicity of composition before a rigid critick, I should not select the *Essay on Man*; for it contains more lines unsuccessfully laboured, more harshness of diction, more thoughts imperfectly expressed, more levity without elegance, and more heaviness without strength, than will easily be found in all his other works.

The *Characters of Men and Women* are the product of diligent speculation upon human life; much labour has been bestowed upon them, and Pope very seldom laboured in vain. That his excellence may be properly estimated, I recommend a comparison of his *Characters of Women* with Boileau's Satire;[64] it will then be seen with how much more perspicacity female nature is investigated, and female excellence selected; and he surely is no mean writer to whom Boileau shall be found inferior. The *Characters of Men*, however, are written with more, if not with deeper, thought, and exhibit many passages exquisitely beautiful. The *Gem and the Flower* will not easily be equalled. In the women's part are some defects; the character of *Attossa* is not so neatly finished as that of *Clodio*; and some of the female characters may be found perhaps more frequently among men; what is said of *Philomede* was true of *Prior*.

In the Epistles to Lord Bathurst and Lord Burlington, Dr. Warburton has endeavoured to find a train of thought which was never in the writer's head, and, to support his hypothesis, has printed that first which was published last. In one, the most valuable passage is perhaps the Elogy on *Good Sense*, and the other the *End of the Duke of Buckingham*.[65]

The Epistle to Arbuthnot, now arbitrarily called the *Prologue to the Satires,* is a performance consisting, as it seems, of many fragments wrought into one design, which by this union of scattered beauties contains more striking paragraphs than could probably have been brought together into an occasional work. As there is no stronger motive to exertion than self-defence, no part has more elegance, spirit, or dignity, than the poet's vindication of his own character. The meanest passage is the satire upon *Sporus.*

Of the two poems which derived their names from the year, and which are called the *Epilogue to the Satires*, it was very justly remarked by Savage, that the second was in the whole more strongly conceived, and more equally supported, but that it had no single passages equal to the contention in the first for the dignity of Vice, and the celebration of the triumph of Corruption.[66]

The Imitations of Horace seem to have been written as relaxations of his genius. This employment became his favourite by its facility; the plan was ready to his hand, and nothing was required but to accommodate as he could the sentiments of an old author to recent facts or familiar images; but what is easy is seldom excellent; such imitations cannot give pleasure to common readers; the man of learning may be sometimes surprised and delighted by an unexpected parallel; but the comparison requires knowledge of the original, which will likewise often detect strained applications. Between Roman images and English manners there will be an irreconcileable dissimilitude, and the work will be generally uncouth and party-coloured; neither original nor translated, neither ancient nor modern.

Pope had, in proportions very nicely adjusted to each other, all the qualities that constitute genius. He had *Invention*, by which new trains of events are formed, and new scenes of imagery displayed, as in the *Rape of the Lock*; and by which extrinsick and adventitious embellishments and illustrations are connected with a known subject, as in the *Essay on Criticism*. He had *Imagination*, which strongly impresses on the writer's mind, and enables him to convey to the reader, the various forms of nature, incidents of life, and energies of passion, as in his *Eloisa*, *Windsor Forest*, and the *Ethick Epistles*. He had *Judgement* which selects from life or nature what the present purpose requires, and, by separating the essence of things from its concomitants, often makes the representation more powerful than the the reality: and he had colours of language always before him, ready to decorate his matter with every grace of elegant expression, as when he accommodates his diction to the wonderful multiplicity of Homer's sentiments and descriptions.

Poetical expression includes sound as well as meaning; *Musick*, says Dryden, *is inarticulate poetry*;[67] among the excellences of Pope, therefore, must be mentioned the melody of his metre. By perusing the works of Dryden, he discovered the most perfect fabrick of English verse, and habituated himself to that only which he found the best; in consequence of which restraint, his poetry has been censured as too uniformly musical, and as glutting the ear with unvaried sweetness. I suspect this objection to be the cant of those who judge by principles rather than perception: and who would even themselves have less pleasure in his works, if he had tried to relieve attention by studied discords, or affected to break his lines and vary his pauses.

But though he was thus careful of his versification, he did not oppress his powers with superfluous rigour. He seems to have thought with Boileau, that the practice of writing might be refined till the difficulty should overbalance the advantage. The construction of his language is not always strictly grammatical; with those rhymes which prescription had conjoined he contented himself, without regard to Swift's remonstrances,[68] though there was no striking consonance; nor was he very careful to vary his terminations, or to refuse admission at a small distance to the same rhymes.

To Swift's edict for the exclusion of Alexandrines and Triplets he paid little regard; he admitted them, but, in the opinion of Fenton, too rarely; he uses them more liberally in his translation than his poems.

He has a few double rhymes; and always, I think, unsuccessfully, except once in the *Rape of the Lock*.

Expletives he very early ejected from his verses; but he now and then admits an epithet rather commodious than important. Each of the six first lines of the *Iliad* might lose two syllables with very little diminution of the meaning; and sometimes, after all his art and labour, one verse seems to be made for the sake of another. In his latter productions the diction is sometimes vitiated by French idioms, with which Bolingbroke had perhaps infected him.

I have been told that the couplet by which he declared his own ear to be most gratified was this:

> Lo, where Moeotis sleeps, and hardly flows
> The freezing Tanais through a waste of snows.[69]

But the reason of this preference I cannot discover.

It is remarked by Watts,[70] that there is scarcely a happy combination of words, or a phrase poetically elegant in the English language, which Pope has not inserted into his version of Homer. How he obtained possession of so many beauties of speech, it were desirable to know. That he gleaned from authors, obscure as well as eminent, what he thought brilliant or useful, and preserved it all in a regular collection, is not unlikely. When, in his last years, Hall's Satires[71] were shewn him, he wish'd that he had seen them sooner.

New sentiments and new images others may produce; but to attempt any further improvement of versification will be dangerous. Art and diligence have now done their best, and what shall be added will be the effort of tedious toil and needless curiosity.

After all this, it is surely superfluous to answer the question that has once been asked, Whether Pope was a poet? otherwise than by asking in return, If Pope be not a poet, where is poetry to be found? To circumscribe poetry by a definition will only shew the narrowness of the definer, though a definition which shall exclude Pope will not easily be made. Let us look round upon the present time, and back upon the past; let us enquire to whom the voice of mankind has decreed the wreath of poetry; let their productions be examined, and their claims stated, and the pretensions of Pope will be no more disputed. Had he given the world only his version, the name of poet must have been allowed him: if the writer of the *Iliad* were to class his successors, he would assign a very high place to his translator, without requiring any other evidence of Genius.

THOMSON

As a writer, he is entitled to one praise of the highest kind: his mode of thinking, and of expressing his thoughts, is original. His blank verse is no more the blank verse of Milton, or of any other poet, than the rhymes of Prior are the rhymes of Cowley. His numbers, his pauses, his diction, are of his own growth, without transcription, without imitation. He thinks in a peculiar train, and he thinks always as a man of genius; he looks round on Nature and on Life, with the eye which Nature bestows only on a poet; the eye that distinguishes, in every thing presented to its view, whatever there is on which imagination can delight to be detained, and with a mind that at once comprehends the vast, and attends to the minute. The reader of the *Seasons* wonders that he never saw before what Thomson shews him, and that he never yet has felt what Thomson impresses.

His is one of the works in which blank verse seems properly used; Thomson's wide expansion of general views, and his enumeration of circumstantial varieties, would have been obstructed and embarrassed by the frequent intersection of the sense, which are the necessary effects of rhyme.

His descriptions of extended scenes and general effects bring before us the whole magnificence of Nature, whether pleasing or dreadful. The gaiety of *Spring*, the splendour of *Summer*, the tranquillity of *Autumn*, and the horror of *Winter*, take in their turns possession of the mind. The poet leads us through the appearances of things as they are successively varied by the vicissitudes of the year, and imparts to us so much of his own enthusiasm, that our thoughts expand with his imagery, and kindle with his sentiments. Nor is the naturalist without his part in the entertainment; for he is assisted to recollect and to combine, to arrange his discoveries, and to amplify the sphere of his contemplation.

The great defect of the *Seasons* is want of method; but for this I know not that there was any remedy. Of many appearances subsisting all at once, no rule can be given why one should be mentioned before another; yet the memory wants the help of order, and the curiosity is not excited by suspense or expectation.[72]

His diction is in the highest degree florid and luxuriant, such as may be said to be to his images and thoughts *both their lustre and their shade*; such as invest them with splendour, through which perhaps they are not always easily discerned. It is too exuberant, and sometimes may be charged with filling the ear more than the mind.

These Poems, with which I was acquainted at their first appearance, I have since found altered and enlarged by subsequent revisals, as the author supposed his judgement to grow more exact, and as books or conversation extended his knowledge and opened his prospects. They are, I think, improved in general; yet I know not whether they have not lost part of what Temple calls their *race*; a word which, applied to wines, in its primitive sense, means the flavour of the soil.

Liberty, when it first appeared, I tried to read, and soon desisted. I have never tried again, and therefore will not hazard either praise or censure.

The highest praise which he has received ought not to be supprest; it is said by Lord Lyttelton in the Prologue to his posthumous play, that his works contained

No line which, dying, he could wish to blot.[73]

AKENSIDE

Akenside is to be considered as a didactick and lyrick poet. His great work is the *Pleasures of Imagination*; a performance which, published, as it was, at the age of twenty-three, raised expectations that were not afterwards very amply satisfied. It has undoubtedly a just claim to very particular notice, as an example of great felicity of genius, and uncommon amplitude of acquisitions, of a young mind stored with images, and much exercised in combining and comparing them.

With the philosophical or religious tenets of the author I have nothing to do; my business is with his poetry. The subject is well-chosen, as it includes all images that can strike or please, and thus comprises every species of poetical delight. The only difficulty is in the choice of examples and illustrations, and it is not easy in such exuberance of matter to find the middle point between penury and satiety. The parts seem artificially disposed, with sufficient coherence, so as that they cannot change their places without injury to the general design.

His images are displayed with such luxuriance of expression, that they are hidden, like Butler's Moon, by a *Veil of Light*;[74] they are forms fantastically lost under superfluity of dress. *Pars minima est ipsa Puella sui* [The woman herself is the least part of

herself].[75] The words are multiplied till the sense is hardly perceived; attention deserts the mind, and settles in the ear. The
reader wanders through the gay diffusion, sometimes amazed,
and sometimes delighted; but, after many turnings in the flowery
labyrinth, comes out as he went in. He remarked little, and laid
hold on nothing.

To his versification justice requires that praise should not be
denied. In the general fabrication of his lines he is perhaps
superior to any other writer of blank verse; his flow is smooth,
and his pauses are musical; but the concatenation of his verses is
commonly too long continued, and the full close does not recur
with sufficient frequency. The sense is carried on through a long
intertexture of complicated clauses, and as nothing is distinguished, nothing is remembered.

The exemption which blank verse affords from the necessity of
closing the sense with the couplet, betrays luxuriant and active
minds into such self-indulgence, that they pile image upon image,
ornament upon ornament, and are not easily persuaded to close
the sense at all. Blank verse will therefore, I fear, be too often
found in description exuberant, in argument loquacious, and in
narration tiresome.

His diction is certainly poetical as it is not prosaick, and elegant
as it is not vulgar. He is to be commended as having fewer artifices
of disgust than most of his brethren of the blank song. He rarely
either recalls old phrases or twists his metre into harsh inversions.
The sense however of his words is strained; when *he views the
Ganges from Alpine heights*; that is, from mountains like the Alps.
And the pedant surely intrudes, but when was blank verse without pedantry? when he tells how *Planets* absolve *the stated round of
Time.*[76]

GRAY

Gray's Poetry is now to be considered; and I hope not to be
looked on as an enemy to his name, if I confess that I contemplate
it with less pleasure than his life.

His ode on *Spring* has something poetical, both in the language
and the thought; but the language is too luxuriant, and the

thoughts have nothing new. There has of late arisen a practice of giving to adjectives, derived from substantives, the termination of participles; such as the *cultured* plain, the *daisied* bank; but I was sorry to see, in the lines of a scholar like Gray, the *honied* Spring. The morality is natural, but too stale; the conclusion is pretty.

The poem on the *Cat* was doubtless by its author considered as a trifle, but it is not a happy trifle. In the first stanza *the azure flowers* that *blow*, shew resolutely a rhyme is sometimes made when it cannot easily be found. *Selima*, the *Cat*, is called a nymph, with some violence both to language and sense; but there is good use made of it when it is done; for of the two lines,

> What female heart can gold despise?
> What cat's averse to fish?

the first relates merely to the nymph, and the second only to the cat. The sixth stanza contains a melancholy truth, that *a favourite has no friend*; but the last ends in a pointed sentence of no relation to the purpose; if *what glistered* had been *gold*, the cat would not have gone into the water; and, if she had, would not less have been drowned.

The *Prospect of Eton College* suggests nothing to Gray, which every beholder does not equally think and feel. His supplication to father *Thames*, to tell him who drives the hoop or tosses the ball, is useless and puerile. Father *Thames* has no better means of knowing than himself. His epithet *buxom health* is not elegant; he seems not to understand the word. Gray thought his language more poetical as it was more remote from common use: finding in Dryden *honey redolent of Spring*, an expression that reaches the utmost limits of our language, Gray drove it a little more beyond common apprehension, by making *gales* to be *redolent of joy and youth*.

Of the *Ode on Adversity*, the hint was at first taken from *O Diva, gratum quae regis Antium* [O Goddess who rules pleasing Antium];[77] but Gray has excelled his original by the variety of his sentiments, and by their moral application. Of this piece, at once poetical and rational, I will not by slight objections violate the dignity.

My process has now brought me to the *wonderful Wonder of*

Wonders, the two Sister Odes; by which, though either vulgar ignorance or common sense at first universally rejected them, many have been since persuaded to think themselves delighted. I am one of those that are willing to be pleased, and therefore would gladly find the meaning of the first stanza of the *Progress of Poetry*.

Gray seems in his rapture to confound the images of *spreading sound* and *running water*. A *stream of musick* may be allowed; but where does *Musick*, however *smooth and strong*, after having visited the *verdant vales, rowl down the steep amain*, so as that *rocks and nodding groves rebellow to the roar*? If this be said of *Musick*, it is nonsense; if it be said of *Water*, it is nothing to the purpose.

The second stanza, exhibiting Mars's car and Jove's eagle, is unworthy of further notice. Criticism disdains to chase a school-boy to his common places.

To the third it may likewise be objected, that it is drawn from Mythology, though such as may be more easily assimilated to real life. Idalia's *velvet-green* has something of cant. An epithet or metaphor drawn from Nature ennobles Art; an epithet or metaphor drawn from Art degrades Nature. Gray is too fond of words arbitrarily compounded. *Many-twinkling* was formerly censured as not analogical; we may say *many-spotted*, but scarcely *many-spotting*. This stanza, however, has something pleasing.

Of the second ternary of stanzas, the first endeavours to tell something, and would have told it, had it not been crossed by Hyperion: the second describes well enough the universal prevalence of Poetry; but I am afraid that the conclusion will not rise from the premises. The caverns of the North and the plains of Chili are not the residences of *Glory and generous Shame*. But that Poetry and Virtue go always together is an opinion so pleasing, that I can forgive him who resolves to think it true.

The third stanza sounds big with *Delphi*, and *Egean*, and *Ilissus*, and *Meander*, and *hallowed fountain* and *solemn sound*; but in all Gray's odes there is a kind of cumbrous splendor which we wish away. His position is at last false: in the time of Dante and Petrarch, from whom he derives our first school of Poetry, Italy was over-run by *tyrant power* and *coward vice*; nor was our state much better when we first borrowed the Italian arts.

Of the third ternary, the first gives a mythological birth of Shakespeare. What is said of that mighty genius is true; but it is not said happily: the real effects of this poetical power are put out of sight by the pomp of machinery. Where truth is sufficient to fill the mind, fiction is worse than useless; the counterfeit debases the genuine.

His account of Milton's blindness, if we suppose it caused by study in the formation of his poem, a supposition surely allowable, is poetically true, and happily imagined. But the *car* of Dryden, with his *two coursers*, has nothing in it peculiar; it is a car in which any other rider may be placed.

The Bard appears, at the first view, to be, as Algarotti and others have remarked, an imitation of the prophecy of Nereus.[79] Algarotti thinks it superior to its original; and, if preference depends only on the imagery and animation of the two poems, his judgement is right. There is in *The Bard* more force, more thought, and more variety. But to copy is less than to invent, and the copy has been unhappily produced at a wrong time. The fiction of Horace was to the Romans credible; but its revival disgusts us with apparent and unconquerable falsehood. *Incredulus odi* [Unbelieving, I hate it.][79]

To select a singular event, and swell it to a giant's bulk by fabulous appendages of spectres and predictions, has little difficulty, for he that forsakes the probable may always find the marvellous. And it has little use; we are affected only as we believe; we are improved only as we find something to be imitated or declined. I do not see that *The Bard* promotes any truth, moral or political.

His stanzas are too long, especially his epodes; the ode is finished before the ear has learned its measures, and consequently before it can receive pleasure from their consonance and recurrence.

Of the first stanza the abrupt beginning has been celebrated; but technical beauties can give praise only to the inventor. It is in the power of any man to rush abruptly upon his subject, that has read the ballad of *Johnny Armstrong,*

Is there ever a man in all Scotland—

The initial resemblances, or alliterations, *ruin, ruthless, helm or hauberk*, are below the grandeur of a poem that endeavours at sublimity.

In the second stanza the *Bard* is well described; but in the third we have the puerilities of obsolete mythology. When we are told that *Cadwallo hush'd the stormy main*, and that *Modred* made *huge Plinlimmon bow his cloud-top'd head*, attention recoils from the repetition of a tale that, even when it was first heard, was heard with scorn.

The *weaving* of the *winding sheet* he borrowed, as he owns, from the northern Bards; but their texture, however, was very properly the work of female powers, as the art of spinning the thread of life in another mythology. Theft is always dangerous; Gray has made weavers of his slaughtered bards, by a fiction outrageous and incongruous. They are then called upon to *Weave the warp, and weave the woof*, perhaps with no great propriety; for it is by crossing the *woof* with the *warp* that men *weave* the *web* or piece; and the first line was dearly bought by the admission of its wretched correspondent, *Give ample room and verge enough*. He has, however, no other line as bad.

The third stanza of the second ternary is commended, I think, beyond its merit. The personification is indistinct. *Thirst* and *Hunger* are not alike; and their features, to make the imagery perfect, should have been discriminated. We are told, in the same stanza, how *towers* are *fed*. But I will no longer look for particular faults; yet let it be observed that the ode might have been concluded with an action of better example; but suicide is always to be had, without expence of thought.

These odes are marked by glittering accumulations of ungraceful ornaments; they strike, rather than please; the images are magnified by affectation; the language is laboured into harshness. The mind of the writer seems to work with unnatural violence. *Double, double, toil and trouble*. He has a kind of strutting dignity, and is tall by walking on tiptoe. His art and his struggle are too visible, and there is too little appearance of ease and nature.

To say that he has no beauties, would be unjust: a man like him, of great learning and great industry, could not but produce something valuable. When he pleases least, it can only be said that a good design was ill directed.

His translations of Northern and Welsh Poetry deserve praise; the imagery is preserved, perhaps often improved; but the language is unlike the language of other poets.

In the character of his Elegy I rejoice to concur with the common reader; for by the common sense of readers uncorrupted with literary prejudices, after all the refinements of subtilty and the dogmatism of learning, must be finally decided all claim to poetical honours. The *Church-yard* abound with images which find a mirrour in every mind, and with sentiments to which every bosom returns an echo. The four stanzas beginning *Yet even these bones*, are to me original: I have never seen the notions in any other place; yet he that reads them here, persuades himself that he has always felt them. Had Gray written often thus, it had been vain to blame, and useless to praise him.

NOTES

1. Cf. Aristotle *Poetics* 8 (implicitly: the exact phrase is not to be found).

2. *Essay on Criticism* 11. 297–98.

3. Manilius *Astronomica* 1. 142.

4. Cf. *Paradise Lost*, 4. 343–44.

5. *Lycidas*, 11. 27–29.

6. Le Bossu, *Traité du poëme épique*, 1. 7.

7. *Paradise Lost*, 6. 221–23. Read: ". . . the least of whom could wield/These elements . . . ."

8. Cf. Addison, *Spectator* 303, and John Clarke, *Essay upon Study* (1731), p. 204.

9. *Spectator* 273.

10. Aristotle *Poetics* 15. 10.

11. Milton calls it a poem on the title page to the second edition, and an heroic song, *Paradise Lost*, 9. 25.

12. Cf. Dryden's *Dedication of the Aeneis* (1697).

13. *An Essay of Dramatic Poesy* (1668).

14. Torquato Tasso.

15. Cf. *Paradise Lost*, 11. 8–9.

16. See Richard Bentley's preface to his edition of *Paradise Lost* (1732).

17. *Preface to Sylvae* (1685).

18. *Spectator* 297.

19. Milton, in his introductory comments to *Paradise Lost*, affirms that rhyme is "no necessary Adjunct or true Ornament of Poem or good Verse, in longer Works especially . . . ."

20. William Locke.

21. Edmund Waller's *Divine Poems* (1685) stimulated this passage on devotional poetry. Some may suspect Johnson of confusing here the limitations of the poetic imagination with the limitations of Waller, but Dante, *Paradiso* 33, is of a similar persuasion: the ineffable simplicity of divine truth eludes all ingenuity of diction or metaphor.

22. These are: William Webbe, *A Discourse of English Poetrie* (1586); George Puttenham, *The Arte of English Poesie* (1589); Ben Jonson, *Timber*; Cowley's prefaces; Dryden, *Essay of Dramatic Poesy* (1668).

23. Cf. Longinus, *De sublimi* 16; Demosthenes *De corona* 263. 11.

24. Joseph Trapp, *Praelectiones poeticae* (1722), p. 386 (1742 translation, p. 348). Johnson's transcription of the Latin omits a few clauses.

25. Joseph Spence, *Essay on Mr. Pope's Odyssey* (1737 edition), p. 121.

26. Dryden's parallel, in the preface to *Dryden's Second Miscellany*, was criticized by George Sewell in his preface to Ovid's *Metamorphoses* (1724).

27. Statius *Sylvae* 1. 1. 1.

28. *Threnodia Augustalis* 11. 337 ff.

29. For Dryden on translation, see his *Discourse concerning Satire* (1693), *Dedication of the Aeneis* (1697), and *Preface to the Fables* (1700). Barton Holyday was an early seventeenth-century translator of Juvenal, Persius, and Horace; George Sandys published his version of the *Metamorphoses* in 1626.

30. *Dedication of the Aeneis*.

31. *Absalom and Achitophel* 1. 1028. Read "time."

32. *Tyrannic Love*, 2. 3, quoted with minor inaccuracies.

33. *A Parallel of Poetry and Painting* (1695). The play being discussed is Otway's *Venice Preserved*.

34. Sir John Davies (1565–1618) published several rhymed treatises on morality and metaphysics.

35. Suetonius *Augustus* 29.

36. The villain in Samuel Richardson's *Clarissa* (1747–48).

37. See the conclusion of *Don Quixote*.

38. Cf. *Spectator* 232; this essay is of uncertain authorship.

39. Addison devoted eighteen *Spectator* papers to an extensive criticism of Milton.

40. Tibullus 4. 2. 14. Johnson's preceding sentence captures the thought.

41. Cf. *Essay on Criticism*, 1. 155.

42. Cf. *Verses on the Death of Dr. Swift*, closing couplet.

43. Cf. *Pastorals* 4. 49.

44. *Remarks upon Mr. Pope's Translation of Homer* (1717).

45. *The Campaign* 1. 470.

46. The *Pollio* is Virgil's fourth eclogue; the "original" is Isaiah.

47. Horace *Odes* 4. 2. 11.

48. *Essay on Criticism*, 11. 219–32.

49. *Aeneid* 5. 144–47.

50. *Metamorphoses* 1. 533–38.

51. *Essay on Criticism*, 11. 337–83.

52. Pope's *Odyssey*, 11. 735–38 (this part was translated by William Broome).

53. *Essay on Criticism*, 11. 370–73.

54. *Imitations of Horace, Epistles*, 2. 1. 267–69.

55. As was customary, Johnson employs the word in its Latin sense of *playful*.

56. Joseph Warton, *Essay on the Genius and Writings of Pope* (1756, 1782).

57. *Remarks on Mr. Pope's Rape of the Lock* (1728). Boileau's *Lutrin* (1674) is generally considered the first modern mock-epic poem.

58. Joseph Warton.

59. G. A. Dell' Anguillara's *Metamorphoses* (1548) is in ottava rima; A. M. Salvini's *Iliad* and *Odyssey* (1723) are in blank verse.

60. Juvenal *Satires* 1. 5.

61. Cf. *Dunciad*, 2. 35–50, 109–20. For Johnson's opinion of Theobald, see *Preface to Shakespeare*, pp. 168–69. Though aware of Bentley's limitations, Johnson always respected his learning and intellectual power.

62. Cf. *Dunciad*, 4. 293–336, 403–36.

62.3. For the passages referred to in these two paragraphs, see *Essay on Man*, 1. 43–50, 60–68, 235–46; 2. 293–94.

64. *Satire* 10.

65. Cf. *Moral Essays*, 4. 39 ff; 3. 299 ff.

66. *Epilogue*, 1. 114, 142.

67. *Preface to Tyrannic Love* (1670).

68. Swift to Pope, 28 June 1715.

69. *Dunciad*, 3. 87–88.

70. Isaac Watts, *The Improvement of the Mind* (1741), chap. 20, sec. 36.

71. Joseph Hall published his rhymed verse satires, *Virgidemiae*, in 1597.

72. Cf. Johnson's remarks on Pope's *Windsor Forest*, p. 253.

73. George Lyttelton, *Prologue to Coriolanus*.

74. Cf. Samuel Butler's *Hudibras*, 2. 1. 905–8.

75. Ovid *Remedia amoris* 1. 344.

76. See *Pleasures of Imagination*, first version, 1. 177, 194; revised version, 1. 232, 252.

77. Horace *Odes* 1. 35.

78. See Horace *Odes* 1. 15.

79. Horace *Ars poetica* 1. 188.

Selected Bibliography

Of general interest:

Bate, W. J. *The Achievement of Samuel Johnson*. New York: Oxford University Press, 1955.

Crane, R. S. "English Neoclassical Criticism: An Outline Sketch." In *Critics and Criticism: Ancient and Modern*, edited by R. S. Crane. Chicago: University of Chicago Press, 1952.

————."On Writing the History of English Criticism, 1650–1800." *University of Toronto Quarterly* 22 (1953): 376–91.

Eliot T. S. "Johnson as Critic and Poet." In *On Poetry and Poets,* by T. S. Eliot. London: Farrar, Strauss and Cudahy, 1957.

Fussell, Paul. *Samuel Johnson and the Life of Writing*. New York: Harcourt, Brace, Jovanovich, 1971.

Hagstrum, Jean H. *Samuel Johnson's Literary Criticism*. Chicago and London: University of Chicago Press, 1967.

Keast, W. R. "The Theoretical Foundations of Johnson's Criticism." In *Critics and Criticism: Ancient and Modern*, edited by R. S. Crane. Chicago: University of Chicago Press, 1952.

Krutch, Joseph Wood. *Samuel Johnson*. New York: Harcourt, Brace and World, 1963.

Leavis, F. R. "Johnson as Critic." *Scrutiny* 12 (1944): 187–204.

Raleigh, Walter. *Six Essays on Johnson*. Oxford: Clarendon Press, 1910.

On special subjects

Boyce, Benjamin. "Samuel Johnson's Criticism of Pope in the *Life of Pope*." *Review of English Studies*, n. s. 5 (1954): 37–46.

Elledge, Scott. "The Background and Development in English Criticism of the Theories of Generality and Particularity." *PMLA* 62 (1947): 147–82

Evans, Bergen. "Dr. Johnson's Theory of Biography." *Review of English Studies* 10 (1934): 301–10.

Fleischauer, Warren. "Johnson, *Lycidas*, and the Norms of Criticism." In *Johnsonian Studies*, edited by James L. Clifford and D. J. Greene. Cairo: Société Orientale de Publicité, 1962.

Jones, W. Powell. "Johnson and Gray: A Study in Literary Antagonism." *Modern Philology* 56 (1959): 243–53.

Keast, W. R. "Johnson's Criticism of the Metaphysical Poets." *ELH* 17 (1950): 59–70.

Lipking, Lawrence. *The Ordering of the Arts in Eighteenth-Century England*. Princeton: Princeton University Press, 1970. (Part 4 discusses *The Lives of the Poets*).

Perkins, David. "Johnson on Wit and Metaphysical Poetry." *ELH* 20 (1953): 200–217.

Rhodes, Rodman D. "*Idler* No. 24 and Johnson's Epistemology." *Modern Philology* 64 (1966): 10–21.

Sherbo, Arthur. *Samuel Johnson, Editor of Shakespeare. With an Essay on The Adventurer. Illinois Studies in Language and Literature*, vol. 42. Urbana: University of Illinois Press, 1956.

Sledd, James H., and Gwin J. Kolb. *Dr. Johnson's Dictionary: Essays in the Biography of a Book*. Chicago: University of Chicago Press, 1955.

Smith, D. N. *Shakespeare in the Eighteenth Century*. Oxford: Clarendon Press, 1928.

Stock, R. D. *Samuel Johnson and Neoclassical Dramatic Theory: The Intellectual Context of the Preface to Shakespeare*. Lincoln: University of Nebraska Press, 1973.

Index

Academy of the English language, 102, 124, 126

Addison, Joseph, ix, x, 1, 2, 17, 43, 66, 159, 187, 204, 206, 217, 218, 253; as critic, 245–47; Roger de Coverley, 244–45; his style, 247–48; on Tate's *Lear*, 189; *Cato*, 159, 245; *Spectator*, 1, 7, 89

Aeschylus, 225

Ainsworth, Robert, 112

Akenside, Mark, 271–72

Algarotti, 275

Amelot, A. N., 124

Anacreon, 160

Anguillara. *See* Dell' Anguillara

Aquinas, Thomas, 136

Ariosto, 221, 227

Aristotle, 31, 79–81, 84, 114, 151, 218

Ascham, Roger, 157

Bacon, Francis, 85, 118, 127

Bailey, Nathaniel, 101, 112

Bate, Walter Jackson, 203

Bentley, Richard, 180, 222, 227, 254, 263, 279

Biography, 40–44

Boccaccio, Giovanni, 124

Boileau-Despréaux, Nicolas, 61, 259, 266, 268, 279

Bolingbroke, Henry St. John, First Viscount, 268

Boswell, James, 137

Boyle, Robert, 127, 162

Broome, William, 263

Budgell, Eustace, 244

Busby, Dr. Richard, 235

Butler, Samuel, 19, 271

Carlyle, Thomas, 137

Caro, Annibale, 124

Catiline, 42

Chambers, Ephraim, 101, 102

Chapman, George, 235

Chaucer, Geoffrey, 158, 162, 180, 234, 253

Cheke, Sir John, 157

Cibber, Theophilus, 201

Cicero, 22, 33, 114

Clarke, Samuel, 217

Claudian, 52, 235

Cobb, Samuel, 254

Coleridge, Samuel Taylor, 136

Comedy, 53–57, 144–46

Condel, William, 167

Congreve, William, 17, 165

Conjectural criticism, 177–81

Cooper, Anthony Ashley, Third Earl of Shaftesbury, ix

Cooper, Elizabeth, 201

Corneille, Pierre, 152

Cowley, Abraham, xii, 69, 202, 207–10, 211, 269, 232, 235, 239

Davies, Sir John, 242

Definitions, 113–16

Dell' Anguillara, G. A., 260

Demosthenes, 233

Denham, Sir John, 17, 238, 239

Dennis, John, 143, 164, 189, 253, 259

De Wit, Jean, 42

"Dick Minim," ix, 2–3, 16–22, 102, 205

Didacticism. *See* Morality and art

Discordia concors, 202, 208

Donne, John, 203, 207

Dramatic illusion, 152–55

Dramatic unities, 59–60, 79–80, 151–56, 243

Dryden, John, ix, x, xi, xii, 2, 6, 17, 67, 71, 134, 182, 190, 191, 204, 207, 219, 220, 226, 254, 255, 261, 263, 267, 273, 275, 278; comic passages in his tragedies, 54–57; as critic,